The Russia complex

The means have been terrible, the result commonplace. [John St Loe Strachey's final verdict on the Soviet Union, *The Strangled Cry* (London, 1962), p. 21]

If we are to cure the 'Russia' complex, instead of becoming anti-Communist or fellow-traveller neurotics, we must do two things. On the rational level we must change the yardstick by which we measure Left and Right; and on the irrational level we must break down the fixation of Russia as Utopia. [R.H.S. Crossman, *New Statesman and Nation*, 24 January 1948]

The Russia complex
THE BRITISH LABOUR PARTY and THE SOVIET UNION

Bill Jones

MANCHESTER
UNIVERSITY PRESS

© W. D. A. Jones 1977

Published by Manchester University Press
Oxford Road, Manchester M13 9PL

British Library cataloguing in publication data

Jones, Bill
   The Russia complex.
    1. Labour Party 2. Russia — Foreign opinion,
   British.
   I. Title
   301.15'43'9470842   JN1129.L32

ISBN 0 7190 0696 1

Typeset by Computacomp (UK) Ltd.,
Fort William, Scotland
and printed in Great Britain
by Unwin Brothers Ltd.,
The Gresham Press, Old Woking, Surrey

Contents

ACKNOWLEDGEMENTS page vi

PREFACE vii

1 Origins of the enchantment 1

2 The enchantment 11

3 Collapse of an image: the pact, Poland and the attack on Finland 33

4 Image repaired: Russia as heroic ally 58

5 Help Russia! The Second Front campaign 74

6 Doubts renewed: the case of Poland 89

7 Triumphant Labour: a new dawn in Anglo-Soviet relations? 103

8 Russia and the case for a socialist foreign policy: the left-wing rebels 121

9 Abandonment of an image 147

10 The genesis of NATO, I. The coup in Czechoslovakia 174

11 The genesis of NATO, II. The Berlin blockade and its aftermath 190

CONCLUDING COMMENTS 209

SELECTIVE BIBLIOGRAPHY 219

INDEX 224

Acknowledgements

Pride of place in these acknowledgements belongs to Dr Brian Porter, Senior Lecturer in International Politics, University College of Wales, Aberystwyth, who supervised the doctoral thesis upon which this book is based. His meticulous advice helped to correct many factual errors, not to mention infelicities of written style. His wisdom frequently tempered the judgements made, although final responsibility for them belongs to me. I owe a considerable debt of thanks to Professor Bernard Crick, who urged the publication of the thesis and whose comments and advice made it more worthy of the conversion.

I was helped considerably during the earlier period of my research by personal interviews with Labour Party politicians, journalists and academics, a full list of whom appears in the bibliography. I would like to thank them all for their generosity in giving of their time and recollections. I spent more time than I care to remember in the libraries of the London School of Economics, UCW Aberystwyth, the National Library of Wales and the British Newspaper Library; I must thank all their staffs, whose help and co-operation served to make the time usefully spent. For typing the major part of the original thesis and the manuscript for this publication with great speed and accuracy I thank Mrs Alison Flynn, and finally a special word of thanks to Wendy, my wife, who sympathised, helped and encouraged during the years of research and writing with a generosity and patience few husbands have the right to expect.

Preface

What impressions does the British socialist have of the Soviet Union sixty years after the Bolshevik revolution? Quite possibly he sees a country with a worryingly large military establishment or perhaps a bleak, highly centralised bureaucratic machine; certainly he sees a State with the unpleasant, not to say unsocialist habit of suppressing dissident views. It was not always so. Today most socialists still view the USSR through the harshly uncomplimentary lens of the Cold War period, softened here and there by the afterglow of *détente* and — who knows? — the occasional gymnastics display. It is hard to appreciate that during the 'thirties a typical member of the Labour Party might have described Soviet Russia in glowing terms, as a hugely successful experiment in planned economics and advanced approaches to social, political and legal questions; in short, as the hope of the world. The ashes are now cold, but for thirty years or so after 1917 the Labour Party had a "love affair" with the Soviet Union, and the story of the relationship — never an easy one — is an integral part of the history of the party. In this book I examine the rise and decline of the enchantment, concentrating my attention upon the late 'thirties and the 'forties.

A major theme is the part played by Labour perceptions of Soviet Russia in the development and post-war decline of the idea of a distinctive 'socialist foreign policy' which rejected traditional power-political approaches. Close attention is paid to the conflicts generated by issues connected with the Soviet Union, and the book also reflects an awareness that Labour's involvement with the idea of a worker's State in Russia had a subtle but profound effect upon British socialism at home. Naturally, some attempt is made to answer the much debated question "Why?" Why did so many British socialists, often brilliant men and women, ignore all the evidence to the contrary and insist upon seeing Stalin's Russia as a Utopia to be visited, marvelled at and defended against its detractors? The study also shows how the focus of Labour interest shifts from one facet of the Soviet Union to another. In the 'twenties it was seen as the custodian of the first socialist revolution and its struggle for survival was watched with close fraternal interest. In the 'thirties it was the astonishing transformation of the Soviet economy that attracted interest, together with its apparent attempt to create a new enlightened socialist society with an advanced political system. Dismay at Stalin's foreign-policy *volte-face* in 1939 gave way, after 1941, to an uncritical acclaim for the Soviet war effort, whereas in the post-war world it was Soviet foreign policy intentions which became the major interest of the party and the principal bone of contention within it.

Sources for this study have been plentiful, possibly too plentiful; one of the major problems has been to sift through the welter of information effectively. Some twenty personal interviews provided valuable background information, and use has been made of the available biographies, autobiographies, collections of private papers and diaries. The Labour Party is a vast organisation with hundreds of thousands of constituency members and millions of affiliated trade union members, and, inevitably, recording Labour Party views has been a selective process. The concentration has been upon the tip of the iceberg: the Parliamentary Labour Party, the National Executive Committee, the Trade Union Congress, the Annual Conference, socialist books and pamphlets and, in particular, the left-wing press. The *Daily Worker* spoke for the Communist Party, the *New Leader* for the Independent Labour Party, and the *Daily Herald* (with occasional deviations) for the trade union and Labour Party leadership. *Reynolds News*, the Sunday organ of the Cooperative movement, represented a left-wing point of view which tended to be pacifistic and sympathetic to the fellow-travelling position. *Forward*, the Glasgow-based weekly, edited by Emrys Hughes (a son-in-law of Keir Hardie) also pursued a pacifist editorial line as well as carrying regular articles by Harold Laski. *The New Statesman and Nation* (*N.S. and N.*) and *Tribune*, both left-wing weekly journals, were vitally important as the voices of intellectual socialist points of view. On foreign policy they were of major importance, both for the influence they exerted within the party and for the luminaries associated with their editorial policies.

The *N.S. and N.*, founded by the eminent Fabians Sidney and Beatrice Webb, was edited by Kingsley Martin from 1930. His close association with Harold Laski and Lowes Dickinson during his academic career contributed to a position which straddled the radical and Marxist traditions in the Labour Party. Martin brought a curious, erratic genius to his job, turning the 'paper of sect into one of world reputation and interest' selling nearly 100,000 copies per week.[1]

It was commonly rumoured that Martin tended to express the opinions (in his superbly written editorials) of the last person he had spoken to. Certainly there was no lack of advisors around the editorial chair. G. D. H. Cole, H. N. Brailsford, Leonard Woolf, Richard Crossman and Aylmer Vallance were regularly employed by the paper, and Martin, a gregarious and much liked man, had constant contacts with a wide spectrum of leading left-wing intellectuals, including the Webbs, Maynard Keynes (who was also a director

1 C. H. Rolph, *Kingsley*, p. 268.

of the *N. S. and N.*), Laski, Lowes Dickinson and C. E. M. Joad. Konni Zilliacus, the foreign policy expert, frequently described as a fellow traveller, had a particularly formative influence upon Martin's thinking.[2] Zilliacus was a regular contributor, under a variety of pseudonyms, to the *N. S. and N.*'s sister, or rival paper, *Tribune* (the two journals seemed to observe a convention of not attacking each other even when in violent disagreement). *Tribune* was founded in 1937 by two wealthy socialists, Sir Stafford Cripps and George Strauss, to advance the arguments for a Popular Front against fascism. After a period during which it fell under the control of fellow-travellers it was edited successively by Raymond Postgate, Aneurin Bevan, Evelyn Anderson and Michael Foot. *Tribune's* circulation was never more than half that of the *N. S. and N.* but its influence was nevertheless considerable, appealing rather more effectively to working-class socialists. Like the *N.S. and N.*, *Tribune* also commanded a retinue of intellectuals which included George Orwell, Barbara Castle and Ian Mikardo as well as Cripps and Strauss. During the 'forties these two journals are seen to embody the continuation, with Marxist adaptations, of the radical tradition in foreign policy imported for the Liberal Party during and after the first world war. This tradition established the prevailing 'idealist' school in Labour approaches to foreign policy during the inter-war years. A distinction is made between idealist and 'realist' approaches in this study. Realists are seen to emphasise the importance of military and economic power in international relations, whilst idealists stress the appeal of ideas, the importance of accepting the good faith of other countries and the possibilities of changing the international system for the better. Whilst sympathetic to the idealist position, I recognise that I, along with Ernest Bevin, have tended to share the realist perspective.

Bill Jones
Manchester, 1977

2 *Ibid.*, p. 163.

To Wendy and Mandy

1 *Origins of the enchantment*

> When the revolution came in 1917 it was like the coming of a new Messiah. It was the great event of the century; it seemed like the prelude to world wide revolution. [Maurice Orbach, MP, in interview with author]

The fall of the Tsar in March 1917 occurred when the Great War seemed, after two and a half tragic and intractable years, to be no nearer a conclusion. To the Labour Party the death of the ancient Russian tyranny was a welcome and unhoped-for bonus of war; a glimpse of the light that might lie beyond it. Moderates liked the sound of the Mensheviks, who spoke and thought like Western parliamentarians, whilst more militant socialists were impressed by the role played in the revolution by workers and soldiers and excited by the growing power of both in the local committees known as Soviets. Under their influence the moderate government of Prince Lvov declared itself to be in favour of a just, negotiated peace, at this time the policy of the ILP but not the Labour Party as a whole. It was the ILP, in association with the Marxist British Socialist Party, that summoned a convention at Leeds on 3 June urging delegates to 'Follow Russia'.[1] This convention marked the catalytic effect which events in Russia were having upon Labour's thinking, particularly on foreign policy.

i

Such ideas had hitherto drawn upon the matrix of dissenting radical views on foreign policy developed during the nineteenth century. From Richard Cobden was drawn a belief that the fictitious and dangerous notion of balance of power should be abandoned in favour of a system of arbitration between

2   The Russia complex

States which had renounced armaments. Behind this argument lay the assumption that 'ordinary' people had no cause to fight each other. Governments alone caused wars. Cobden also argued that foreign policy should be wrested from the secretive conclave of the Cabinet and made subject to open diplomacy under parliamentary control. This idea was later developed by E. D. Morel, whose book on the Agadir crisis *Morocco in Diplomacy* (1912) brought the clamour for an end to the diplomats' deadly charade into the forefront of radical complaint.

However, Cobden's belief that free trade would engineer a peaceful revolution in inter-State relations was rejected by J. A. Hobson, who argued, in his book of the same name (1902), that *Imperialism* was the inevitable corollary of *laisser-faire* economic systems. Such economies produced surplus capital which financiers invested abroad and pressed their governments to protect with armed force and the superstructure of imperial control. Norman Angell added his gloss to the analysis by perceiving self-interested commercial interest groups, particularly armaments producers, who induced a gullible public to accept the *Great Illusion* that economic advantage could accrue from acts of war.[2]

Whilst radical intellectuals were producing these remarkably neo-Marxist analyses, the loose, domestically orientated coalition between trade unionists and socialist societies called the Labour Party was contributing to the vague deliberations of the Second International, lending its support at the 1907 conference at Stuttgart to the resolution that in the event of war the working classes should intervene to 'bring it promptly to an end'. And yet in the summer of 1914 the military machines of Europe proved firmer of purpose, more swift in motion than the ponderous political armies of socialism. One by one the major socialist parties of Europe accepted the *fait accompli* of war and rallied to their respective national causes. On Saturday 2 August over 100,000 British socialists demonstrated against the war, but on 15 October a Labour Party manifesto duplicated the Liberal view of the war as a struggle between democracy and military despotism. Labour leaders added their voices to the recruitment campaign, called a halt to industrial action and, finally, took their place in the government. Socialism had briefly stood up to nationalism, but the end result had been a pushover.

Determined minorities in the Liberal and Labour parties refused to admit defeat, and their pre-war convergence of thinking found an institutional expression in the form of the Union for Democratic Control, founded in September 1914 with E. D. Morel as its energetic secretary. Here radicals like Hobson, Angell, C. R. Buxton, Charles Trevelyan, Bertrand Russell, Lowes Dickinson and G. P. Gooch collaborated closely with ILP-ers like the author and journalist H. N. Brailsford and the nationally known Philip Snowden and Ramsay MacDonald.

The UDC sought to make out of the necessity of war the virtue of a worthwhile peace; no territories should be transferred without plebiscite, parliaments should ratify treaties, armaments industries should be nationalised and nations disarmed, balance-of-power policies should be abandoned and international co-operation between States inaugurated through the establishment of an International Council. The latter point was elaborated brilliantly in a series of books and articles by Brailsford, Hobson, Leonard Woolf and Lowes Dickinson, who in 1916 formed the League of Nations Society.

Within six months the ILP conference had endorsed the UDC proposals, but the bulk of the Labour Party proved more resistant. In January 1917 the Labour Party Conference witnessed exchanges between the ILP and the pro-war majority in the Labour Party; Snowden excoriated Labour for joining Lloyd George's coalition, whilst Clynes retorted that Snowden and his 'immovable minority' acted as if there were no war.[3] Resolutions calling for international socialist action to produce a negotiated settlement were heavily defeated. But within a year the views of the immovable minority had been wholly accepted; events in Russia had played a major part in the radicalising process.

On behalf of the War Cabinet Arthur Henderson visited Russia in May and returned to urge support for a negotiated peace as the most likely means of keeping the new Russian government in the war and preventing a Bolshevik take-over. His consequent support for Labour representation at the Dutch-sponsored socialist peace conference in Stockholm cost him his Cabinet place but freed his redoubtable energies to transform Labour from a pressure group into a viable alternative government. His concern to produce a broad-based moderate party, resistant to the revolutionary left, was influenced by his Russian experiences.[4]

Henderson's fear of the left was not shared by many of his colleagues at the Leeds convention in June, where enthusiasm for the March revolution coincided with opposition to the war. All sections of the Labour movement were represented at what developed into a euphoric demonstration; resolutions emerged hailing the Russian revolution, endorsing the foreign policy of the provisional government and urging the establishment of workers' and soldiers' councils in Britain. Reacting to the mood of their audience, mild trade unionists talked like Bolsheviks and for a few hours, within the crowded hall, a socialist revolution in Britain seemed a viable proposition.

In the event, practical outcomes were slight; for example, few workers' and soldiers' councils were ever formed and Parliamentary Labour Party leaders cautiously retraced their steps towards constitutional action. But, despite the rapid evaporation of revolutionary feeling, a fundamental movement to the left had occurred within their political attitudes. While the Labour Party shied away from revolution it had, under the spur of the Russian example, contemplated it, if only briefly. A few weeks later a special conference adopted a policy memorandum on the war which accorded closely with the ILP–UDC line, and in December 1917 another conference overwhelmingly endorsed a similar document.

More than ideas were transfused into the Labour Party at this time. Radical intellectuals crowded into the party from the UDC to dominate the Advisory Committee on International Questions, Leonard Woolf being made its chairman. This committee was soon deeply engaged in matters concerning Russia which were destined to add a further element to Labour Party foreign policy. In November the Bolsheviks took over.

Disappointment was felt in the Labour Party that the frail flower of Western-style democracy should have been crushed so soon and Russia plunged once more into violence. The direct and muscular Marxism of the Bolsheviks was alien to the Fabian gradualists of the Labour Party and the socialist pacifists who led the ILP, whilst J. R. Clynes expressed a typical trade unionist view of Bolshevik methods as 'vicious, unjust, tyrannical and dictatorial'.[5] The British Socialist Party (BSP), however, was jubilant at the Bolshevik success, perceiving in it the unravelling of the Marxist analysis of capitalist society. Apart from the ideologically committed, there were small minorities in all sections of the Labour Party, particularly among its younger members, who were either blind to Bolshevism's less pleasant aspects or were prepared to justify them as necessary but temporary expedients. For them the Russian revolutions were apocalyptic events which presaged victory for socialism in other countries, not least Britain itself.

Maurice Orbach, later a left-wing MP, described it in this way: 'When the revolution came in 1917 it was like the coming of a new Messiah. It was the great event of the century; it seemed like the prelude to world-wide revolution.'[6] The mixture of high ideals and rapid shifts of events laced with violence gave the 1917 revolutions a drama and romance which proved irresistible to many left-wing intellectuals in the West; they could not fail, either, to be excited by the fact that the revolution itself was led by intellectuals. Even the majority, who were disturbed by the violence of Bolshevism, felt an identity with its objectives and an immense sympathy for the hardships the new regime was suffering in resisting counter-revolution from within, and, thanks to the Western powers, invasion from without.

The Bolsheviks' determination to withdraw from the war led to their acceptance of the harsh treaty of Brest Litovsk (3 March 1918) as the cost of peace. Allied governments condemned Russian withdrawal, and rumours began to circulate that they might intervene to depose the Bolsheviks and reopen the Russian front.

The Labour Party reacted to these rumours by expressing sympathy with the Bolsheviks, although the ACIQ was divided over the issue of intervention. On 30 May the committee considered a memorandum by H. N. Brailsford which strongly opposed any intervention in Russian affairs. He maintained that despite its faults the Bolshevik revolution was fundamentally progressive and that the Bolsheviks had a right to solve their own problems. His views were resisted by elements within the committee which justified intervention as militarily advantageous to the allies and as the only way to save Russia from the Germans.[7]

When British troops actually landed at Murmansk on 2 August 1918 the question became more sharply defined. While the war lasted the more cautious trade union element of the Labour Party tended to be receptive to the military advantage argument, but when the Armistice was signed on 11 November trade unionists added their voices to those who denounced the British presence.

In the face of the post-war right-wing backlash the hard-pressed Bolsheviks seemed to symbolise the beleaguered spirit of socialism in Europe, and social democrats firmly identified the Bolsheviks as being on their side. It was a widely shared determination within the Labour Party that the spark of socialism in Russia should not be extinguished by the 'interests of financial capital'.[8]

Britain and France recalled their troops from Russia in October 1919, but Labour feelings ran high against the military aid still being rendered to anti-Bolshevik forces in Russia. Feeling ran higher still in April 1920 when Poland invaded Russia under the stimulus, Labour believed, of French and British diplomacy. Direct action was sparked by the refusal of workers at the East India Docks to load a ship, the *Jolly George*, with munitions bound for Poland. Ernest Bevin, the dockers' leader, backed up their stand. The Labour Conference of 1920 passed a resolution favouring a general strike to prevent government assistance to Poland.

By August the Poles had been pushed back by the Red Army, and war fears grew when Lloyd George warned Russia that unless an immediate armistice was signed Britain would have to come to Poland's aid. War seemed imminent; *The Times* called for unity in face of danger. The Labour Party was thrown into ferment by these developments. Rapid consultations among the Labour leadership in the trade unions and in Parliament produced the idea of councils of action to mobilise 'the whole industrial power of the organised workers' against the war. Within a few days over three hundred of these extraordinary councils existed. On 10 August Lloyd George met the members of the Central Council with soft words. Military action was never contemplated, he explained, it was only invoked as a diplomatic weapon. A trial of strength was avoided when the Poles managed to repel the Russians without further assistance from Britain, but Labour allowed themselves to feel that they had won a remarkable victory. Under the leadership of the Labour Party the threat of a general strike had been seriously made and seriously regarded. The idea that united working-class action had foiled a capitalist attack upon the first workers' State became a potent element in Labour mythology which nourished the emotional identification Labour would feel with Russia in ensuing decades.

Understandably when the USSR was under attack, Labour reservations tended to diminish. Sympathy gave birth to an enthusiasm which acted as an antidote to doubt. Labour also developed a partisan interest in refuting Conservative critics whose vilifications of the Soviet Union were intended to belittle its supporters in the Labour Party. The progress of the Soviet experiment therefore became a highly contentious element in the party debate and support for the Soviet Union something of a tenet of left-wing faith. Even when deeply disappointed by Russian behaviour, Labour organs of opinion did not fail to defend Russia against Tory attacks.

Sad to say, Labour party concern for the fledgling Soviet State was not reciprocated. In the international field the ILP, dismayed by the anti-Bolshevik mood of the resuscitated Second International applied, in 1920, for membership of the newly formed Third International (or Comintern) which had been formed, under the dominant influence of Lenin, to disseminate and popularise the Bolshevik recipe for revolution. The ILP made one condition: that the aims of the Comintern be peaceful. The published reply was such a fierce and abrasive condemnation of the ILP and its leaders that much support was alienated. MacDonald and Snowden were stung by these attacks, and did not forgive or forget. This helps to explain why throughout the 1920s the Labour leadership tended to be less enthusiastic about Russia than rank-and-file supporters. In 1929 Hugh Dalton, then a junior Minister at the Foreign Office, observed that Russia 'is still, in the whole field of foreign affairs, the subject on which we are under most pressure from our own Party for quick action'.[9]

Labour had further opportunity to observe the Russian brand of socialism after 1 August 1920, when the BSP, in association with other smaller parties, formed the Communist Party of Great Britain (CPGB). Lenin's directions to his British *protégés* were founded upon Russian experience. In the same way as the Bolsheviks had permeated and won over the Menshevik-dominated Petrograd soviet, so the CPGB was to begin by affiliating to the Labour Party. By boldly denouncing the treachery of reformist Labour leaders, who were secretly controlled by big business interests, the Communist Party would convert the bulk of the Labour Party. Similarly communists would form cells in every possible working-class organisation to form the forward positions of the assault upon the consciousness of the working classes. Thus, from the outset, communist policy was founded upon the propaganda of exhortation and denunciation and the tactic of infiltration into existing organisations.

The members of Labour's National Executive Committee (NEC) were sufficiently aware to appreciate the danger posed by the communist application for affiliation: it was turned down. At the 1921 Conference Henderson sought to identify the new party as agents of Bolshevism. He doubted the sincerity of the communist promise to adhere to the recently agreed Labour Party constitution; in the vote an overwhelming majority shared his doubts and endorsed the NEC rejection.

During the next year communists and their sympathisers worked hard to reverse this decision, but the Edinburgh Conference of 1922 set the seal upon their exclusion. The miners' leader, Hodges, roundly condemned the tyranny of the communist creed, describing its British adherents as the intellectual slaves of Moscow; Ramsay MacDonald weighed in with more denunciations of their political bondage to a foreign country. The CPGB's application was again rejected by a massive majority and in the 1925 Conference a constitutional resolution proscribed all dealings with it.[10]

At first glance it may seem intolerant of Labour to have excluded a party dedicated to similar goals, but the hostility between the two was simply an extension of the traditional conflicts between revolutionaries and social democrats. The Labour Party maintained that peaceful though piecemeal reforms could achieve socialism without entering into the volatile, unpredictable spectrum of violence. Communists argued that such reforms were an illusion obscuring the fact that the underlying capitalist system would survive intact. Social democrats, they argued, were confidence tricksters employed by the capitalists to lull the masses into quiescence with meaningless reforms. The only answer was a revolution that would sweep away the rotten capitalist structure and establish, through the temporary dictatorship of the proletariat, a true communist democracy. The primary task of communists, therefore, was to destroy social democracy and then root out the shady figures who manipulated it. Given that both movements competed for the same audience, these fundamental doctrinal differences were bound to set them apart.

The BSP had never commanded a following in the trade unions, and even by 1922 not one major trade union had been won over to the communist cause. Trade unionists tended to be more interested in immediate material gains rather than the speculative gains of a revolution. But, whilst opposed to communism at home, trade union leaders in the early 1920s were keen to see it succeed in Russia. Following the visit of a British delegation to Russia, the TUC had set its face against majority opinion in the International Federation of Trade Unions (IFTU) and had established in April 1925 a bilateral Advisory Committee with the Soviet trade unions. This committee issued several joint declarations, but the honeymoon was brought to an abrupt end when British trade unions called off the General Strike on 12 May 1926, leaving the miners to fight on by themselves. The difficulties of collaboration between revolutionaries and domestic reformists were starkly presented. Soviet trade union leaders regarded the General Council's action as a pusillanimous retreat from what should have been the decisive British revolutionary struggle. When their offer of financial assistance was turned down the Russians called on the British working classes to cleanse their traitorous leadership. The British trade unions reacted by reaffirming their loyalty to Thomas, Hicks and Purcell, who had been singled out for criticism.

The Advisory Committee became an irritating embarrassment; the 1927 Conference at Edinburgh witnessed its formal burial and, significantly, the adoption of a tougher attitude by the TUC towards communism at home. TUC fingers had been badly burned, and Congress's cautious, pragmatic leadership did not forget the lesson of 1926. The TUC, however, did not abandon its protective interest in the Soviet Union. It objected strongly, for example, to the action of the Conservative government in breaking off diplomatic relations with the USSR following the raid on the premises of 'Arcos' and the Soviet trade delegation on 12 May 1927.[11]

The Advisory Committee episode demonstrates how inappropriate Leninist propaganda was to British conditions. Denunciations of their leaders as traitors moved the traditionally loyal British trade unionists to even greater loyalty and stimulated measures which made infiltration more difficult. Labour leaders learned that their most effective answer was to invoke the strong patriotism of their followers by accusing communists of being a Trojan Horse for sinister Russian influence — the mirror image, ironically, of the accusation made by Conservatives about the Labour Party. Indeed, the experiences of the short-lived minority government in 1924 brought home to the Labour leadership the grave electoral disadvantages of being too closely associated with the Moscow-orientated CPGB.

Rather against his inclinations MacDonald had accorded *de jure* recognition to the USSR shortly after coming to power, but had been unable to settle a dispute over pre-1917 Russian debts to Britain. Conservatives made great play of the fact that left-wing MPs had intervened to mediate successfully a settlement whereby the Bolsheviks would receive a British loan. Coinciding with the ensuing political storm, a dubious prosecution case against the communist journalist J. R. Campbell for allegedly seditious writings was withdrawn at the behest of the Labour Attorney General. MacDonald lost the resultant motion of censure, but more was to come. In the election campaign that followed a mysterious letter was published, supposedly written by Zinoviev, president of the Comintern, which gave various subversive instructions to the CPGB. It was widely supposed that the 'Red Letter Scare', which played on Labour's link with Russia and strove to identify it with the subversive CPGB, lost Labour thousands of votes in an election which put them out of office.

In reality the triangular relationship between Labour, the CPGB and the USSR was asymmetrical. Certainly, indirect Russian interference in the British Labour movement was resented, and the new proximity of the communist creed caused many to reject it and look unfavourably upon its source. But it would be a mistake to regard the Labour Party's attitude towards the CPGB as a reliable barometer of its attitude towards Russia; rejection of the communist application for membership, for instance, occurred at a time when Labour had only recently supported Russia, with some passion, against the dangers of Western intervention. Support for Russia at this time was distinguished by a different set of motivations.

Russia was sufficiently distant to be a comfortable object for Labour's moral support. In Britain socialism was still a theory; in Russia it was a fact, and socialists everywhere felt their political *raison d'être*, to some extent, to be on trial. Communism might be inappropriate within the civilised, traditionally peaceful British system of government, but in a backward society accustomed to harsh rule, then, maybe it could legitimately be argued, communism was the only form socialism could take. At least communism seemed to be an improvement upon the regimes of the tsars, and the Labour Party was determined that Lenin should be allowed a fair chance to conduct his experiment in government free from external interference. Whilst opposing the export of communism, the British Labour Party was a firm advocate of its internal consumption.

The intellectuals of the party were divided in their assessment of Bolshevism. The ACIQ had been split over the desirability of intervention whilst the war lasted, Sidney Webb being a supporter. Beatrice too had no time for the regime during the 'twenties, being repelled by its 'transcendent impulse to violence' and 'crude dogmatism'.[12] Bertrand Russell visited Russia

10 The Russia complex

in 1920 and returned to prophesy that the 'oppressive methods of Bolshevism would destroy the idealism of the revolution and produce a Napoleonic imperialism with ensuing centuries of darkness and futile violence'.[13] H. N. Brailsford, however, who went at the same time, was more sanguine; his book *The Russian Workers' Republic* (1920) was full of praise for the Bolshevik efforts to civilise their backward country. Many of the younger intellectuals flocked into the CPGB and even those who left towards the end of the decade remained strongly pro-Soviet. Such 'refugees' from the CPGB as W. N. Ewer, Raymond Postgate, Margaret Cole, William Mellor and Ellen Wilkinson carried their protective admiration for the USSR back into the mainstream of the Labour Party. Their voices helped to generate the crescendo of Labour Party admiration and support for the Soviet Union in the early part of the next decade.

Notes

1 S. R. Graubard, *British Labour and the Russian Revolution, 1917–24*, pp. 36–40.
2 N. Angell, *The Great Illusion: a study of the Relationship of Military Power to National Advantage* (London, 1911).
3 *LPCR 1917*, pp. 125–9.
4 David Howell, *British Social Democracy: a Study in Development and Decay* (London, 1976), p. 31.
5 Graubard, p. 68.
6 Interview with Maurice Orbach.
7 Graubard, pp. 61–2.
8 A phrase used at the party conference in 1918, *LPCR 1918*, p. 156.
9 Hugh Dalton, *Call Back Yesterday: Memoirs, 1887–1931*, p. 230.
10 The application was rejected by 3,086,000 votes to 261,000.
11 *TUCR 1927*, pp. 213–15.
12 Margaret Cole (ed.), *The Diaries of Beatrice Webb, 1912–24*, p. 176.
13 Bertrand Russell, *The Practice and Theory of Bolshevism* (London, 1920), p. 6.

2 *The enchantment*

Sidney and I have become ikons in the Soviet Union. [Beatrice Webb to Malcolm Muggeridge, in his *Chronicles of Wasted Time*, Vol. I (London, 1972), p. 206]

I am never surprised at anything. [Clement Attlee, Granada Historical Record interview (London, 1967), p. 32]

At the end of the twenties the Labour Party was in close sympathy with the policy objectives of the Bolshevik regime, which it stoutly defended from Tory attacks, but retained reservations about its illiberalism and revolutionary internationalism. Out of this fundamental empathy there developed, during the early 'thirties, a remarkable idealised view of the USSR which became widely disseminated and which proved resistant to change. The most important reason for the growth of this enchantment was the coincidence of economic disaster in the West with an apparent economic miracle in the Soviet Union.

i

The Labour Party, confident in opposition and full of hope after its election successes of 1929, was unable to halt the drift towards even greater economic stagnation. In 1929 unemployment stood at 10·6 per cent. By 1930 Snowden's Gladstonian economic remedies had proved hopelessly inadequate; unemployment rose to 16·2 per cent, and in the following year to an unbelievable 22 per cent. In the shipbuilding and mining industries the figure was often as high as 50 per cent. The fact that the disease of depression originated in America merely emphasised to socialists that the whole system, rather than capitalism at home, was the real enemy. Many socialists felt a sense of decay and disintegration, felt that the world was spiralling out of control. The capitalist era, it seemed, was grinding to a halt. Its factories stood idle, its workers lounged around the streets.

In the fertile soil of these economic conditions drastic remedies proliferated and visions of Utopia flourished; the Soviet Union began to be seen as such a vision. The New Economic Policy, swan song of free enterprise in Russia, had given way in 1928 to a highly centralised Five Year Plan which aimed to transform production by collectivising farm holdings and laying the foundations of a new industrial system. For socialist observers, agricultural failures were overshadowed by the massive upsurge in industrial production combined with full employment. The Labour Party had always argued, in the teeth of anti-Soviet Tory propaganda, that the experiment in Russia should be allowed to proceed without external interference. Now it seemed clear that this experiment was proving successful, and a large proportion of the Labour Party felt a personal identification with this success, felt in a sense that their *protégé* had proved the critics wrong.

Such vital advances combined with a bold attempt to engineer a new society provided striking vindication of Marxist remedies. Influential elements in the Labour Party began to regard Soviet Russia as the only progressive economic force in a world cluttered with the wreckage of a declining capitalist system. The *débacle* of 1931 served to sharpen this admiration.

The 'betrayal' of the Labour Party by MacDonald and Snowden precipitated a crisis of faith and political alignment unknown before or since in Labour history. In the elections that followed the formation of the coalition government the Labour Party returned a mere forty-six MPs, of whom only Cripps, Lansbury and Attlee were politicians of stature. MacDonald's gradualist policies were discredited along with his own reputation, and the Labour Party cast around for alternative routes to socialism. Mosley set off on a road which was to end in the British Union of Fascists. Splinter groups abounded, but in the void of disappointment which followed 1931 the confident assertions of the Marxists proved more influential than ever before. As they had predicted, the social democrat leaders had betrayed the masses, whilst reformist policies had achieved nothing but open collaboration with the capitalist party. By successfully insisting on the lowering of the unemployment benefit, capitalism had revealed its reserves of strength and its determination to thwart a socialist government. The communist analysis fitted the facts and suited the mood of the time. The proof of the communist thesis, the breathtaking transformation of Russian society and the Russian economy, now became the object of intense interest in the Labour Party. "No longer was social disgrace the penalty for visiting Russia, as it had been in certain circles during the nineteen-twenties. Now, one was much more likely to be ostracised if he criticised the country of the Bolsheviks."[1] The Soviet travel agency, Intourist, conducted a brisk trade. Awe-struck visitors from the Western world were carefully shepherded around, content for the most part to see only what they were allowed to see. The newspaper reports of Louis Fischer and Walter Duranty were keenly followed. Information and travel books were widely circulated. Maurice Hindus, the author of many works on Russia during the inter-war period, would have appreciated Malcolm Muggeridge's comment that 'the road to world revolution is paved with best sellers'.[2] Books like *Humanity Uprooted* and *Red Bread* by Hindus provided romantic, dramatic, though substantially accurate, accounts of life in Russia, presenting communism as a noble crusade against the social and physical environment. Furthermore new Soviet culture, particularly the films of Eisenstein, received great applause in left-wing circles. Communism received legions of new recruits, particularly from the intelligentsia, and, as was observed by R.H.S. Crossman, 'The conversion of so many men of letters expressed feelings which were dimly shared by the inarticulate millions who felt that Russia was on the side of the workers.'[3]

Many of the recruits were young. The early 'thirties witnessed an eruption of radical feeling in British universities. Politics in Britain had reached a state of economic and intellectual immobilism. Marxism alone, by combining a profoundly theoretical analysis of society with an urgent call to action, satisfied the intellectual appetites of this new generation as well as its desire to change the world for the better. Unlike other causes, communism seemed already to have achieved a major success in Russia. By joining its ranks either as CPGB members or as 'fellow-travellers' the young idealists could feel that they were contributing their effort in the most effective way. Moreover alignment with a force which claimed to be inexorably on the side of 'good' was a haven of refuge to many a bemused young liberal faced with the realities of facism abroad and poverty at home.

The connection with Russia, the source of communist political weaknesses, was also one of its greatest strengths. It was to Moscow that the communist made his pilgrimage, there that the high priests of communism resided, and where the shrine of communism's Russian saint was to be found. It was in Moscow that heretics were denounced, the official texts of communism interpreted, and the laws of history applied to the present. The very distance of Moscow enhanced the authority of its directives and added to the aura of infallibility that surrounded its decisions.

By surrendering himself to communism the new convert found spiritual anchorage and a cause to fight for and defend. Yet he risked an awful dilemma, for in so doing he made his conscience a hostage to whatever policies the Kremlin might choose. The price of obedience might involve, on the one hand, a compromise of his most deeply rooted humanitarian principles, or, on the other, the loss of faith, certainty and the respect of his friends. By committing himself so totally the communist had a vested interest in preserving his faith. As this faith depended for its survival upon a sanctified image of the USSR, communists tried desperately hard to think only the best of events in Russia and to convince the Labour Party that anything less was mere Tory fabrication. For many communists and left-wing intellectuals the USSR existed only in their imaginations; it was an escape, a necessary fantasy land. Many dismissed stories of police terror, executions and slave labour simply because these things were inconceivable; they were totally alien to British practice. But what of those who, despite their public denials, must have known what was going on? They present a puzzle. No doubt some assumed the draconian regime would eventually be ameliorated by the socialist environment which it was creating; after all, Marx had thought that environment determines consciousness. But who knows, perhaps others derived a macabre satisfaction, a vicarious omnipotence, through identifying, at a safe distance, with a man who ruthlessly ground his opponents under foot?

Membership of the CPGB was 2,500 in 1931, but by 1937 it stood at over 12,000 and the *Daily Worker*, then in its seventh year, was selling around 70,000 copies per day. But more important than party membership were the number of people who espoused communist doctrine without actually joining the party. An impressive array of intellectual talent can be found amongst those who, temporarily at least, identified themselves with the communist position and who, by subscribing to pro-Soviet attitudes, helped perpetuate and strengthen Russian prestige within the Labour Party. Most of the professions came to contain vociferous minorities of such fellow-travelling communists.

In journalism, for instance, there were Claud Cockburn, Philip Toynbee, Tom Driberg and, incomparably, John Strachey. In the law there was D. N. Pritt, John Platts-Mills and Dudley Collard. Among academics there were Maurice Dobb (an influential don at Trinity College, Cambridge), Eric Hobsbawm and Christopher Hill. Even the Church had its representative in the form of the 'Red Dean', Hewlett Johnson.

Certain eminent British scientists were also influenced by communism. Bourgeois doctrines of pure science, the communists argued, were merely a sham which concealed the scientist's subservience in capitalist society to the ruling classes. Communist society recognised the true importance of science and harnessed it directly to the interests of the masses. The novel appeal of communism was thus to enhance the importance of science whilst investing it with a moral purpose. J. B. S. Haldane responded by joining the CPGB and writing regularly on science in the *Daily Worker*. Several other distinguished scientists became communists in all but name. They included Alan Nunn May, Hyman Levy, J. D. Bernal, Joseph Needham and the Nobel prizewinners P. M. S. Blackett, C. F. Power and R. L. M. Synge. Young writers like Spender, Auden and Isherwood also made their singular contributions to what has become known as the 'Red decade'. Orwell believed that during the 'thirties the CPGB exercised an 'almost irresistible fascination for any writer under forty' and that the central stream of English literature had come under communist control.[4]

Such gifted men proved valuable members of communist 'front' organisations. Some twenty of these were used by the communists in the 'thirties to maximise support on particular issues. The 'Friends of the Soviet Union', for instance, was an organisation devoted to the dissemination of the 'perfect' communist image of Russia. At its height it claimed a membership of 50,000 and its journal *Russia Today* was widely circulated. The Society for Cultural Relations and the Anglo/Soviet Parliamentary Committee were similar set-ups. The latter was formed in 1924 as a development of the 'Hands off Russia' movement. Under its indefatigable secretary W. P. Coates (author of several books on Russia) this organisation produced a fortnightly bulletin and many publications. In December 1935, for example, when Eden was in Moscow, a National Week of Peace and Friendship with the USSR was organised and the committee produced an appeal for friendship with the USSR signed by communists (Haldane), fellow-travellers (Pritt and Dobb), ex-members of the wartime Union for Democratic Control (Noel Baker, J. A. Hobson, Seymour Cocks), left-wing socialists (H. N. Brailsford, G. D. H. Cole and Harold Laski), as well as a few Liberals and Conservatives.

Pre-eminent amongst the fellow-travellers of the 'thirties was John St Loe Strachey, an ex-Etonian and an ex-Labour MP. The betrayal of 1931 cast him adrift from the Labour Party. After a brief flirtation with Mosley's New Party he applied himself to relating the intricacies of the Marxist dialectic to contemporary conditions with a force and clarity which made him the foremost communist idealogue of his day. His aim was simply, a Marxist revolution, violent or otherwise, in Great Britain. He sought not to implant the new Soviet civilisation in Great Britain but to defend all that was best in Western culture against the menace of a decaying capitalism and its most dangerous mutation, fascism.[5] Strachey drew heavily on the Soviet example, supporting his theories with evidence drawn from Soviet experience. For instance, to support his proposition that in a world of socialist States war would become obsolete, he cited the example of Soviet foreign policy. Whereas territorial expansion was the companion of economic expansion in capitalist countries, Strachey pointed out that unparalleled economic growth in the Soviet Union had produced no encroachment on border States.[6] To Strachey the perceived performance of the Soviet Union was the touchstone of communism's efficacy.

Closely connected with the communists (though by no means a front organisation) was the Socialist League. This was a body born of I. L. P. dissentients who wished to remain within the Labour Party and who fused in 1933 with G. D. H. Cole's creation, the Socialist Society for Information and Propaganda. Composed of several hundred mainly middle-class Marxists[7] led by Sir Stafford Cripps, this body preached a diluted form of communism. Though often less credulous than communists, Socialist Leaguers shared a similar image of Russia, which their visits to that country generally reinforced. The knowledge that extreme left-wing remedies had succeeded in Russia was a great source of strength to those who advocated similar measures in Great Britain. They closely identified their brand of socialism with the cause of the USSR. To criticise that country or to doubt its achievements was to betray socialism itself. It was logical, therefore, for Stafford Cripps to brave a violently anti-Soviet House of Commons in 1933 to defend the right of the Soviet Union to imprison five MetroVick engineers accused of sabotage. At Labour Party Conferences the Socialist League became the ablest champion of class conflict at home and friendship with Russia abroad.

The Socialist League was greatly influenced by the political thinking of Harold Laski, a man whose thought is frequently reflected throughout the span of this study. Unlike Strachey, who argued that revolution was necessary and desirable, Laski argued that revolution was undesirable and still possibly avoidable.[8] Laski, in fact, had great difficulty in reconciling his Marxism with his libertarianism. He was nervous about pawning freedom for revolution in exchange for a greater amount at some distant and speculative date. In the 'thirties Laski's Marxism gained the upper hand, and, once having accepted the probability of violence in the overthrow of capitalism, he came to regard the Soviet Union with great favour. 'Russia,' he declared, 'is the one effective centre of creativeness in a world which otherwise does not seem to know how to turn its feet from the abyss.'[9] He admired in particular the singleness of purpose of communism in Russia, the confidence and exhilaration it inspired.[10] Laski believed that 'the defence of the Soviet Union is one of the highest duties a society can fulfil'. Being Jewish moreover lent an added impetus — as it did for so many other Jewish members of the left — to his faith in Russia as a bulwark against the anti-Semitism of fascism.

Paradoxically some of the most fervent support for Russia in this decade came from the founder members of the Fabian Society, the very architects of the Labour Party's gradualist philosophy. George Bernard Shaw had always been an admirer of Lenin, but during the 'twenties his support for the Soviet system (apart from a public contretemps with Zinoviev in 1925) had matured into passionate admiration.[11] In July 1931, in the midst of famine and enforced collectivisation, he celebrated his seventy-fifth birthday in Moscow; he was received with a wealth of acclaim which did not disappoint his very considerable vanity. Throughout his carefully choreographed nine-day visit he tirelessly played to the gallery, on one occasion pleading with a Moscow audience not to 'blame' Lady Astor and Lord Lothian (his incongruous fellow-travellers) for being capitalists.[12] An American journalist who covered the visit was unimpressed.

> His performance was not amusing to the Russians, I happen to know. It was macabre. The lengthening obscenity of ignorant or indifferent tourists, disporting themselves cheerily upon the aching body of Russia, seemed summed up in this cavorting old man, in his blanket endorsement of what he could not understand.[13]

Shaw returned to declare that 'the society which has established itself and is being worked out in Russia is a Fabian society'.[14] Two years later he attempted to justify the extermination of the Russian peasantry in one of his famous prefaces. Capitalism, he maintained, had long been indirectly and indiscriminately exterminating people through the caprices of market forces and the absurd criminal code which underpinned it. In Russia, on the other hand, extermination was carried out on a scientific and humane basis. 'For a Communist Utopia,' he wrote 'we need a population of Utopians.' 'Peasants will not do,' pronounced Shaw, and it followed that it was perfectly sensible to liquidate them.[15] He also mentioned how the Soviet Commissar for Transport had been 'obliged' personally to shoot stationmasters who disobeyed his orders. Such liquidation, carried out usually by the secret police, was not punishment — the Soviet criminal code, after all, had abolished the death penalty — but merely 'weeding the garden'.[16]

Apart from the wholesale abandonment of the notion that human life had any intrinsic sanctity, how did Shaw imagine that the Cheka's power over life and death would not be abused? His only answer to this crucial question was feeble and almost incomprehensible: 'The Cheka had no interest in liquidating anybody who could be made publicly useful, all its interests being in the opposite direction.' One can only imagine how the millions of Russian citizens imprisoned by the Cheka would have reacted to this line of reasoning. The truth was that Shaw lived a life of privileged comfort, in which he could indulge his eccentricities and irresponsible moralising; indeed, he was even expected to by an adoring public. He was totally removed from the harsh realities upon which he dilated so cheerfully and nonsensically. He was for ever confusing dictators like Mussolini, Hitler and Stalin with his lofty notions of 'Supermen', as embodiments of his 'Life Force'. One of his biographers has written: 'There were times when one felt that even[17] Al Capone would have met with his approval'. Another biographer provides an insight into how Shaw reacted when unpleasant realities were forced upon him. During a trip to China in 1933 his aeroplane approached the scene of a fierce battle in Manchuria between Chinese and Japanese forces. 'Turn back, turn back!' he shouted to his pilot. 'I don't like wars.'[18]

Shaw's currency as a political commentator had been devalued for the left by his acclaim of Mussolini. The conversion of Sidney and Beatrice Webb to a pro-Soviet standpoint is of greater importance and interest. Unlike Strachey and Laski, whose views on Russia were closely involved with their intellectual theorems, the Webbs' conversion had little to do with their political attitudes; indeed, they tended not to urge upon Britain the sort of development followed by the Bolshevik revolution, but remained more or less true to their gradualist policies. Their conversion is the more remarkable because they had earlier viewed Bolshevism as no different from fascism.[19] Searching Beatrice's diaries for clues it seems that the Webbs' interest was first aroused on 20 February 1930, when they were very favourably impressed by the ascetic and dedicated Soviet ambassador Sokolnikov (later shot in the 1937 purges).[20] Two days later Beatrice read two 'first rate' books on the Soviet Union (one by Hindus) which seemed to influence her greatly; she now doubted the 'superior virtue of British over Russian socialism'.

After reading another Hindus book the following June, she wrote of the massive Soviet attempts to quell in men 'the acquisitive instinct upon which capitalism was founded'.[21] When it came to a choice between the profit motive of the United States and the public service rationale of Soviet society, she declared that it was 'useless to deny we are prejudiced in its favour'.[22] Sidney joined Beatrice (following his retirement from active politics in 1931) in making an exhaustive three-month study of Soviet society and economics. Their favourable impressions were confirmed by a three-week visit to the USSR in 1932, during which they were treated like royalty. In 1935 they produced a massive two-volume study entitled *Soviet Communism: a New Civilisation?* In 1937 a second edition appeared without the question mark. The work represents the apotheosis of Labour's favourable image of the USSR. Throughout it is permeated by a bubbling enthusiasm punctuated by numerous exclamation marks of joyful amazement and studded with reverent capital letters for such Webbsian notions as the 'Remaking of Man' in the Soviet Union or the 'Companionship' or 'Order' known as the Communist Party.[23] At the time it was reviewed with great favour on the left and had a tremendous impact. Even one of its critics, C. E. M. Joad, allowed that it was a 'great book', but since then 'preposterous' is one of the kinder epithets that have been used to describe it.²⁴ Forty years or so on, is it time for a rehabilitation of the Webbs' mammoth work? Certainly the book was a work of great scholarship, drawing upon an enormous body of literature. Furthermore there were genuine achievements to admire in the Soviet Union; breathtaking feats of engineering, the establishment of a State-owned industrial system which ended unemployment and doubled production between 1928 and 1933, the establishment of a welfare State which had halved infant mortality, improved health and hygiene standards and virtually abolished illiteracy. These were immense steps forward, and the Webbs were justified in directing the West's attention to them. They were on shakier ground, however, when they demanded the loudest applause for the Soviet political and legal system. Even allowing that the true facts about Stalin's terror did not emerge conclusively until 1956, the Webbs' handling of these subjects still makes *Soviet Communism* a very silly book.

A careful reading reveals that they were not unaware of the repression, though scarcely of its extent and intensity. There was no reason, they feared, to doubt the reality of the 'Red Terror' in the early days of Bolshevik rule or the ubiquity of the OGPU, with its 'ghastly secretiveness'.²⁵ They accepted that the kulaks had been 'liquidated' but — the Webbs could not identify with the kulaks — asserted that this was necessary to improve production.²⁶ The persecution of the intelligentsia — with whom they could identify — they accepted as a fact but could not justify. They primly disapproved of the 'disease of orthodoxy' and pointed out that suppression of original thought was a waste of a national asset. But the reader was not to worry too much; they were confident that 'in due season' the USSR would come around to their own point of view.²⁷ The OGPU, moreover, was not just a repressive organisation; led by the 'idealist fanatic' Djerjinsky, it was more concerned these days with 'constructive work' than with prosecutions and death sentences.²⁸

We know that the feats of 'human regeneration' which the Webbs drew from such sources as the *Moscow Daily News* referred in reality to the widespread use of prisoners as slave labour.²⁹ They wrote of the model prison they had visited at Bolsevo; prisoners there, it seemed, were so completely reformed that they were reluctant to leave even when their sentences were complete. The reintroduction of the internal passport system restricting freedom of movement — Lenin had denounced it as the 'worst stigmata of Tsarist backwardness and despotism'³⁰ — the Webbs welcomed as an 'extraordinary' step forward. It would enable accurate manpower statistics to be kept.³¹ The Webbs were great ones for statistics.

Was the Soviet Union a dictatorship? On the contrary, the Communist

Party operated through 'persuasion', not coercion; it was an ascetic and devoted body of men dedicated to leading Russia towards the goal of a classless society. Democratic debate flourished in the million or so meetings of the local soviets. But if the Webbs accepted the reality of the repression, what sort of debates did they think were being conducted? Was Stalin a dictator? Not according to them; nowhere in the constitution was authority vested in one man.[32] But what of the tens of thousands of busts, pictures and statues, the endless outpourings of praise? The result, reassured the Webbs, of a 'tacit understanding' within the 'ruling junta' that Stalin should be 'boosted' as a hero figure to exploit the traditional Russian reverence for a personal autocrat. Naturally this would make it virtually impossible to dismiss Stalin as long as he wanted the job.[33] They did not amend this section in their second edition, despite the fact that, in the meantime, the 'ruling junta' had been wiped out following the Moscow trials. The Webbs would not be denied their Utopia.

There were other anomalies between the two editions. The first had applauded the ease with which women could achieve liberation from the family through legal abortions;[34] the second applauded the 'courage and decisiveness' of the Bolsheviks in making abortions illegal, even though they were 'not clear what were the facts or arguments on which this change of policy was based'. What had happened to women's liberation? The Webbs speculated that possibly some women had still felt in their hearts that abortion was a 'sin' and in consequence suffered remorse and a 'subtle deterioration in character'. Whatever the reason, the overall health of society was bound to be the overiding concern of the Communist Party.[35]

In the second edition they agreed that inequalities in income had increased, but these, they claimed, were transient and unimportant because unrelated to differences in social status or education.[36] But how transient were the differences, and how long would it take for them to produce a new elite class? No mention appeared of the fact that on 17 April the death penalty had been made applicable to children over the age of twelve.[37]

And what of the Moscow trials? To many Western sympathisers the spectacle of prominent Bolsheviks meekly admitting to sabotage, conspiracy to assassinate and collusion with foreign agents was the final point of departure. Not so for the Webbs. 'Whatever changes of personnel may occur,' they had written, 'no careful observer can doubt the essential stability of the government as a whole.'[38] There must have been strong grounds, they argued, for actions which placed the Soviet government in such a bad light.[39] Stalin would have agreed. It was inevitable, they continued, that a revolutionary movement weaned on secrecy, deceit and even murder should produce opposition movements which employed these same methods.

The enchantment 21

Westerners, moreover, used to our farcical legal procedures, were unable to comprehend Soviet justice. 'Why should not a conspirator,' they asked, 'who is caught out by the government, degrade himself uselessly by a mock defence instead of at once facing the facts and discussing his part in them candidly with his captor?'[40]

If you are battle-hardened revolutionary, used to deceit and subterfuge, and if your life is at stake, then the reasons for not indulging such 'candid' (a favourite Webb word) confessions, except under duress, are so obvious that they need explaining only to those besotted with a false image of the USSR. In the postscript to the second edition they exultantly explained why they believed developments in that country constituted a new civilisation.

Why? Why did these two relentless searchers after truth and exposers of evil in British society make such a calamitous series of naive and mistaken judgements about the USSR? The first reason was almost certainly their age; by the time of their pro-Soviet twilight their minds were not as clear, their judgements not as sound. For example, the Webbs minimised the terror but they did accept its existence and they did not shrink, on some occasions, from condemning it. Indeed, it almost seems that having condemned the repression they could then forget about it and not bother to allow it to affect their judgement that the USSR was a new civilisation. Yet part of their infatuation derived from traits that had always been discernible in their characters. They were Plato's Guardians personified; they gloried in the orderly arrangement of the masses by a dedicated and capable elite. In the USSR social planners like the Webbs had been allowed the freedom which the British political system denied them; the Soviet Union thus represented a wish fulfillment. Moreover the Webbs lacked warmth and were remote from the common people; Margaret Cole recalls that Beatrice was, in addition, a fearful snob.[41] Both of them were the sort of socialists who were keener on planning for people than upon people themselves, an outlook making for a tolerant approach to those plans which had to be forced upon a reluctant citizenry: collectivisation, for example. And they were both perhaps a little vain, as elderly people often are. When they visited the USSR they were received with rapture — no doubt well rehearsed rapture — as the authors of the work Lenin had praised: *The History of Trade Unionism*. Upon her return Beatrice proudly commented to her nephew Malcolm Muggeridge, 'Sidney and I have become ikons in the Soviet Union.'[42]

But it was not just the economic and social advances of which the Webbs approved, nor the Soviet constitution, which accorded so closely to their own draft socialist constitution.[43] Whereas they had shrunk from the 'creed-autocracy' of Bolshevism in the 'twenties, they now looked towards it with hope. Beatrice saw clearly that communism was akin to a religion, but it was now the spiritual side that attracted her: 'Personally, being a mystic and a moralist, I always hankered after a spiritual power.'[44] Rather like her nephew in his later years, the Webbs clung to a form of religious belief as mankind's only hope of salvation. Beatrice was not unaware of the dangers. 'All I know is that I wish Russian communism to succeed, a wish that tends to distort one's judgment. To be for or against Soviet communism is today a big gamble of the intellect'.[45]

The publication of their book revealed how much of their spiritual capital they had wagered. They followed the logic of the gamble, and in the second edition, ignoring events which should have increased their doubts, declared them dispelled. They felt that the Soviet approach would spread to other countries but they wished the USSR would eschew violence in favour of the 'shining example' approach.[46] Ironically many of those who had sown the seeds of the Webbs' pro-Sovietism — W. H. Chamberlain, Hindus, Louis Fischer — later lost their faith, but until the end of their days the Webbs could see only the glow in the east. They spoke and thought of little else. They lectured, wrote articles and pamphlets, receiving the endless propaganda from Moscow with a credulity that provided perfect insulation from adverse criticism of the Soviet Union.

Their hymn of praise was echoed during the middle years of the decade, with varying degrees of enthusiasm, by other elements of the Labour Party. Admiration for the Soviet Union permeated the party; it was all things to all kinds of socialists. Trade unionists could look to it as the country of the seven-hour day, no bosses and equal pay; to socialist planners it was the home of planned economic growth; to feminists it seemed the home of birth control and female emancipation; to international socialists it appeared as the focus of proletarian solidarity, to pacifists as the home of peace and disarmament, to opponents of fascism as their ally in the east. Frustrated revolutionaries could ventilate their zeal in admiration of a revolution in practice. Each group tended to perceive the fulfilment of its objectives; the Soviet Union thus became the mirror image of socialist demands at home. Political theory and an image of another country had fused to produce a Utopia, or nowhere land. The theory was socialism, the image was projected by Soviet propagandists. The link between the two was the deep desire of Western socialists to see their theories proved in practice. Small wonder that, having committed so much of themselves, admirers of Russia in the Labour Party were reluctant to jettison an enthusiasm so closely connected with personal beliefs.

It should not be assumed, however, that the rising chorus in favour of the Soviet Union was unaccompanied by discordant voices.

ii

The Soviet system of justice had come in for some Labour scrutiny as early as 1931, when the party published a Labour and Socialist International Report on the 1930 Menshevik trials in Moscow which described the "fantastic methods of lying and calumny used by the Bolsheviks". The MetroVick trial also caused grave concern, but unease was compensated by Labour's opposition to the trade reprisals which the government imposed. The speedy release of the engineers seemed to support left-wing assertions of Soviet reasonableness. Soviet prestige in the Labour Party soon recovered.

The Tory-owned press continued its policy of hostility, accentuating Soviet failures and belittling successes. On the left of the Labour Party such propaganda was probably counter-productive. Claud Cockburn, once a *Daily Worker* columnist, has written that he was so used in the 'thirties to hearing anti-communist lies that he automatically disbelieved them.[47] Under these conditions the truth about events in Soviet Russia became the thinnest of phantoms, invisible to left and right alike.

Criticism from the Tories was easily explained, but criticism from the left itself was harder to digest. Some early travellers to Russia returned with less reassuring impressions. Malcolm Muggeridge served a spell as the Moscow correspondent of the *Manchester Guardian*. In his *Winter in Moscow* (1934) he provided possibly the most eloquent statement of those 'who had gone to Moscow to bless and stayed to curse'.[48] He wrote of the people terrorised by an insidious secret police into acceptance of an absurd proletarian mysticism, and of a leadership composed of a 'few vain old men grouped around a maniac'.[49] He concluded, 'The poor little frightened soul of the Dictatorship of the Proletariat is what I despise, not its works.'[50] He reserved his most abrasive criticisms for those worthy but myopic visitors who believed Soviet propaganda and sedulously duplicated it upon their return home. No doubt he viewed his aunt by marriage, Beatrice Webb, as one of the most myopic of this credulous band. She magnanimously chose to excuse him his fulminations, as 'an artist, anarchist and aristocrat by temperament'.[51]

Trade union attitudes towards Russia were yet another brake upon Labour's rising pro-Soviet euphoria. Since the *débâcle* of the Anglo-Soviet Trade Union Advisory Committee the TUC had become concerned lest favourable attitudes towards the Soviet Union assist the intensified communist attempts to penetrate British trade unions. The General Council at this time was consequently 'pressing the Labour leadership for a firmer stand on the Soviet regime'.[52] The distance of rank-and-file membership from the problems of infiltration and international contacts with communism tended on the whole to create among them more favourable attitudes towards the USSR than those of their leadership. Among the miners in particular there was a feeling of solidarity and gratitude dating back to the Russian support for their cause in 1926.[53] Sir Walter Citrine (General Secretary of the TUC) visited Russia in 1936, and his minutely observed study revealed that the Soviet worker, whilst nominally his own boss, in reality did exactly as he was told. He lived under a dictatorship where secret police had destroyed his freedom of speech and where a single-party system made nonsense of his right to vote.[54] Citrine saw no basis for contact between Russian and British trade unions until Russia displayed convincing proof of her progress towards democracy. However, he praised the genuine efforts to dispense with capitalism and unemployment. He was not alone among trade union leaders. Even as militant an anti-communist as Ernest Bevin could plead in 1932 for an open mind upon this 'superhuman effort to rebuild a State on socialistic lines'.[55]

Soviet foreign policy in the mid-'thirties won more positive endorsements from trade unionists and appealed powerfully to most elements of the Labour Party. Soviet propagandists concentrated heavily upon the need for peace, and the powerful pacifist trend in a Labour Party led by the pacifist Lansbury responded to this emphasis by identifying Russia as a force for peace. Stalin's decision to join the League of Nations — Lenin had dismissed it as a 'thieves' kitchen' — won still more Labour applause from an even broader spectrum. Labour's foreign policy was founded upon a passionate belief in collective security; the accession of the USSR was welcomed as a strengthening of League sinews as an endorsement of an organisation brought into disrepute by the Manchurian affair in 1931. Stalin's motives were essentially practical.

As the menace of German fascism grew in the 'thirties, Soviet leaders decided that it could be resisted only by a re-entry into the arena of European politics. The 'Popular Front' idea was an extension of this policy. It sought to fuse the anti-fascist forces of the centre with a communist-led left wing in a governing coalition which would join hands with Russia in resisting German expansion. However suspicious Soviet legal procedures might appear, not to mention the activities of the secret police, the bulk of the Labour Party regarded the growing symptoms of Nazi dictatorship — summary arrest and execution, the persecution of Jews and socialists — as more sinister omens. The Soviet action in taking up the standard of the anti-fascist cause won Labour admiration and attracted increased support for Russia within the penumbra of left-wing opinion surrounding the Communist Party.

Russia gained still more friends through her attitude towards the Spanish civil war. To European socialists the conflict in Spain was the supreme event of the 'thirties, anticipating in miniature the impending clash between fascism and democracy. General Franco's revolt in 1936 against the newly elected coalition Republican government (which included the Spanish Communist Party) roused the organised forces of fascism to its aid and the irregular forces of socialism in fierce opposition. Whilst German armaments and Italian troops helped Franco destroy the Republican forces and the Western democracies stood nervously on one side, the Soviet Union boldly supplied material assistance to the Republicans. Scores of left-wingers, including writers and poets as well as trade unionists, who joined the Communist-led International Brigade, felt a new and more intense kind of comradeship with the Soviet Union. One intellectual who fought in Spain, however, returned a 'socialist' but deeply disillusioned with the Soviet Union.

Initially George Orwell supported the communist line of postponing social revolution until the defeat of Franco but changed his mind when he realised that left-wing opponents of this line, like the anarchist party POUM, were being labelled 'Trotskyists' and ruthlessly wiped out by arbitrary arrest, imprisonment and execution. He believed the Spanish Communist Party, its political strength inflated by its control over the supply of Soviet arms, was following Moscow's instructions and levering out the left-wing opposition in the Republican government.[56]

In the pro-Soviet atmosphere of the British left, Orwell's heretical assertions were unpopular; he never forgave Kingsley Martin for refusing to let him 'blow the gaff' on the Spanish situation in the pages of the *New Statesman and Nation*.[57] 'It is an unfortunate fact,' he wrote, 'that any hostile criticism of the present Russian regime is liable to be taken as propaganda *against socialism*; all socialists are aware of this and it does not make for honest discussion.'[58] Honesty was Orwell's obsession. Whilst others used their talents to advance socialism, Orwell always tempered his contributions with an unerring nose for the truth, even if it showed socialism in a bad light, and even if no one immediately wanted to listen to him. Until his death in 1950 his cogent, fearless voice spoke up for the values which the theories of the the British left-wing intelligentsia often threatened to erode. Never an enthusiast for the Soviet regime — 'all people who are morally sound have known since 1931 that the Russian regime stinks' — he now set about destroying the 'Soviet mythos' in the Labour Party.[59]

From mid-1936 onwards he was assisted by events which were in no way congruent with the view that Russia was the home of a benevolent and developing democracy. In August 1936 the first of the show trials began in Moscow. Zinoviev, Kamenev, Smirnov and thirteen others openly confessed that they had organised a terrorist group to murder Stalin. In January 1937 another group including Radek, Piatokov and Sokolnikov confessed to similar crimes. In the following March it was the turn of Bukharin, Rhykov, Yagoda and nine other highly respected old Bolsheviks. Of the seventy-one members of the Central Committee elected in 1934 only 21 were destined to see the year 1939.[60] All those convicted were shot or imprisoned, and it was widely reported that thousands had been affected by these purges. As Malcolm Muggeridge observed, 'Stalin was his own counter-revolution.'[61]

These events were greeted with incomprehension and dismay by Russia's friends abroad. Before the trials left-wing apologists could deny that such anomalies existed in a legal system which had abolished the death penalty. They now faced the choice of explaining, justifying or condemning events which they had previously believed impossible. The 'perfect' image which the communists had successfully disseminated was seriously impaired. Confessions extracted in prison cells from brainwashed subjects began to intrude into the popular view of Russia.

The Webbs' easy acceptance of the trials has already been mentioned, yet others proved equally gullible. D. N. Pritt, QC, MP, one of the country's leading lawyers, was so impressed by Soviet legal showmanship that he declared himself 'completely satisfied ... that the accused were fairly and judicially treated';[62] he never gave up his belief in the legitimacy of the trials even after Khrushchev revealed the truth in 1956.[63] The NS and N, however, was bewildered.

In early 1936 ecstatic editorials spoke about the 'sensational' Soviet economic performance.[64] Articles appeared by Pearl Binder describing how 'everyone' loved the new socialist opera and how Moscovites bought 'gourmet' fish.[65] Louis Fischer wrote of this 'new land of opportunity' in which 'the human units' (curious phrase) 'are inspired by an impulse towards greatness'.[66] In August 1936 he reviewed the new Soviet constitution, which guaranteed paid employment, leisure, free education plus freedom of speech, the press and demonstration. Fischer foresaw a 'new era in civil liberties for Soviet citizens in which 'dictatorship would yield to democracy'.[67] A new era was certainly on the way.

The confessions were 'too abject to be convincing',[68] mused the journal when the first news of the trials came through, but there was 'no reason to think that torture is now used by the GPU'.[69] Perhaps this was the GPU's last fling before the new constitution curbed its power?[70] There was no doubt about it, the trials were wholly unconvincing, but 'very likely there was a plot'. All in all, there was a great deal amiss'; of the Bolshevik leaders only Stalin now remained, but this did not alter the essential fact that Russia was a country with an 'overwhelming desire for peace'.[71] The Russian revolution with its economic innovations was still the greatest achievement of its generation; the power of the GPU and the Russian bureaucracy was only a secondary consideration. Even after the second round of purges the 'only honest course' for Kingsley Martin was to give general but critical support to the one country which had adopted a planned socialist economy.[72] 'Environment determines consciousness,' said Marx; it was only a matter of time, it was assumed, before new economic realities ameliorated the superstructure of the State. *Tribune*, the journal founded by Cripps and George Strauss, MP, in 1937 was also disturbed, and called for an explanation from the USSR. H. N. Brailsford, an old friend of the Bolsheviks, condemned a 'terror based on lies',[73] *The Daily Herald* spoke of 'judicial methods worthy of Tsarism'[74] and Laski calculated that the trials cost Labour some half a million votes.[75]

The later years of the decade saw several influential intellectuals reassessing their attitudes towards Russia. For a few euphoric years they had discerned in her the successor civilisation to the decaying capitalism of the West. They now realised that Lenin's leap in the dark had left Russia still very much in darkness. The initial idealism of the revolution had been choked by the extension of authoritarian control and the elevation of its chief manipulator, Stalin. Trotsky's claim that Stalin had betrayed the revolution began to receive consideration in the West. André Gide returned from a visit in 1937 sickened by a sycophantic welcome and dilated upon his disappointments in an influential book.[76] Max Eastman, an American ex-communist, pronounced upon the *End of Socialism in Russia*,[77] whilst Arthur Koestler returned from Spain no longer a communist. Stephen Spender also parted company with the party, saying it was impossible to believe that communists or any other party would produce 'dictators, bureaucrats and police who would willingly wither away'.[78] Louis Fischer was privately disillusioned but restrained his public parting, as he still had faith in Soviet foreign policy.[79]

iii

But whilst these distinguished erstwhile pro-Soviet intellectuals were making their rueful journey back from Moscow many more eager young hopefuls were embarking on the first leg of the pilgrimage, attracted by Russia's foreign policy stance and the related United and Popular Front campaigns. The declared aim of the latter, supported chiefly by the leaders of the Socialist League, was to replace the National Government with a coalition which would join Russia in opposing fascism. Collaboration with the CPGB carried the penalty of disaffiliation, and in 1937 the Socialist League preferred to disband rather than deny its members a Labour Party audience. They remained in the party to develop the arguments of their communist friends. They were greatly aided by the Left Book Club, founded in May 1936 by Victor Gollancz. The club regularly supplied its 56,000 members with cheap books chosen by Gollancz, Laski and Strachey, mostly on international affairs and many written by communist authors like Strachey, Palme Dutt, Pat Sloan and Page-Arnot. The bond between the Labour left and the CPGB was never stronger than during these years, and through the LBC and *Tribune* the communists were able to direct much pro-Soviet propaganda into the body of the Labour Party.

Labour and trade union leaders were highly resistant to the United and Popular Front ideas; they feared the electoral consequences and suspected the communists of an ulterior subversive intent. Alliance with Russia against Germany, however, was one element of the Popular Front programme which appealed to the leadership. Just when the conciliatory policies of the Baldwin administration were succeeded by Chamberlain's appeasement the 'realists' of Transport House, Bevin, Dukes and Citrine, together with Hugh Dalton, were beginning to conclude that Hitler could be contained only by a policy involving a clear threat of force. Closer co-operation with Hitler's enemy in the east was increasingly seen by the Labour leadership as a political necessity. Despite their reservations about dictatorship in the USSR and their awareness of its similarities with Hitler's regime, Labour leaders found a brutally imposed economic experiment infinitely less repellent than national aggrandisement and racialism. Munich brought the question to a head.

On the eve of the crisis the National Council of Labour (which contained representatives from the TUC, the NEC and the Parliamentary Labour Party) urged the government to 'leave no doubt in the mind of the German government that they will unite with the French and Soviet governments to resist any attack upon Czechoslovakia'.[80] In reaching the Munich settlement Chamberlain completely ignored Russia, despite the fact that she was both an ally of Czechoslovakia and a member of the League of Nations Council. With some justice Russia could feel that Hitler had been handed the key to the door of Eastern Europe.

The intensity of the European crisis between Munich and the outbreak of war significantly altered Labour Party images of Russia. As foreign affairs became the dominant ingredient in Labour's political thinking, concern with Russia's domestic regime declined. After Munich virtually no criticisms of the Soviet Union appeared in Labour organs of opinion. The emphasis was now squarely on Russian foreign policy, which virtually every section of the party had come to support with passion. In the same way that the intellectuals had perceived a new civilisation evolving in Russia during the dark days of the depression, so, ironically, did the realists of the Labour Party, when faced with the threat of Hitler, perceive a powerful, resolute anti-fascist bulwark of peace. The *Daily Herald* of 21 February 1939 summed up the new attitude: 'It is above all now that the full co-operation of Russia is needed. Russia is both powerful and peaceful. Not even the severest critics of her government could fairly say that her policy threatens or disturbs any nation. Russia is a peace Keeper.' At the Southport Conference the party chairman declared that 'Moscow is the custodian of peace'.[81]

One of the side effects of this new enthusiasm was to resolve the factional dispute over the Popular Front, which had reached a climax in 1939 when Cripps, Bevan and Strauss had been expelled from the party. Cripps and his friends, realising that their hopes of a Popular Front government were futile and irrelevant in the face of Hitler, campaigned outside the Labour Party for direct co-operation with Russia. Ideological conviction and political expedience now combined to intensify their efforts.

The clamour for an alliance grew in volume when, in March 1939, Hitler dropped all pretence and marched into Czechoslovakia. The National Council of Labour reacted immediately by calling for a peace pact with France and Russia to resist further acts of aggression by Germany.[82] Chamberlain now belatedly responded to Soviet overtures and opened up negotiations, but his heart was never really in it. His aim was to maximise potential support from Russia whilst avoiding reciprocal commitment. Consequently the low-ranking delegation he sent to Moscow, at a leisurely sea-borne pace, did not make much headway. The Labour Party was horrified by Chamberlain's dilatory approach.

Throughout the summer of 1939 Labour spokesmen mounted an importunate campaign to extract from Chamberlain the reasons for his procrastination. Left-wingers tended to interpret his half-hearted responses as evidence of a latent ambition to attack Russia in alliance with Germany. In June yet another delegation of the National Council of Labour visited him to emphasise the necessity of speeding up the Moscow talks. Chamberlain revealed that the breakdown of the negotiations would not be the 'end of the world'.[83] For their part Soviet leaders continued to exhort Britain and France to rally to the anti-fascist cause, and anti-Nazi propaganda blared out from Moscow throughout the early weeks of August. It was consequently with some mystification that Labour greeted the news on 21 August that Ribbentrop had been invited to Moscow.

Labour Party members (not to mention those of the Communist Party) must have awaited the outcome of this meeting with a tense admixture of feelings. Despite its recently tarnished domestic image the Soviet Union was, after all, the pioneer of a planned socialist economy, the historic friend of the Labour Party, and the recipient of its benign partisan protection. The Soviet record in foreign policy had been impeccable in terms of support for peace, collective security, opposition to fascism and to the growing threat of Hitler. It was more than the containment of Hitler which hung upon the result of this

30 *The Russia complex*

meeting; also on trial was the Labour Party's faith in Socialist Russia together with its conception of what constituted a socialist foreign policy.

Notes

1 Neal Wood, *Communism and British Intellectuals*, p. 43.
2 Malcolm Muggeridge, *Chronicles of Wasted Time*, Vol. I, p. 244.
3 R. H. S. Crossman, *The God that Failed: Six Studies in Communism*, p. 8.
4 Sonia Orwell and Ian Angus, *The Collected Essays, Journalism and Letters of George Orwell*, Vol. I, p. 512.
5 For the best exposition of his ideas see John St Loe Strachey, *The Theory and Practice of Socialism*.
6 *Ibid.*, pp. 250–6.
7 Members included: R. Mitchison, Charles Trevelyan, William Mellor, H. N. Brailsford, R. H. Tawney, T. Horrabin, D. N. Pritt, George Strauss, Aneurin Bevan, Ellen Wilkinson.
8 B. Kingsley Martin, *Harold Laski, 1893–1950: a Biographical Memoir*, p. 88.
9 Harold J. Laski, 'The possibilities and prospects of communism', *Foreign Affairs*, XI, October 1932, p. 104.
10 H. A. Deane, *The Political Ideas of Harold J. Laski*, p. 218.
11 William Irvine, *The Universe of G.B.S.* (London, 1948), p. 355.
12 R. J. Minney, *The Bogus Image of Bernard Shaw* (London, 1969), p. 141.
13 Eugene Lyons, *Assignment in Utopia* (New York, 1937), p. 429.
14 *The Times*, 6 August 1931. Also of interest, his letter to *The Times*, 13 August 1931.
15 *Prefaces by Bernard Shaw* (London, 1934), p. 361.
16 *Ibid.*, p. 359.
17 St John Irvine, *Bernard Shaw: his Life, Work and Friends* (London, 1972).
18 Minney, p. 143.
19 Margaret Cole (ed), *The Diaries of Beatrice Webb, 1912–24*, p. 106.
20 Margaret Cole (ed), *The Diaries of Beatrice Webb, 1924–32*; see also David Caute, *The Fellow Travellers*, pp. 78–83.
21 *Diaries, 1924–32*, p. 257.
22 *Ibid.*, p. 298.
23 Sidney and Beatrice Webb, *Soviet Communism: a New Civilisation*, pp. 69 and 41.
24 C. E. M. Joad, *N.S. and N*, 8 February 1936, and A. J. P. Taylor, *English History, 1914–45*, p. 348n.
25 *Soviet Communism*, pp. 574 and 581.
26 *Ibid.*, p. 563.
27 *Ibid.*, p. 1042.
28 *Ibid.*, pp. 588 and 594.
29 *Ibid.*, p. 591.
30 Robert Conquest, *The Red Terror: Stalin's Purge of the Thirties*, p. 25.
31 *Soviet Communism*, p. 594.
32 *Ibid.*, p. 438.
33 *Ibid.*, pp. 438–40.

34 *Ibid.*, p. 827.
35 *Ibid.*, pp. 1202–5.
36 *Ibid.*, p. 1211.
37 Conquest, p. 86.
38 *Soviet Communism*, p. 101.
39 *Ibid.*, pp. 1152–62.
40 *Ibid.*, p. 1153.
41 Interview with Margaret Cole.
42 Malcolm Muggeridge, *Chronicles of Wasted Time*, Vol. I, p. 206.
43 Beatrice and Sidney Webb, *A Constitution for a Socialist Commonwealth of Great Britain* (London, 1920).
44 *Diaries, 1924–1932*, p. 298.
45 *Ibid.*, p. 305.
46 *Soviet Communism*, p. 1116.
47 Claud Cockburn, *I Claud*, p. 263.
48 *Ibid.*, p. 357.
49 Malcolm Muggeridge, *Winter in Moscow* (London, 1934), p. 47.
50 *Ibid.*, p. 234.
51 Kitty Muggeridge and Ruth Adam, *Beatrice Webb: a Life, 1858–1943* (London, 1967), p. 243.
52 Michael R. Gordon, *Conflict and Consensus in Labour's Foreign Policy, 1914–1965*, p. 30.
53 Interview with Ernest Ferryhough, MP.
54 Walter Citrine, *I Search for Truth in Russia*, pp. 306–12.
55 Allan Bullock, *The Life and Times of Ernest Bevin (1881–1940)*, p. 507.
56 Sonia Orwell and Ian Angus, vol. I, p. 272.
57 *Ibid.*, pp. 281 and 288.
58 *Ibid.*, p. 373.
59 *Ibid.*, p. 583.
60 G. D. H. Cole, *A History of Socialist Thought*, Vol. V. ˙Socialism and Fascism, 1931–1939*, p. 252.
61 Muggeridge, vol. I, p. 262.
62 Letter to *News Chronicle*, 26 August 1936.
63 Interview with D. N. Pritt in 1968. He still apparently believed the trials were valid.
64 *N.S. and N.*, 29 February 1936.
65 *Ibid.*, 7 March 1936.
66 *Ibid.*, 22 February 1936.
67 *Ibid.*, 1 August 1936.
68 *Ibid.*, 22 August 1936.
69 *Ibid.*, 12 September 1936.
70 *Ibid.*, 22 August 1936.
71 *Ibid.*, 5 September 1936.
72 *Ibid.*, 6 November 1937.
73 *Tribune*, 17 July 1937.
74 *Daily Herald*, 25 August 1936.
75 *LPCR 1937*, p. 161.
76 André Gide, *Back from the USSR* (London, 1937).

77 Max Eastman, *The End of Socialism in Russia* (London, 1937).
78 R. H. S. Crossman, *The God that Failed*, p. 266.
79 *Ibid.*, p. 223; see also his article "Russia's new expansion" in *Reynolds' News*, 1 October 1939.
80 *Daily Herald*, 22 March 1938.
81 *LPCR 1938*, p. 215.
82 *Daily Herald*, 22 March 1938.
83 Dalton, Diaries, 28 January 1939.

3 Collapse of an image: the pact, Poland and the attack on Finland

> The Union of Soviet Socialist Republics is dead. Stalin's new imperialist Russia takes its place. [*Daily Herald*, 1 December 1939]

Never an enthusiast for an Anglo-Soviet alliance, Chamberlain could only appear unperturbed when it passed finally out of his reach. The British guarantee to Poland was formally endorsed on 25 August, but behind the scenes he was pressing Poland to make concessions to Hitler. Hitler invaded on 1 September. Reluctantly shuffling behind the mood of Parliament, Chamberlain announced on 3 September that a state of war now existed between Britain and Germany.

On 17 September Russia invaded Poland's eastern territories, proving that the agreement of the previous month had provided for Russian collusion as well as 'neutrality' in the German attack upon Poland. By 22 September Poland was once more effectively partitioned by her historic enemies, the Russian boundaries being drawn to coincide roughly with the Curzon line of 1920. A week later Russia joined Germany in offering the West peace terms based upon this *fait accompli*, warning that rejection of them would involve responsibility for the continuance of an 'imperialist' war.

Within a month Russia had dramatically reversed her policies of diplomatic and ideological opposition to Hitler and had adopted a species of appeasement which made Chamberlain's efforts seem primitive. British hopes of denying Germany essential war supplies through naval blockade were torpedoed by reports that Russia had undertaken to supply Germany with oil, wheat and iron ore. Her neutrality thus operated strongly against Britain's war effort.

The worst was yet to come, for Stalin now appeared to join Hitler in carving up Eastern Europe. On 30 November when Finland refused to cede certain territories, the Red Army invaded Finland. An ex-Comintern official, Otto Kuusinen, was established as the head of a provisional workers' government which Russia acclaimed as the only legitimate government of Finland. Her intervention was ostensibly to free Finnish workers from an oppressive capitalism which was planning, in collaboration with Western capitalist imperialists, to attack and destroy the home of socialism.

Finland, however, offered stout resistance and repelled the massive but inept Russian attacks. The War Cabinet considered sending an expeditionary force to relieve the embattled Finns.[1] Had this initiative come to pass, Britain would have been at war with Russia and a firm military alliance would have been forced out of the dubious diplomatic understanding which then existed between Stalin and Hitler. Finnish resistance collapsed on 13 March, when an armistice was signed. The impact of these events upon Labour images of Russia was immense.

i

For Labour and trade union leaders, co-operation with Russia had become the corner-stone of their faith in collective security against Hitler. On the very eve of the Nazi-Soviet pact the *Daily Herald* declared that there should be 'an immediate attempt to speed up the negotiations, both political and military, with Russia'.[2] The *Herald*'s wise and experienced diplomatic correspondent, W. N. Ewer, had detected a chilly breeze when the pro-Western Jewish Litvinov had been replaced by the austere, unbending Molotov, but the news of the pact shocked him greatly.[3] On 2 September his paper's editorial grimly reviewed the extent of the betrayal.

At the critical junction she has left the line. She chooses to make friends with aggressive Nazism. It is her affair. We fight without her. But we shall not forget.

Seeking an explanation, Greenwood and Dalton visited Maisky at the Russian embassy. Maisky, who, according to Dalton, seemed himself bewildered by this development, assured them both that all Soviet non-aggression pacts contained an escape clause in the event of aggression by either party against a third — an assurance shortly to be disproved. One of Maisky's aides sourly explained that his government had taken this step 'in order to teach your government and the French a lesson'.[4]

The Trades Union Conference meeting at Bridlington on the day before war was declared reflected feelings of bitter reproach. Citrine delivered a scathing indictment of the USSR. Several speakers from the floor offered a defence, one rhetorically asking whether it was 'likely that a government of

Collapse of an image 35

working people could throw in its forces on the other side of world imperialism?'.[5] Citrine's reply suggested a certain relish in being able at last to speak his mind. The apologists for the Soviet Union had blinded themselves for years, he declared. 'They have seen a dictatorship in Russia as severe and cruel as anything that has happened in Germany.' Had Russia acted through fear of being double-crossed by the West? Citrine ridiculed the morality of a pre-emptive stab in the back and asserted that Russian action had 'precipitated this war'.[6]

The Soviet invasion of Poland called down more anathema from the right and centre of the party. The *Daily Herald* diagnosed 'naked territorial gain' in Soviet foreign policy.[7] Arthur Greenwood compared the pretext for the attack with Hitler's 'monstrous outrages'.[8] The pact of a few weeks before was now widely regarded as a simple carve-up between two imperialist powers. The trade unionist MP David Grenfell declared that Russia had 'kicked Poland when she was prostrate and shook hands with the aggressor'.[9]

Dalton was less concerned with Russia's eastern slice of Poland as long as the latter could receive, after the war, some territorial compensation in the west. As a hard-headed foreign affairs specialist he was more concerned lest 'high pique' should affect the handling of Russian relations. Visiting Butler at the Foreign Office, he received assurances that this would not be the case. Nevertheless Dalton emphasised to Eden (then at the Dominions Office) the need to send a 'high personage' to Moscow to pre-empt any further hardening of Soviet-German friendship. Eden was not convinced of the wisdom of such a course.[10]

On 5 October a photograph in the *Daily Herald* of Stalin and Ribbentrop joking together tended to harden Labour suspicions that Germany and Russia had joined hands against the Western democracies. Gone now was any tendency for the Labour right and centre groupings to defend Soviet action from Tory attacks; rather their condemnations tended to be even more bitter in reaction to the betrayal of trust. The erosion of the favourable Soviet image, well under way in the right and centre by the time of the Moscow trials, arrested temporarily by events in Spain and the need to ally with Russia against Hitler, had proceeded at a dramatic pace. Dalton privately reflected that the Russians had long since parted company with anything that could be called communism. They had become first nationalists and now, after Poland, imperialists. Whilst appreciating that British and French diplomacy had mishandled Russia he had no illusions about Soviet diplomacy: 'They are double-crossers by nature.'[11] This conclusion was widely shared within the Labour Party, and yet the *Daily Herald* could hardly believe on 30 November that Russia, as it was rumoured at the time, could invade Finland. 'If such an attack were actually delivered on her tiny neighbour,' ran the editorial, 'it would be as glaring and inexcusable a crime as Hitler's invasion of Czechoslovakia and Poland.'

When invasion duly followed the next day the *Herald*'s editorial read:

Now finally Stalin's Russia sacrifices all claim to the affection and respect of the world-wide working class movement which Lenin's USSR had as a right ... The Union of Soviet Socialist Republics is dead. Stalin's new imperialist Russia takes its place.[12]

The virulence of the rebuke marked a severance of the umbilical cord of socialism which had formerly connected the right and centre to Russia. The *Daily Herald*'s image of the Soviet Union now tended to be that of a huge, bleak totalitarian State led by a cynical dictator. W. N. Ewer, for example, could liken Stalin to the modern Genghis Khan: a great Asiatic imperial chieftain with ambitions to avenge Europe's conquest of Asia.[13]

The National Council of Labour reacted with 'profound horror and indignation. In the House of Commons Dalton spoke of an 'indefensible' act of aggression. Finland's prolonged and gallant defensive action, at a time when no other hostilities were taking place, focused full attention on Russia's unheroic role. All the national dailies carried stories and pictures of Russian urban bombing, at that time regarded as an atrocity. Feeling against Russia intensified. In mid-December *Daily Worker* attacks on certain trade union leaders — Conley, Citrine, Hicks, Kaylor, Hancock and J. Brown — were met with libel actions rather than the usual indifference. The courts decided that the articles had been deliberately written with bias and inaccuracy for the purpose of casting discredit upon trade union members. The judge commented that the libel had been 'inspired from abroad'.[14]

Responding to a joint invitation from the Finnish TUC and Social Democratic Party a Labour Party delegation, comprising Philip Noel Baker, J. Downie and Citrine, left for Finland on 26 January 1940. The visitors examined the widespread damage caused by Russian air attacks and were greatly impressed by Finnish defensive efforts. They returned to urge that more military aid should be sent.[15] Yet despite their intense sympathy the delegation 'indignantly' denied in its official report that Britain should physically enter the war on the side of Finland. 'In our view,' it emphasised, 'war between this country and Russia would be a grave misfortune.'[16]

Stalin was now firmly established in Labour minds as Hitler's accomplice: the Labour Party actually published a pamphlet entitled *Finland: the Criminal Conspiracy of Stalin and Hitler*. Yet whilst urging the greatest possible support for the Finns[17] the Labour leaders, in common with the report of the Finnish delegation, did not lend their voices to any demand for the 'spreading of the war', as plans to open hostilities with Russia were euphemistically described at this time. It should be emphasised, however, that it was a realistic appreciation of Britain's war potential and not sympathy with the Soviet Union which led them to oppose such a course of action.

The ILP, the party with the worst record for political effectiveness during the 'thirties, at least salvaged over these months the consolation of having the most consistent attitude towards Hitler, the war and the Soviet Union. The ILP's attitude towards Russia had already been determined by the Moscow Trials and by communist actions in Spain, so that Soviet foreign policy in the autumn and winter of 1939 merely confirmed its suspicions and increased its conviction that Russia had ceased to be a friend of the working classes. Short of rank-and-file membership, the ILP concentrated its efforts in Parliament, where its spokesmen took colourful but unco-ordinated lines. One of its members, John McGovern, hated Hitler and Stalin with equal venom; on 24 August he condemned the 'bloodstained handshake of Stalin and Ribbentrop'.[18]

The ILP was passionately opposed to the war, Maxton urging Chamberlain on the eve of hostilities that even 'war postponed is something gained'.[19] The ILP had applauded Munich and Chamberlain's policy of appeasement, but its support of Chamberlain ceased once the war with Hilter had been enjoined.[20] McGovern viewed it as a 'grinding materialist struggle for human gain',[21] no different from the first world war. ILP-ers continued to call hopefully for spontaneous revolution to overthrow capitalism, thus keeping alive the spirit of the Second International nearly three decades after its demise. The ILP's ideological approach was not devoid of insight. Its analysis of Russian foreign policy as cynical expansionism anticipated Soviet behaviour both in the early and later phases of the war. Its opposition intensified after the attack on Finland, but the threat of British involvement in a war against Russia elicited a revealing response. The ILP declared that it would 'resist war with Russia to the last ounce of our strength. Many of the achievements of the October Revolution remain in Russia despite Stalinism and we shall certainly not line up with British capitalism to destroy them.'[22]

The ILP and the CPGB found themselves in a strange position in the early years of the war. The former United Front colleagues together provided the principal opposition to the war, both labelling it as 'imperialist' and both lending their efforts to bring it to an end. They were no less energetic, however, in indulging in the most virulent of mutual denunciations. The source of their animosity, of course, lay in their respective attitudes to Stalin's regime.

Stalin himself sorely tried communist faith in these months. In August J. R.

Campbell (editor of the *Daily Worker*) had described the idea of a pact between Stalin and Hitler as a 'vile slander'.[23] Yet when the pact was announced the paper hailed it as a 'master stroke of Soviet peace policy', as a humiliating defeat of Germany's anti-Comintern policy, as a recognition of the Soviet Union's formidable strength and 'as a victory for peace and socialism against the war of fascism and the pro-fascist policy of Chamberlain'.

British communists refused to believe that the situation had been essentially changed. 'Now is the time and the hour,' the *Daily Worker* exhorted, 'to develop the mass movement for the immediate signing of the Anglo-Soviet Pact.'[24] In Parliament Gallacher underlined the increased necessity for such a pact and blandly assured the House that 'any attack on France by Germany would immediately bring the Franco-Soviet Pact into operation'.[25] Pollitt added to this argument, 'there is nothing incompatible between promising not to attack a man and promising to help another man if he is attacked'.[26] 'Now that the war has come,' declared the editorial of the *Daily Worker* on 4 September, "we have no hesitation in stating the policy of the Communist Party. We are in support of all necessary measures to secure the victory of democracy over fascism.' The Soviet invasion of Poland the paper billed as a pre-emptive counter-blow against the Nazis, but the joint Soviet-German agreements over Poland reversed the situation and threw the Communist Party into confusion.

The Kremlin decreed that those countries which continued to fight would expose their aims as imperialistic. The *Daily Worker* understood the riddle; it duly changed its tune. Britain, according to the Communists, was now concerned 'not to rescue Europe from fascism, but to impose British imperialist peace upon Germany' before fomenting war against the Soviet Union.[27] On 5 October the CPGB called for negotiations to end the war.

This *volte-face* is arguably the most important event in the history of the CPGB — in the short term inaugurating a period of intense political discomfort and in the long term irrevocably destroying the party's chance of mass support through association with the Labour Party. Those leaders who had championed the anti-fascist war now stood down. Pollitt, who had actually written a pamphlet in support of the war, was replaced by Palme Dutt as secretary of the party and William Rust, a man whose 'thoughts were moulded almost completely by Moscow',[28] took over from Campbell as editor of the party newspaper. Arthur Horner, the miners' leader, refused to believe that the defeat of fascism was not now the foremost aim of communism. However, he later joined Pollitt and Campbell in refuting their 'mistaken' analyses.[29]

For the majority of the Central Committee of the CPGB allegiance to Moscow exceeded the appeals of logic and patriotism. J. B. S. Haldane even managed to describe Soviet foreign policy as 'fantastically consistent'.[30] The CPGB had been thrown back upon the bedrock of its faith and its organisation had been seriously shaken. Yet the illusion of unity still had to be maintained. Gallacher declared to readers of the *Daily Worker* that 'talk of splits in the Party is without foundation, the Party is united on policy'.[31] In Parliament, not for the first time, he was given an extremely rough passage, particularly by the ILP's John McGovern, but Gallacher steadfastly maintained that Britain's final objective was an imperialist attack upon the worker's government of the USSR.

The CPGB developed this theme with mounting conviction as Russia attempted to intimidate Finland. Here, alleged the communists, was the vital 'jumping-off base'[32] for 'Butcher Mannerheim and his masters Chamberlain and Daladier'.[33] Yet even allowing for Finland's aggressive intent, were Soviet demands unreasonable? The *Daily Worker* comfortably asserted that the loss of one naval base and a few miles of territory was unlikely to make the Finnish position any worse.[34]

For the CPGB the decisive turning point was the Soviet-German arrangement over Poland. Once this had been assimilated, the attack on Finland was accepted without much apparent difficulty. An interesting deviation appeared, however, in the views of Hewlett Johnson, at that time one of Britain's most prominent champions of Russia, his book *The Socialist Sixth of the World*, published in November 1939, having made a considerable impact. On 16 December a letter from the Red Dean was published in the *New Statesman*, describing the actions of the USSR as indefensible and 'bitterly regretted by her warmest friends. No honest man believes that the Soviet Government acted because Soviet soldiers had been attacked by the Finns and that the Finns had appealed for help against their own government.' This public attack from a future member of the *Daily Worker* Board is quite unique. Significantly no mention of it appears in Hewlett Johnson's autobiography.[35]

As if in reply, a letter from Archibald Robertson appeared two weeks later, which expressed precisely the total commitment which communists made to the Kremlin leadership:

We support the war [against Finland] because we consider that the future of socialism depends first and foremost on the success and prestige of Soviet Russia. The USSR is the embodiment of socialism in action while the West has so far exhibited only socialism in talk. Whatever therefore advances the power of the Soviet Union advances socialism.[36]

It is significant that Russia's actions now required such a frank and all-inclusive endorsement, stripped as it was of any lip service to the Comintern, to international law or to any other pretext.

For the next eighteen months the CPGB faithfully pursued its anti-war policy, at one stage exhibiting an almost 'perverted' political enthusiasm for rubbing shoulders with the political creed it had formerly opposed so vehemently. Following an article by Walter Ulbricht, the German communist, in *Die Welt*, the party veered suspiciously close to direct support of Hitler.[37] Ulbricht had stated that 'Those who intrigue against the friendship of the German and Soviet people are enemies of the German people and are branded as accomplices of British imperialism'. The *Daily Worker*, although not openly supporting Hitler, now apparently banished from its pages any critical comment on Germany. In France communist opposition to the war became a contributory factor to the rapid collapse of French resistance; in Britain communism was too weak and action by the Labour Party too prompt for the CPGB to exert any comparable influence.

As its erstwhile friends on the left began to melt away the CPGB responded by attacking former comrades. An article in the *Daily Worker* on 6 December reflected this mood of good-riddance. Kingsley Martin, W. N. Ewer, Vernon Bartlett, Fenner Brockway and H. N. Brailsford were critically singled out as people who had been 'always anti-Soviet'. For the communist it was not enough to declare support for the Soviet Union with qualifications; public commitment had to be unequivocal and one hundred per cent. To publicise one's reservations was regarded as the weak indulgence of a liberal conscience, not the action of the 'true' Marxist. According to this yardstick Martin and company had long ago fallen by the Marxist wayside, and the break over Finland enabled communists to express the contempt they had always felt.

The Popular Front alliance between communists and left-wing intellectuals was beginning to fracture. Loyal communists closed their eyes and ears to all but the Moscow's interpretation of events. Within Labour's left wing, determined fellow-travellers began to sort themselves out from those Popular Fronters who were dismayed by Soviet behaviour and who chose to travel with the body of the Labour Party. D.N. Pritt and H. N. Brailsford were fairly representative of these two groups, and a comparison of their thinking throws some light upon that of their respective alignments.

ii

Brailsford had never been 'anti-Soviet'. Although his criticisms of Bolshevik illiberalism were frank, his sympathy during the inter-war years remained strong; he lent his support to the Popular Front campaign. On 26 August he analysed the Nazi-Soviet pact.³⁸ He could see that much blame lay with France and Great Britain throughout this period, but their 'crime' had been to pursue half-heartedly an alliance which would prevent war, whereas Stalin's action had virtually invited Hitler to invade Poland. Furthermore the trade agreement would nullify the threat of a British blockade. 'Europe,' he concluded, 'had become a finishing school for cynics. Munich was the kindergarten; Moscow is the graduates' class.' Following Russia's invasion of Poland, Brailsford concluded that Stalin's policy of neutrality merely masked a policy of national aggrandisement, but he cautioned against the premature assumption that Russia was the fast friend of Germany. The government's best course would be to cultivate a 'friendly' neutrality by withholding public judgement of Russian actions, by sending Eden to Moscow, by accepting the Curzon line as Russia's western boundary and by attempting to negotiate a trade agreement.³⁹ He was less sure of this analysis after the Soviet-German agreement of 29 September.

The USSR he once knew, even as a potential ally for Britain's war against Germany, had become unrecognisable. Brailsford now seemed to invest an almost hysterical importance in India. By granting independence, Brailsford believed, Britain could provide the proof of her commitment to freedom, thus encouraging the masses to rise against their tyrannical rulers. In this way, Brailsford seemed to believe, Britain could win the war.

Brailsford's reaction to the Finnish attack revealed how socialists extended attitudes on Soviet foreign policy to make judgements upon the character of the regime itself. Stalin's unprovoked attack upon Finland, he now judged, had 'compelled us to pass the judgement we had hitherto refused to register. His Russia is a totalitarian State, like another, as brutal towards the rights of others, as careless of its plighted word'. However, the attack on Finland paradoxically suggested that German-Soviet unity was not as strong as he had formerly supposed. Stalin was obviously frightened of Germany and sought greater security by his invasion of Finland. Brailsford reminded his readers that the breaking of Nazi power was the only justification of the war. Talk of a Holy War against Russia was dangerous. It would be folly to turn a doubtful friend of Hitler into a 'decided and belligerent ally'. Furthermore it would be dangerous to ask the workers of Europe to supply arms against Russia, where, for the first time in history, private property had been ended and the foundations of a classless society laid: 'bid them march against Russia and you will arouse in some bewilderment, in others revolt'.⁴⁰

Dennis Noel Pritt, KC, had always been an enigma even to some of his closest colleagues. Whereas advancing years encouraged a more cautious and pragmatic attitude in most of his contemporaries, Pritt moved ever leftwards. In the autumn of 1939 he was foremost among those of the Russophile left who remained to be counted with the communists. A brilliant lawyer, he had been considered in 1930 for Solicitor General in the Labour government. His subsequent career made him something of a left-wing equivalent of Oswald Mosley. A visit to the Soviet Union in 1932 seems to have impressed him greatly. He wrote that he returned to Britain with a 'big jolt forward in my political thought'.[41] Elected in 1935 for Hammersmith North, he quickly made an impact, becoming successively a member of the PLP executive and of the NEC. He formed part of the militant left wing of these committees, being a passionate advocate of co-operation with Russia. The decisive moment arrived in August 1939. 'I was shocked when I first heard it,' he recalls, 'but within a few hours I soon realised what it meant.'[42] The West had been trying to settle with Germany, he believed, whilst ostensibly negotiating with the USSR. Stalin had merely jumped in first and pre-empted an Anglo-Franco-German attack on his country. Far from stabbing Poland in the back, Stalin's subsequent occupation of that country had saved her from falling completely under Nazi rule.

In October Pritt produced, very rapidly, a Penguin Special entitled *Light on Moscow* which so flagrantly vindicated Soviet behaviour that, in the atmosphere of the time, his publishers refused to accept the manuscript without alterations, and a legal dispute ensued, settled eventually in Pritt's favour.[43] Following the Finnish war another Penguin by Pritt entitled *Must the War Spread?* was a similar duplication of the communist approach.

The Labour Party Executive was in no mood to accept such a maverick attitude in wartime and felt strongly enough to expel him from its midst.[44] Pritt claimed that the real reason was not his views on Finland, which he had a constitutional right to express (no Conference decision having been taken), but his left-wing socialist point of view, which the right-wingers on the NEC found intolerable. Defending the Executive's decision at the 1940 Conference, Philip Noel Baker allowed that Pritt's intentions were to promote a better understanding between Britain and Russia, but he claimed that all Pritt's efforts had been designed to 'vilify the government of Finland and defend the Soviet attack'.[45]

Admiration for Russia first led Pritt in the direction of communism, and his continued loyalty to Russia finally robbed him of his political future in the Labour Party. He now became, in the words of a Labour MP, 'the amateur champion of communist propagandists',[46] finally finding a focus for his redoubtable energies in the People's Convention Movement.

Compared with Brailsford, he was an innocent in politics.[47] Brailsford applied his socialist analysis with the sophistication of forty years' scrutiny of international relations. Unlike Pritt, he displayed an acute awareness of the political dynamics behind the verbiage of politics. His analysis of the defensive motive behind Stalin's Finnish attack was shrewd, and his firm opposition to war with Russia sensible. Pritt, on the other hand, was essentially a lawyer in politics, the free services of whom the USSR was indeed fortunate to retain. Like all good advocates he handled his brief with great ability, but unlike other good advocates he appeared genuinely to believe his own rhetoric. Brailsford's analysis was wholly his own; Pritt's was a dull repetition of the official communist line, displaying clearly that his judgement had been surrendered to that of the Soviet leaders. Brailsford's views were not without influence on the left; Pritt's were treated with scant respect; Dalton described him as 'of little account ... a lightweight in the party'.[48] It is significant that Pritt claimed to have reached his conclusions independently; their perfect congruence with the communist line was apparently a 'coincidence'. He was always quick to point out that he had never been a member of the Communist Party.[49]

That a man of such evident intellectual distinction could reach such naive judgements upon such scanty evidence raises once again the general question of why communists and certain of their sympathisers within the Labour Party followed the Moscow line with such unswerving fidelity.

iii

In mid-September 1939, according to Claud Cockburn, at that time close to the inner counsels of the CPGB, there was great dismay when the news of the 'anti-war' line was received over the telephone from Dimitrov.[50] But the prestige of the hero of the Reichstag fire trial proved decisive. 'No one can have any notion', wrote Cockburn, 'of what Dimitrov was to us in the way of a symbol, a flame in the darkness.'[51] Yet loyalty to individual leaders is only part of the answer; for a fuller explanation one has to look at the overall political and social contexts within which communist beliefs are formed.

Initially shifts in the party line might cause a communist some disquiet, but the effectiveness of his party work, the comradeship of his colleagues, encourage him to find reasons for accepting the new policy. Official explanations, however thin, gain credence when the alternative to acceptance might involve the loss, for the communist, of any purpose in life. The first suppression of doubt may be difficult, but the next time it is easier, until the point is reached where acceptance becomes virtually automatic. A nucleus of belief has been formed at the centre of the communists' political attitudes which is now impregnable to all but the most serious of assaults. Charlotte Haldane, at this time a communist, later wrote that in defence of his way of life and certainty of his convictions a communist learns to 'believe lies in his own soul'.[52] Orwell, of course, in *Nineteen Eighty Four*, suggested that the ultimate development of this tendency is a state of 'double-think', when a proposition and its converse can be accepted simultaneously without difficulty.[53] Few, if any, would fall into this paradigm category, but all communists were a prey to the rationalisation process, and those on the left who collaborated closely with them, particularly in the Popular Front campaign, were to some degree similarly affected.[54]

The news of the Nazi-Soviet pact did not explode with the same damaging force within the left wing of the Labour Party as it had within the party proper. *Tribune* duplicated the communist line on the pact, presenting it as the outcome of Chamberlain's procrastination and as a 'great reinforcement for peace in Eastern Europe'.[55] The *New Statesman* followed suit, agreeing that alliance with Russia was still not only possible but now even more necessary.[56] In Parliament Ellen Wilkinson pointed out that in recognising Soviet strength, and reaching an agreement, Hitler had been forced to 'swallow all his bile' about Russia. In the light of the past British attitudes towards her, Russia had no moral obligation to save the British Empire.[57] Blaming Chamberlain for this new situation, Aneurin Bevan urged continuing efforts to reach an agreement with Russia.[58]

The vessel of the Popular Front, therefore, survived the storm, but one or two leaks had appeared which were to prove fatal. The *New Statesman*, which, if it reflected communist policies, had never adopted their propagandist style, was quite prepared to describe Stalin's action as a 'double-cross', and did not, like *Tribune*, echo communist claims that Chamberlain had been planning with Hitler to attack the Soviet Union.[59]

The underlying differences in perception between the editors of the two journals become more apparent on the eve of the war. *Tribune* regarded this 'masterstroke of diplomacy' as the signal for a nation-wide effort to turn out the 'double-dealing Chamberlain gang' and to co-operate with the only country which would not give a free hand to German aggression.[60] The editors dissociated themselves from Zilliacus's expressed regret, published in *Tribune*, that the Soviet Union had not waited a little longer for an agreement with the Western democracies.[61] In contrast Kingsley Martin revealed at this point that he had long regarded Stalin as the 'astute and unscrupulous ruler of a great nation whose help we needed'. He saw the pact as an attempt to protect purely national Soviet interests.[62]

Following Russia's invasion of Poland, Cripps produced a line of defence worthy of any communist rationalisation. Stalin, he asserted, realising that war was inevitable, had signed the pact to preserve his immediate safety. Once Hitler had invaded Poland, then Stalin had no choice but to take pre-emptive action in the East. Cripps reiterated the basic tenet of Popular Front thinking on Russia: 'Russian policy is the continued development of socialist power in Russia'.[63] Yet this new development caused fissures to widen within the

Popular Front alliance. There now existed a considerable gulf between those who, like Zilliacus, Cripps and George Bernard Shaw,[64] believed that Stalin had stepped in to check further German aggression, and those like Maurice Edelman who were in no doubt that the 'dearly beloved leader of the working class — Comrade Stalin — made a non-aggression pact with party comrade Hitler to partition Poland'.[65] Vernon Bartlett, whose election to the House on a Popular Front ticket had been a great triumph for the left, now confessed that he found it difficult to accept the moral excuses put forward by the Soviet government for the invasion of Poland.[66] The highly respected American journalist Louis Fischer now made public his criticisms of Russia. Fischer, an ex-communist, had long before realised that socialism had been crushed and perverted in Russia, but now he parted company with the remnants of his confidence in Russia:

As long as the Soviet government behaved like a sincere advocate of world peace and helped the victims of fascist aggression, I was willing to moderate my criticisms of its deeds. But now the Russians have made a deal with Hitler. Now I am afraid Russia has set out on the road to Pan-Slavic expansion.[67]

Following this new development the *New Statesman* for the time being steered a middle course between the newly disenchanted and the still communist-oriented left. The journal raised no real objection to Russia's slice of Poland (most of which Poland had seized twenty years before from Russia) and censured the *Times* for attacking the Soviet Union at a time when a friendly attitude was vital. On the other hand Russia bore the responsibility for (in Citrine's phrase) 'precipitating the war'. Kingsley Martin noted the demise of left-wing belief in Stalin's infallibility and took some pleasure in the discomfiture of those 'arrogant and unctuous pundits' who had helped propagate the myth.[68] That this discomfiture was keenly felt is supported by the (unverified) rumour recorded in the Glasgow pacifist weekly *Forward* that following these events a prominent member of the Left Book Club had cut his throat![69]

Up to this point all elements of the Labour and non-Labour left, except for the ILP and certain pacifists, had expressed strong support for the war, but the offer of peace terms by Germany and Russia threw their loyalties into turmoil. Their confusion was accompanied by a desperate investment of hope in utopian remedies. Home rule for India,[70] world federation,[71] a resuscitated League of Nations,[72] universal disarmament, and world peace conferences[73] were all rediscovered, embellished, elaborated and presented both as the only alternative to war with Hitler and as tentative counter-proposals to Hitler's sinister offer of 'peace'. The Labour left did not follow the communist line of openly calling for an end to war; they did not even agree, at first, that it was an imperialist conflict, but they were responsive to suggestions that Hitler's proposals should be considered, and they opposed precipitate rejection. In this confused situation Lloyd George's recommendation in the House of Commons on 3 October that peace proposals should be considered seriously was eagerly taken up and echoed on the left. In the same debate left-winger George Buchanan retraced Lloyd George's argument, adding (amid scornful laughter) that if the 'Russians were prepared to trust the Germans then why not us?'[74] The *New Statesman* pleaded for a 'cool assessment'[75] of Hitler's offer, endorsing Lloyd George's plan for a secret session of Parliament. Stafford Cripps advised *Tribune* readers on 6 October, 'Don't turn down the peace offer,' but he did not favour anything as simple as acceptance. Instead he believed his own personal programme should be presented as a counter-offer. This entailed the ending of imperialism and the substitution of some kind of international authority which could organise the resources of the world. Cripps's perceptions of the Soviet Union, however, were clearly changing; he was now concerned to argue that the implementation of his plan would help 'detach the Soviet Union from the line-up of our potential enemies'.

George Bernard Shaw was less wary of Hitler's proposals. 'Our business now,' he believed, 'is to make peace with him and all the world instead of making more mischief and ruining our people in the process.'[76] *Tribune's* editor, furthermore, was writing at this time of this 'widespread demand for peace'.[77]

The paradoxes of left-wing arguments were pithily and memorably summarised by J. M. Keynes in a letter to the *New Statesman* which deserves to be quoted in full

The Intelligensia of the left were loudest in demanding that the Nazi aggression should be resisted at all costs. When it comes to a showdown, scarce four weeks have passed before they remember that they are all pacifists and write defeatist letters to your column, leaving the defence of freedom and civilisation to Colonel Blimp and the Old School Tie, for whom Three Cheers.[78]

The following week, by way of reply, Michael Stewart, the future Foreign Secretary but at that time a mere prospective candidate, pointed out that many Labour supporters had not allowed their 'nerve to fail'. Orwell was similarly scathing of those who were the 'most anti-fascist between 1935–39' and the 'most defeatist now'. He upbraided the British left-wing intelligentisia for being irresponsible, emotionally shallow and unpatriotic.[79] The confusion on the left was due in reality to a frenetic inner conflict of pacifism, patriotism

Collapse of an image 47

and ideology which the behaviour of the Soviet Union had done much to precipitate. Here was an opportunity to end the war, endorsed by the country which until recently the left had regarded as the sole repository of socialist wisdom. Refusal of these terms, Russia had warned, would expose the imperialist nature of Western capitalism. Such an appeal was bound to provoke some response from a political group long accustomed to regard war as the expression of imperialist economic forces. Finland resolved these conflicts.

Despite wide disagreements among former supporters of the Popular Front there had been a real attempt to understand and explain Soviet conduct. The Left Book Club had not protested openly at Soviet actions, and John Strachey had accepted the Russian rationale of her invasion of Poland. On the eve of the attack Cripps managed to produce enough good reasons to acquit Soviet foreign policy was 'no more exalted'[81] than national aggrandisement and for blaming Russia in the situation into which she has been driven by the capitalist governments of the world, for taking every step that she can to strengthen her position.'[80] But the attack upon Finland destroyed the bridge between the Labour left and the Communist Party, revealing to both sides the gulf that in reality had always separated them.

The *New Statesman* even before the attack had concluded that Russia's foreign policy was "no more exalted"[81] than national aggrandisement and security, yet in the light of Russia's maltreatment by the West the journal had tended to condone this *raison d'état* policy as legitimate. The attack upon Finland, however, massively overdrew the credit the *New Statesman* had been prepared to allow. Russian pretexts for invasion were dismissed as pathetic fabrications. 'The flagrant contradiction between Stalin's present aggression and his former pretensions' cleared away an 'incubus of wishful thought' for the *New Statesman*.[82] The collapse of faith in her foreign policy tended to direct attention to Russia's domestic regime. She was now seen to represent, along with Germany and Japan, a 'new totalitarian idea', a grouping hostile to both democracy and socialism, yet the editor still retained a vague feeling that in the last resort the USSR would be the enemy of fascism.[83]

The attack was sufficiently unambiguous, therefore, to disabuse the Labour left of the notion that Stalin's foreign policy was unaffected by narrow national considerations. For Cripps and his lieutenants, Bevan and Strauss, this was a decisive moment. Cripps had needed some agility to preserve intact his image of Russia throughout this difficult period, but the Finnish attack compounded all his doubts and made an open breach with the communists inevitable.

The *Tribune* Board, along with 'Vigilans', dismissed as nonsense the Russian claim that their attack was in the interests of the Finnish workers;

socialism could not be 'expected to take root if its seeds are sown by means of bombing raids'. In answer to the Soviet claim that Finland was planning to attack Russia, *Tribune* pointed out grimly that 'chickens do not hunt wolves'. 'Vigilans' declared Kuuisinen to be a Soviet puppet and ridiculed Cockburn's suggestion in *The Week* that Finland was being prepared as a bridgehead for invasion of the Soviet Union by the USA and Sweden. Yet *Tribune* was not prepared, like other disenchanted elements, to condemn Russia as totalitarian. 'We deplore her aggression, but we support her for her socialism.' Bevan opposed the sending of British arms to Finland on the grounds that full-scale capitalist intervention against Russia might recur.[84]

R. Palme Dutt, possibly the dominant figure in the CPGB at this time, was quick to censure *Tribune*'s deviation from the communist line. Writing *in the same edition* on 8 December, Dutt made an earnest appeal 'to all those who have been associated with the *Tribune* to take their places in this fight and to cease to attempt to cover up the policies of betrayal with phrases of confusion'. Something curious now began to happen to *Tribune*. A breach opened up between the editorship of the journal and its controlling Board; the publication of Dutt's article had itself been a symptom of this division. The gulf widened for several weeks until the Board finally took drastic action.

When *Tribune* had fused temporarily with the Left Book Club it became, in the opinion of Michael Foot (who consequently discontinued writing for it), purely an organ of the CPGB.[85] Apparently under the noses of Cripps, Strauss and Bevan, the editorship fell to a fellow-traveller named Hartshorn. The fact that Dutt should not only have prior knowledge of the policy of the *Tribune* Board and should pronounce anathema upon the paper within its very pages suggested some collusion between its editor and the secretary of the CPGB. Strauss interpreted the article as advice to readers to end their subscriptions, and indeed *Tribune*'s circulation (very much in the hands of communist distributors) dropped to an all-time low of 9,000 copies a week.[86] The already overstaffed journal began to lose money heavily. In addition its pages now carried weekly endorsement of the communist policy of 'revolutionary defeatism'.[87] An article by the editor on 23 February 1940 argued for a negotiated settlement with Germany. This, as it turned out, was his swan song.

Strauss dismissed Hartshorn and, together with Bevan, took over the editorship briefly (Cripps was undertaking a world tour at this time) until Strauss contacted Raymond Postgate and offered him the job. Postgate, who had previously disliked the journal, agreed to take over with a commission to reformulate its policy, alter its layout and to produce in practice a journal similar to the *New Statesman*.[88] Most of the fellow-travellers on the staff were either dismissed or, as Postgate recalls, 'left soon after in dislike of me'.[89]

Perhaps to guard against future splits, Postgate was given a seat on the Board.[90] *Tribune*'s policy now moved into harmony with that of its Board, thus completing the break with the communists. Support for Russia was the *sine qua non* of communist friendship. By opposing the Comintern's policy of revolutionary defeatism and condemning Russia's invasion of Finland, *Tribune* abandoned friendship with the CPGB.

However, it has been clearly shown, that whereas the bulk of the Labour Party cried betrayal at the Nazi-Soviet pact, it required all the events leading up to and including the Russian attack on Finland to induce a similar sense of betrayal in the left wing of the party. The intellectuals on the left, whose support had given some credibility to the Popular Front, now recoiled from their former communist colleagues. Philip Toynbee, for example, made public his withdrawal from the Communist Party, declaring that, as a result of the *Daily Worker's* calm acceptance of the Finnish attack, the 'danger of this almost mystical association of the individual with the organisation had become deplorably obvious'.[91]

Yet an interesting difference persisted between private disillusion and public dissociation. The organisers of the Left Book Club, for instance, had all opposed the Finnish attack, but it was only when they believed that communist obedience to a *pro-German* line had become a danger to Britain's war effort that they made a serious effort to publicise their disagreement with the communists.

iv

In April 1940 Germany attacked Norway and Denmark, and in the *New Statesman* of 27 April letters appeared from both Strachey and Gollancz. Strachey formally dissociated himself from the *Daily Worker's* analysis of this extension of the war.[92] Readers of the paper, he observed, were being persuaded that Britain and France were responsible. The details of the German attack had hardly been mentioned. The *Daily Worker* was now not so much anti-war as pro-German. Communists believed that German success against Britain would pre-empt the imperialist attack upon Russia which Britain intended to launch once Germany had been defeated. Strachey could not condone defeatism against Hitler, even if it was designed to defend the Soviet Union. Strachey's analysis of the *Daily Worker* was indeed correct; the 1 February edition confirmed the following assertion: 'Britain declared war, not Germany. Attempts were made to end the war but Soviet-German peace overtures were rejected by Britain. All through these months the British and French Governments have had the power to end the war. They have chosen to extend it.'

Gollancz's appeal to those who might have been converted by the LBC to the communists was entitled 'Where are you going?'.[93] In this pamphlet he attacked the communist argument that revolutionary defeatism, the policy successfully employed by Lenin in 1917, was the only way out of this imperialist struggle. With a kind of benign ruthlessness he destroyed each proposition in the communist case. The distorting influence of Nazi propaganda, he pointed out, would prevent a popular rising of Great Britain from strengthening anti-Nazi feeling in Germany.[94] The Gestapo would immediately crush such a movement, in any case. Hitler sought to invade, to occupy and establish Nazism in Great Britain. Protest against imperialist conflict would be futile once she had allowed Hitler to defeat her and would be silenced anyway along with the immediate destruction of the working-class movement in Britain. Gollancz listed the articles in *Die Welt* and the *Daily Worker* which, he claimed, revealed that the policies of the CPGB, even if its members were not aware of the fact, were serving to strengthen German Nazism and to weaken British socialism.

The third member of the Left Book Club triumvirate, Harold Laski, developed similar views. Laski had earlier been called upon by the NEC to refute the communist definition of the war as 'imperialist'. He had compromised in his Labour Party pamphlet[95] by agreeing that the way was "imperialist" but judging that German imperialism was the more virulent strain and therefore to be resisted.[96] As for the communist approach to the war and to Russia, he was totally opposed to the policy of revolutionary defeatism founded upon the expectation of a European rising. This was merely a communist attempt to make Stalin's cynical *volte-face* acceptable. 'The communists' first allegiance,' he recognised, 'is the Soviet Union, it can do no wrong.'[97]

Yet Laski was insistent that an immense domestic political and economic achievement had been brought about in Russia and he argued that hostile Western attitudes should bear some responsibility for the unfortunate developments in Soviet foreign policy.[98] He favoured a magnanimous attitude towards Russian misdemeanours. 'She is like a burglar who unintentionally commits murder to prevent a burglarly from being found out.'[99] Yet he feared that Stalin's "supreme psychological blunder"[100] would destroy trust in his good faith for a long time to come. Proof of this observation was provided on 30 January 1940, when Laski's suggestion that a Labour delegation should be sent to the USSR was defeated in the NEC.[101]

The defection of the LBC Board from the communist line precipitated a conflict with the communists within the LBC membership throughout 1940. Gollancz publicly attacked those members who wished to pursue a policy leading to the enslavement of the working classes.[102] All over the country communists reacted by attempting to dominate LBC branches and take them over. Gollancz spoke out against the tactic of turning branches into 'bastard CP locals'; he resolutely refused to allow the LBC to become a 'spearhead of communist propaganda' and declared he would rather see such branches come to an end.[103] The communists' struggle continued well into 1941, but the Board's resolve was unshakable. In emphatic fashion it had joined *Tribune*, the *New Statesman*, the Labour Party and the trade union leadership in supporting the war and opposing the policies of the Soviet Union. The alliance of the Popular Front had finally sundered. The separation of the left from the communist orbit was an event of historic importance to the Labour Party. Richard Crossman commented:

Ever since 1931, the communists and their fellow travellers have had a virtual monopoly of left wing public opinion. Political consciousness has been almost synonymous with the acceptance of the USSR as the leader of world socialism and of Transport House as the home of reaction; and this has led to a disastrous division between the intelligentsia and the Labour electorate.[104]

Within the party the creative dynamic of the left had formerly been pulling away from the rest. Now two of the foremost points of conflict between the left and the party machine had been removed: Labour's official attitude towards Russia, and collaboration with the communists. The valuable intellectual energy of the left could now be used more effectively in the service of the party and in the formulation of its post-war programme.

The divorce of the left from the communists was social as well as political. Middle-class Marxists caught up in the Popular Front campaign had enjoyed an intimacy which was compounded by similar social and educational origins. Gollancz records that, despite their close personal friendship, he never saw Pritt again socially after the Finnish attack. Links with the Maiskys, familiar figures in left-wing social circles, were similarly severed.[105] The Russian embassy did not invite Gollancz on any subsequent occasion to its receptions, even those which included the most reactionary Tories. The Russians seemed to reserve their most lasting hatred for disillusioned friends rather than lifelong enemies.

Disorientated intellectuals were thrown temporarily into limbo, some floating towards the centre of the Labour Party, some dropping out of politics altogether, some forming new groups, the most important of which centred around the charismatic Aneurin Bevan, and others whose political lives were swamped by their involvement in the war effort.

v

John Strachey has written that the convulsions of mind and heart caused by Soviet behaviour are 'impossible to overestimate'; a revulsion had set in against the great secular religion of our time, leaving Gollancz, for example, an 'intellectual and spiritual shipwreck'.[106] In this atmosphere of doubt and disillusion Arthur Koestler's novel *Darkness at Noon*, published in 1940, caused something of an intellectual explosion. The debate between the sincere old Bolshevik prisoner, Rubashov, and his dour Stalinist interrogator, Gletkin, crystalised perfectly the central cause of doubt: how far had Stalinist Russia drifted away from the early ideals of the revolution? In their eagerness to remedy the acute economic and social problems of capitalist society and resist the growing power of fascism, many socialist intellectuals had been prepared to suspend conventional scruples and to condone (if not celebrate) Stalin's draconian imposition of socialism. Some went on to urge its emulation at home. *Darkness at Noon* reminded them how vital were the Christian humanist values which had been built up so painstakingly by the civilisation of Western Europe. It also vividly pointed out how brittle and tenuous were the defences against totalitarianism if these values were ignored.

The fellow-travelling intellectuals had dreamt they were marching confidently along the broad highway of history, in the van of 'progress' and the working class; *Darkness at Noon* awoke them to the facts that this highway was in reality a narrow and discontinuous footpath, flanked by precipices on both sides. Strachey read the book in the spring of 1941; the effect on him was 'stunning'.[107] Its publication, he recalls, caused 'riots, broke friendships, split families and was denounced by many people who were by no means communists'. In an interview with the present writer, Raymond Postgate recalled that the book had been referred to in such blood-curdling terms by left-wing friends that he had not cared to read it. Strachey insisted that he did so. Several other Labour Party figures interviewed recalled the deep effect Koestler's book had upon them. It is fascinating to note that Maurice Orbach only turned to Koestler a decade later, when his own faith in the Soviet Union began to wane. Whilst he wished to preserve his faith he ignored the book; once his doubts set in he turned to it for confirmation.[108] Thus did *Darkness at Noon* become the official textbook of the disillusioned Russophile; as such it must rank as one of the most influential novels ever written.

The break-up of the Popular Front alliance revealed that there had always been three tendencies among its Russophiles. Firstly there were the hard-core communists, close to the inner councils of the CPGB, who had few illusions about the blacker aspects of Stalinism, who accepted them as necessary but who vehemently denied them in public, citing the appropriate Soviet explanations whilst not necessarily believing them. These men accepted without question that the ends of communism justified whatever means were needed to achieve them. Secondly there was an outer group which disbelieved many of the horrific stories coming out of Russia and worked hard to find justifications for those they did believe. This group included members of the CPGB and fellow-travellers like Strachey, Gollancz, and Laski. Its beliefs, however, were founded, in part at least upon liberal values, and when Soviet transgressions were deemed to be both irrefutable and unjustifiable it was outspoken in its condemnation. A third group, made up of people like the Webbs, Pritt and Hewlett Johnson, was similar to the second but steadfastly refused to accept that the Soviet Union had committed any unjustifiable acts. It accepted the thinnest of Soviet explanations with an astonishing credulity.

Soviet behaviour also served to remove some of the veils from Labour eyes regarding the conduct and practice of foreign affairs. The country which the party had defended so stoutly in 1920 and stood by in the inter-war years had flagrantly violated virtually every major tenet in the Labour conception of a socialist foreign policy.

The party was opposed to the system of power politics; Russia had cynically participated in it to the full. Labour invested tremendous hope in a world-wide system of collective security against aggression; by joining hands with Hitler Stalin had betrayed this cause. A socialist foreign policy eschewed secrecy; the Nazi-Soviet pact had been dramatically born out of a background of total secrecy. Labour hoped that the working classes would cooperate to defeat the threat of capitalist war; Russia had ignored this principle and made her peace with capitalism's most virulent expression, Nazism. Socialists believed that socialist States, having abolished the capitalist economic base of imperialism, were incapable of following such a policy; Russia's predatory actions in respect of Poland and Finland brought this thesis painfully into question.

Russian behaviour moreover helped to make clear to the Labour leadership the fundamental fact of international relations, that in the last resort a nation's safety lies in its own hands. Participation by Labour leaders in Churchill's coalition, and its formulation of foreign policy, would serve to sharpen their appreciation of the role of power in international politics and to alienate them further from the idea of a radical idealistic foreign policy.

The collapse of the favourable Russian image helped also to put an end to an era in socialist thought. No longer could the theorists of the left cite the example of Russia as justification for their quasi-revolutionary plans. It is no coincidence that Strachey, the former prophet of Marxist revolution in the 'thirties, should now look for a peaceful evolutionary path to socialism.[109] If the strategy of revolutionary defeatism could work in the West in 1940 as it worked in the East in 1917, then, Strachey believed, 'Leninism, as the doctrine has been developed by the Communist International over the past twenty years, will have proved itself justified. But if not, not.'[110] Strachey gave his own answer to this question by elaborating a third approach to socialism, based upon Keynsian economic controls which would be a 'halfway house' between social democracy and communist policies.[111] Laski too ended his flirtation with violent revolution and began to formulate a theory of 'Revolution by Consent'.[112]

It was no coincidence, either that the left-wing monopoly of progressive socialist thinking should now be broken. Books by such 'right-Wingers' as Hugh Dalton and Evan Durbin began to attract attention, helping to form the basis of the programme which Labour would enact after 1945.[113] Following the cynical concord with Hitler, the future of Russian and British communism parted company with that of British social democracy. Admiration for Soviet economic achievements and military prowess would return and reach new heights during the war, but never in quite the same way. The nexus of innocent enthusiasm which had joined the Labour Party to Russia had been broken by the events of the autumn of 1939.

Notes

1 E. Llewellyn Woodward, *British Foreign Policy in the Second World War*, vol. I, pp. 16–28.
2 *Daily Herald*, 22 August 1939.
3 Interview with W. N. Ewer.
4 Dalton, Diaries, 22 August 1939.
5 J. D. McMillan, *TUCR 1939*, p. 30. Other speakers were W. Zak (pp. 294 and 295) and J. R. Stanley, p. 296.
6 *Ibid.*, pp. 302–6.
7 *Daily Herald*, 18 September 1939.
8 351. H.. Deb., 983–90, 20 September 1939.
9 *Ibid.*, 1882, 3 October 1939.
10 Dalton, Diaries, 18 September 1939.
11 *Ibid.*, 18 October 1939.
12 *Daily Herald*, 1 December 1939.
13 *Ibid.*, 6 December 1939.
14 *TUCR 1940*, p. 153.
15 Citrine was pressed to join the delegation despite his admitted anti-Russian bias. W. Citrine, *Two Careers*, pp. 17–19.
16 *LPCR 1940*, p. 14.
17 A nation-wide Finland Fund was started by the Labour Party. *LPCR 1940*, p. 15.
18 351 H.C. Deb., 37–43, 24 August 1939.
19 *Ibid.*, 285, 2 September 1939.

Collapse of an image 55

20 Fenner Brockway had opposed Munich but had been outvoted on the Executive of the ILP. Fenner Brockway, *Outside the Right*, p. 18.
21 351 *H.C. Deb.*, 702–10, 13 September 1939.
22 *New Leader*, 1 March 1940.
23 See 'Critic's London Diary' (written by Kingsley Martin), *NS and N*, 23 September 1939.
24 *Daily Worker*, 23 August 1939.
25 351 *H.C. Deb.*, 28–31, 24 August 1939.
26 *Daily Worker*, 26 August 1939.
27 *Ibid.*, 5 October 1939; see also H. Pelling, *The British Communist Party*, pp. 109–26.
28 Claud Cockburn, *I Claud*, p. 214. Pollitt's pamphlet was called *How to Win the War*, 14 September 1939.
29 Arthur Horner, *Incorrigible Rebel*, p. 164.
30 In a letter to *N.S. and N.*, 20 September 1939.
31 *Daily Worker*, 14 October 1939.
32 *Ibid.*, 30 November 1939. Mannerheim was the Finnish C.-in-C.
33 In an article by Palme Dutt, *Daily Worker*, 1 December 1939.
34 *Daily Worker*, 25 November 1939.
35 Hewlett Johnson, *Searching for Light* (London, 1968), pp. 155–59.
36 *N.S. and N.*, 20 December 1939. For a similar letter from the same writer see *N.S. and N.*, 4 July 1940.
37 *Die Welt*, 2 February.
38 This account of Brailsford's views is based upon his articles in *Reynolds, News* during autumn and winter 1939–40.
39 *Reynolds' News*, 17 September 1939.
40 *Ibid.*, 3, 17 and 31 December 1939, and 4 February 1940.
41 D. N. Pritt, *The Autobiography of D. N. Pritt*, vol. I. *From Right to Left*, pp. 38 and 190. See also his chapter in Margaret Cole (ed.), *Twelve Studies in Soviet Russia*.
42 Pritt, p. 190.
43 Interview with H. L. Beales, at that time an advisor to Penguin Books.
44 Laski, Ellen Wilkinson and Susan Lawrence voted against Pritt's expulsion.
45 *LPCR 1940*, pp. 164–6.
46 Garro Jones, MP, *Reynolds' News*, 10 March 1940. For a typical example of Pritt's ideas see his article in *Reynolds' News*, 7 March 1940.
47 Pritt did not even study the works of Marx until the late 1940s. Interview with D. N. Pritt.
48 Dalton, Diaries, 15 March 1940. For further evidence see reviews of Pritt's books on *N.S. and N.*, 17 February and 15 June 1940.
49 Interview with D. N. Pritt.
50 Cockburn, p. 214. In an interview with the author the prominent CPGB member Andrew Rothstein denied that such intructions had ever been received.
51 Cockburn, p. 215.
52 *Tribune*, 23 and 30 July 1948. See also Charlotte Haldane, *Truth will Out* (London, 1949).
53 George Orwell, *Nineteen Eighty Four*. See also G. A. Almond, *The Appeals of Communism* (Princeton, N.J., 1954).
54 For verification of this point see V. Gollancz, *The Betrayal of the Left*, pp. 287–91.

56 *The Russia complex*

55 *Tribune*, 25 August 1939.
56 *N.S. and N.*, 26 August 1939.
57 351 *H.C. Deb.*, 46–52, 24 August 1939.
58 *Ibid.*, 55–60.
59 *N.S. and N*, 26 August, and *Tribune*, 25 August 1939.
60 *Tribune*, 1 September 1939.
61 From November onwards, Zilliacus's name disappeared from *Tribune*'s pages. The explanation was that he was engaged upon 'important war work' (*Tribune*, 24 November 1939). His place was taken by 'Vigilans', who wrote regularly in *Tribune* urging co-operation with Russia but also supporting the war and incurring the wrath of the communists. The identity of Vigilans? None other than Zilliacus, who was never happier than when writing under a pseudonym. For this information I am indebted to the late Raymond Postgate.
62 *N.S. and N.*, 2 September 1939.
63 *Tribune*, 24 September 1939.
64 Letter to *N.S. and N.*, 7 October 1939.
65 *N.S. and N.*, 23 Sept 1939.
66 351 *H.C. Deb.*, 1003–7, 20 September 1939.
67 *Reynolds' News*, 17 October 1939. See his contribution to Crossman (ed.), *The God that Failed*, pp. 199–231.
68 *N.S. and N.*, 23 September 1939.
69 *Forward*, 23 September 1939. No verification on this point has been traced.
70 H. N. Brailsford, *Reynolds' News*, 1 October 1939.
71 Charles Trevelyan, in a letter to *N.S. and N.*, 7 October 1939.
72 Stafford Cripps and Zilliacus in *Tribune*, 22 and 15 September 1939.
73 Emrys Hughes, in *Forward*, 23 September 1939.
74 351 *H.C. Deb.*, 1870–1874 and 1888, 3 October 1939.
75 *N.S. and N.*, 7 October 1939.
76 Letter to *N.S. and N.*, 7 October 1939.
77 *Tribune*, 20 October 1939.
78 Letter to *N.S. and N.*, 14 October 1939.
79 Sonia Orwell and Ian Angus, *The Collected Essays, Journalism and Letters of George Orwell*, Vol. 2, p. 70.
80 *N.S. and N.*, 25 November 1939.
80 *Tribune*, 1 December 1939.
81 *N.S. and N.* 25 November 1939.
82 *Ibid.*, 2 December 1939.
83 *Ibid.*, 6 January 1940.
84 *Tribune*, 8 December 1939.
85 Interview with Michael Foot.
86 Interview with George Strauss, MP.
87 The editors ensured that the correspondence columns were filled with letters of criticism of the Board's policy. A letter from Stephen Swingler (later an MP), for instance, completely dissociated him from *Tribune*'s views — *Tribune*, 15 December 1939.
88 Interview with Raymond Postgate.
89 Letter to author from Raymond Postgate. Anthony Hearne, a sub-editor to Hartshorn, and an 'ardent Stalinist', was, however, retained under Postgate.
90 Other members were Strauss, Gollancz and Bevan. Vigilans (Zilliacus) also

attended Board meetings but, according to Postgate, was invariably asleep.
91 Letter to *N.S. and N.*, 16 March 1940.
92 Strachey had still believed Britain should withdraw from the war up to December 1939 — see *Left News*, December 1939.
93 For some reactions to these arguments, see Vigilans, *Tribune*, 10 May 1940, William Rust's reply in *N.S. and N.*, 4 May 1940.
94 For some actual evidence of this provided by the Ministry of Information, see 368 *H.C. Deb.*, 718, 30 January 1941 (written answer).
95 Labour Party pamphlet, *Is this an Imperialist War?*, 1939. Also *Left News*, December 1939.
96 This formulation appealed to many on the extreme left who could not accept revolutionary defeatism. Sidney Silverman expressed Laski's view of the Labour Party Conference (*LPCR 1940*, p. 130); at the same Conference Attlee testily remarked that he had no patience with those 'who talk claptrap about an imperialist war', *LPCR 1940*, p. 124.
97 In the preface of V. Gollancz, *Betrayal of the Left*.
98 See Laski's review of Max Eastman's critical work on the Soviet Union, *N.S. and N.*, 21 December 1940.
99 In a letter to the American Lawyer, Felix Frankfurter, quoted in B. Kinglsey Martin, *Harold Laski: a Biographical Memoir*, p. 131.
100 *Ibid.*, p. 132.
101 Dalton, *Diaries*, 30 January 1940.
102 *Left News*, May 1940, p. 1485. See also Strachey in the same journal July 1940, p. 1489, and December 1940, p. 1573.
103 *Ibid.*, May 1940.
104 R. H. S. Crossman, *N.S. and N.*, 6 April 1940.
105 V. Gollancz, *Reminiscences of Affection*, p. 13.
106 John St Loe Strachey, *The Strangled Cry*, p. 128.
107 *Ibid.*, p. 13. For Orwell's comments see *Tribune*, 10 January 1940, and for Kingsley Martin's effusive review see *N.S. and N.*, 8 February 1940.
108 Interview with the author.
109 See Kingsley Martin's review of Strachey's *A Programme for Progress*, (London, 1940) in *N.S. and N.*, 30 March 1940, also Strachey's chapter in Gollancz, *Betrayal of the Left*, p. 200, and his chapter in *I Believe: Personal Testimonies of Twenty-three Eminent Men and Women of our Time* (London, 1940), pp. 277–93. Strachey himself refused to accept the label 'social democrat' — letter to *N.S. and N.*, 6 April 1940.
110 Gollancz, *Betrayal of the Left*, p. 225.
111 *Ibid*.
112 Kingsley Martin, pp. 138–67.
113 See Crossman's review of two books in *N.S. and N.*, 6 April 1940; Hugh Dalton, *Hitler's War* (London, 1940), and E. F. M. Durbin, *The Politics of Democratic Socialism* (London, 1940)

4 Image repaired: Russia as heroic ally

A country does not cease to be socialist because it follows for a time a radically mistaken policy. [G. D. H. Cole, *Europe, Russia and the Future* (London, 1941), p. 18]

We are convinced that the Soviet Union will re-establish her connections with the main democratic inspiration of the twentieth century. [Aneurin Bevan, *Tribune*, 24 January 1942]

'Who knows,' hinted Attlee at the party Conference in June 1940, 'whether the USSR will continue to sit at the dinner table or will be the next course on the menu.'[1] During the year that was needed to make Attlee's prophecy come true, Labour's relations with Russia were robbed of any real substance.

The conclusion of the Finnish war and the collapse of France had transformed the situation facing Russia. If Stalin had hoped for a war of attrition between France and Germany his hopes had been disappointed. Britain's departure from the Continent at Dunkirk, and Germany's occupation of Norway, Denmark, the Low Countries and France, had given Hitler unparalleled power and freed his hands to fulfil his old territorial ambitions in the east. As in the years before the war, Russia and Britain were in a position to do business. Yet this time it was Russia who was the unwilling partner, who seemed to be desperately pursuing a policy of peace through appeasement. The appointment of Sir Stafford Cripps as ambassador to Moscow was the foot which Churchill diplomatically placed in the door of co-operation with Russia.

The ending of the Finnish war in March 1940 had removed the heat from Anglo-Soviet relations. Russia had abandoned the ideological fiction of the Kuuisinen government (embarrassing still further those friends of Russia in the West who had sincerely supported this regime) and limited her demands to purely strategic requirements. Yet Stalin at this time appreciated the logic of his situation imperfectly. Like Chamberlain, whose weakness he had previously condemned, he seemed to place an inordinate faith in Hitler's sincerity.[2] Stalin would not refuse British overtures, both as an insurance policy against the future and as a hint to an over-ambitious Hitler, but neither would he accept British offers of co-operation lest he should nudge Hitler into ending the precarious Nazi-Soviet accord. On the extreme left in Britain the tense international situation produced a curious political phenomenon, the Convention Movement.

i

The Convention Movement was an artefact which the communists sought to substitute for the defunct Popular Front. Invented in July 1940, its programme carried familiar left-wing demands like friendship with the USSR and independence for India, but the vital ingredient was the demand for a 'People's Peace by the working people of all countries, based on the right of all people to determine their own destiny'. In effect the Convention Movement asked for the overthrow of the Churchill government and the substitution of a workers' government which would appeal for a settlement to the workers of Germany. This policy was an extension in new disguise, of communist policies, but the CPGB, no doubt aware of its unpopularity at this time, was understandably coy about its sponsorship of the movement. It chose instead to utilise the 'front' tactic, emphasising leadership of a 'non-communist' D. N. Pritt rather than party members like Dutt, Pollitt and Page Arnot.

During the next six months the Convention became organised, issuing pamphlets and organising local branches. On 12 January 1941 a public delegate meeting was held, representative, claimed Pritt, of 1,200,000 people.[3] The real figure was probably a fraction of this number.[4]

The whole of the Labour Party now united in hotly opposing the Convention Movement. *Tribune* denounced its activities at the time of Britain's greatest peril as loudly as the *Daily Herald*. Strachey declared that 'it is as certain as that the sun will rise tomorrow that the People's Convention is an anti-war movement, and that its activities are expressly designed to interfere with our complete victory over fascism'. His former colleagues in the CPGB he now dismissed as 'fools with a fixed idea carried to the point of insanity'.[5] What concerned Strachey was that well-meaning people of some prominence on the left had been duped by the ambiguous stance of the movement into lending their support. As an illustration of this an exchange of letters between Victor Gollancz and Hewlett Johnson revealed the extent of the latter's confusion. Whilst regarding Hitler as enemy number one and supporting Churchill's war against him, the Red Dean saw no conflict with his support for the People's Convention movement.[6]

The *New Statesman and Nation* pointed out that the 'people's peace' which the Convention advocated would be a 'fascist peace' and as such an even greater threat to the USSR than a British victory.[7] Herbert Morrison, now Churchill's Home Secretary, publicly dismissed the importance of the movement and the degree of national representation demonstrated by the 12 January meeting. Yet his ban upon the *Daily Worker* and *The Week* belied his apparent lack of concern about communist activity.[8] In fact the NEC convened a special meeting to discuss the Convention movement on 21 January 1941 and applied pressure upon signatories of its manifesto.[9] Some forty withdrew their names. At least two local Labour parties were disaffiliated from the party.[10] An NCL circular distributed to local parties emphasised the communist connections with the movement, and asserted that the CPGB was working for the defeat of the government in the hope of seizing power during the ensuing chaos.[11]

Whilst the left endorsed the party machine's crushing of the People's Convention it cavilled at the banning of the *Daily Worker*; the 'worst mistake of the war', concluded *Tribune*. In Parliament Bevan led the opposition to Morrison's decision, signifying his emergence as a spokesman for a vociferous minority of Labour MPs who were destined consistently to oppose the policies of the coalition government.[12]

At the time of Germany's attack upon Russia the Convention Movement had long ceased to cause the Labour Party any concern. James Griffiths, chairman of the Labour Party, jocularly commented that followers of the Convention ought to be under the jurisdiction of the Ministry of Health.[13] Pritt's assessment of the movement's importance at this time was predictably more generous. He claimed that it had done much to encourage popular sentiment towards the USSR, that when Russia entered the war Churchill, despite his fundamental opposition to Russia, had been forced to welcome her as a friend.

Once the Finnish war ended, the nadir in Labour Party attitudes towards Russia had been passed. Stalin's modest, strictly strategic demands on Finland now placed his country's attack in a more favourable light; perhaps defence against Germany really had been his sole intention. The Labour Party supported government attempts to improve relations with Russia; the realists on the right as a way of bringing pressure to bear upon Hitler, but the support of the left was also a symptom of a tentatively reborn optimism about Russia's future role.

In October 1940 Aneurin Bevan advocated a new diplomatic offensive; he believed the circumstances were now more 'favourable to a rapprochement with Russia than they have been since the war began'.[14] In the same month as Bevan's speech the Soviet government had demanded that the assets of the Baltic States which had been 'accepted' into the USSR in August 1940 should be transferred from London to Moscow. In addition it demanded that shipping belonging to these States, at that time held in British ports, should be handed over.[15]

Further prodding from the left occurred in April 1941 when Hitler moved into the Balkans. The ensuing agreement between the USSR and Yugoslavia was seen by *Tribune* as a golden opportunity to clear up outstanding issues with the Soviet Union and to win her friendly neutrality. The suitability of the Churchill government to negotiate with the Russians was still regarded as suspect. Tory influence, feared *Tribune*, would sabotage better relations, and it was recommended that 'notorious' anti-Soviet officials in the Foreign Office should be transferred to 'innocuous' posts.[16]

By early 1941 much of the left-wing indignation at earlier Russian behaviour had passed away. In retrospect Kingsley Martin could see the logic behind Stalin's move against Poland and the Baltic States. The Finland episode he now regarded as part of a more or less legitimate effort by Stalin to keep his country out of the war.[17] In harmony with other strands of left-wing opinion, Martin did not share the popular view of Soviet military weakness. Part of the left-wing image of Russia had always been a confidence in the strength of the Red Army. The Finnish *débâcle*, it seemed, had suspended left-wing faith in Soviet strength only temporarily. Bevan could even inform the House of Commons that the Soviet Union was capable of ending the war in just one week.[18] Writing to the *N. S. and N.*, Shaw judged that Stalin was strong enough not to fear Hitler. He expressed sympathy for the fate of his potential adversaries and added, with typical irrelevance, that he thought Stalin much the handsomest of all the present rulers in Europe.[19] Labour support for British diplomatic overtures towards the Soviet Union in the autumn of 1940 and the spring of 1941 also owed something to the appointment of Sir Stafford Cripps as British ambassador in May 1940.

ii

Cripps had always maintained that in the pre-war negotiations Britain had failed to pursue Anglo-Soviet co-operation with any sincerity or energy. Generously endowed with both, Cripps was convinced that he could extract a firm accord from Russia's sullen neutrality. His colleagues were less sanguine. Dalton thought him unsuitable; Gallacher, the worst possible choice. 'I didn't kid myself,' Attlee later recalled, 'that our left-wingers would have any more influence on Uncle Joe than a right-winger.'[20] He was right. Molotov was quick to point out that 'Cripps's political views are of no interest to the Soviet Government'.[21] Churchill reflected that he had not fully appreciated that the 'nearer a man is to communism in sentiment, the more obnoxious he is to the Soviets unless he joins the Party'.[22]

Cripps's personality moreover scarcely endeared him to the Soviet leaders; a vodka-drinking extrovert would have inspired more confidence than this humourless ascetic whose only relaxation seemed to be the strange un-Russian habit of taking his dog for long walks. Stalin kept him endlessly waiting, and the eminent QC displayed less than diplomatic patience. When his initiatives, some of them surpassing his Foreign Office instructions, were ignored, he tended to over-react and threaten reprisals, again on his own authority. In January 1940 he wrote to Monckton that he was completely disillusioned with the Russians and that Halifax gave him no cards to play.[23] A few days later Molotov told him that, if anything, he had served to worsen Anglo-Soviet relations.[24] Cripps's sojourn in Moscow 'profoundly altered his political outlook', in Michael Foot's opinion, and removed the 'Marxist veneer which had once supplied a crude cover for his Christian Socialism'.[25] He must also have learned a lesson yet unrealised on the left, that, where the security of great nation States are concerned, ideological affinity is of scant relevance. Ironically, as it turned out, Cripps was given the credit for what he had failed to do. Within a few hours, on 21 June 1941, Britain's position was dramatically altered. The name of Sir Stafford Cripps, the foremost advocate of alliance with Russia before the war, was now associated with the huge upsurge in hope and morale that attended Russia's entry into the war.

Fears on the left that Churchill might now unite with Hitler to crush the workers' government in Russia were at once put to rest by his broadcast on 22 June 1941. This was no class war, said Churchill; 'the Russian danger is our danger.' The left were greatly relieved; Laski wrote that 'Mr Churchill swept an epoch into the lumber room of history by his great speech'.[26] At Churchill's request, Attlee also welcomed Britain's new ally, playing on Labour's traditional pro-Soviet sympathies. Orwell wrote, 'I never thought I should live to say Good Luck to Comrade Stalin, but so I do.' In his private diary he commented bitterly on how the exigencies of war could turn the most repugnant regimes into glorious allies: 'One could not have a better example of the moral and emotional shallowness of our time than the fact that we are all more or less pro Stalin. This disgusting murderer is temporarily on our side and so the purges are suddenly forgotten.'[27] The National Council of Labour, comprising men who, eighteen months earlier, had unreservedly condemned the USSR, offered warm greetings to the 'Russian people'[28] and assured them of support in their efforts to defeat the common enemy. The *Daily Herald* echoed these sentiments but expressed little optimism about

Russia's capacity to survive.[29] After the Red Army's showing against Finland these doubts were certainly justified; they were shared by the Labour leadership. Attlee even hinted at his own doubts in the broadcast mentioned above, Cripps confessed privately that he gave the Russians only a few weeks,[30] and Dalton too held out little hope: 'I am mentally prepared for the headlong collapse of the Red Army,' he wrote in his diary.[31]

These fears were not shared by the left-wing of the party, most of whom were convinced that the entry of Russia into the war left its outcome in no doubt. Bevan, for instance, declared that Hitler had 'played his last card and lost'.[32] So confident did one future Labour MP feel that he and his wife decided to start a family.[33] The left, indeed, tended to refute suggestions that Russia would quickly collapse, interpreting them as indirect slights upon Russia's form of economic organisation.

No doubt mindful of earlier embarrassments, communists were loath to comment on this sudden development. In Parliament, James Griffiths demanded a statement on whether the CPGB would now support the war, and in confusion Gallacher weakly replied, 'I must ask notice of that question.'[34] Once the new line had been unequivocally drawn, British communists were greatly relieved. Many had suffered an excruciating conflict of loyalties since the Nazi-Soviet pact; some had no doubt contemplated a policy of sabotage at home if Churchill had joined hands with Hitler. But now the path of duty was thankfully clear once more, and communists could enjoy the rare political comfort of operating within a vast consensus. Co-operation with their arch-enemy, Churchill, it was true, was almost as difficult for communists as their neutrality towards Hitler had been, but the pill was 'sweetened' by the opposition communists now mounted against the 'Men of Munich' in Churchill's government.[35] For his part, William Rust immediately began an ultimately successful campaign for the legalisation of the *Daily Worker*.

Public enthusiasm for Russia was spectacular. Kingsley Martin noted that the Russian resistance had 'engendered an immense enthusiasm among people everywhere irrespective of party'.[36] Michael Foot recalls that meetings he addressed in support of Russia during these months were among the most fervent and best attended in his experience before or since.[37]

The mass media, accustomed to relaying a generally hostile attitude towards Russia, rapidly adapted itself to feed the public interest. Newspaper articles on Russia abounded, the partisan expertise of *Daily Worker* columnists being in great demand.[38] News of the bitter Soviet resistance, her scorched earth policy, heroic incidents, terrible fighting conditions, now crowded the news columns of the national dailies. The number of broadcasts upon every conceivable aspect of Soviet life increased enormously; in the second half of

1941, for example, nine times more broadcasts on Russia went out than during the first six months.³⁹ Immediately pro-Russian journals and books reappeared on the bookstalls in vast numbers.⁴⁰ *Soviet Communism* was dusted down and reprinted; Maisky obligingly corrected the proofs. The Royal Institute of International Affairs held a series of lectures upon the Soviet Union in the autumn of 1941. The traditional opponents of Russia, furthermore, were silenced; indeed, in many instances they were eager to deliver glowing tributes to Russian valour.⁴¹

All kinds of 'Aid for Russia' societies sprang up all over the country. Mrs Churchill founded a Help Russia Fund. Hewlett Johnson (together with A. T. D'Eye) launched a National Anglo-Soviet Medical Aid Fund which during the war collected £1¼ million for this purpose.⁴² Nantymoel in South Wales was just one little mining village where a Medical Aid for Russia Committee was established which organised fund-raising activities like boxing displays. The anniversaries of the Anglo-Soviet alliance were now occasions to be celebrated, in Onllwyn, South Wales, for example, with silver bands and male voice choirs.⁴³

Communists were given an ideal opportunity to propagate favourable images of Russia and in the process advance their own political cause. Now that patriotism and ideological conviction coincided, they threw themselves into the war effort. Party shop stewards applied themselves to the novel occupation of improving production by co-operating with management on production committees and introducing and carrying through output drives. Workers were exhorted to work yet harder, 'Stakhanovite' workers were publicised and strikes discouraged. The production of war materials for Russia was now the communist's prime objective. Communists found themselves the focus of a vast receptive amphitheatre of public interest, and took full advantage of it. Party members easily manipulated the countless Anglo-Soviet weeks into highly effective propaganda exercises for the Soviet Union. Andrew Rothstein, London correspondent of *Tass*, was, for instance, one of those invited to lecture to the Royal Institute of International Affairs. Party membership increased to 60,000 during the war, but any hopes they had of a change of heart by Labour Party leaders over the question of membership were quickly dashed. The NEC in its report to Conference in May 1942 saw no reason why Labour support for Russia should alter the situation. When Britain's need had been greatest, the NEC pointed out, communist support had been lacking. To rub home the rebuke, the NEC condemned communist attempts to capitalise upon Anglo-Russian solidarity for purely party ends through the creation of such front organisations as the Anglo-Soviet Unity Friendship Committees and the National Conferences for Anglo-Soviet Unity.⁴⁴ Conference accepted the report's advice and rejected the application for affiliation. Morrison's dark references to sinister people behind the CPGB were justified soon after by the conviction of its National Organiser, Springhall, for passing on information to Russia.[45] Some evidence of the climate of the time, however, is revealed in the NEC's decision not to take disciplinary action against Labour Party members who spoke on the same platforms as communists: previously this had been considered a heinous crime. In July 1941, for example, at the Stoll Theatre in London a huge gathering was addressed by left-wingers Bevan, Foot and Frank Owen, together with Harry Pollitt.[46] The left wing of the Labour Party in fact was scarcely less industrious than the communists in the cause of helping Russia. Gollancz once more busied himself with producing pro-Soviet literature and with speaking engagements in support of the USSR. *Tribune* gave an enormous amount of space to articles upon Russia, providing information upon all aspects of the Soviet war effort, her government and economy; one edition was given over wholly to the subject.[47]

iii

Would it be true to say that the old Popular Front alliance between the Communist Party and the Labour left was reforged by this turn of events? Not really. Certainly the principal bone of contention, Soviet behaviour, had been removed and had been replaced by fervent agreement. The Left Book Club was now able to convene a cosy national conference at which Kingsley Martin could even say, 'We need a new Popular Front and maybe we are working towards it'.[48] But despite these familiar appearances the willing wartime co-operation between the CPGB and Labour Party members was not based upon the old pre-war intimacy. Institutionally, too, the communists and the Labour left tended to go their own way. The Anglo-Soviet Public Relations Committee, for example, which was set up in 1941 with old Popular Fronters amongst its membership, did not contain any prominent communists. Rather, it tended to comprise the non-communist element of the old Popular Front, together with some representatives from the centre and right.[49] Victor Gollancz, secretary of the committee, was rather typical of this new alignment. He had been a tireless organiser and publicist for the Popular Front, but when Russia joined the war he could not forgive the communist betrayal of British for Soviet interests. A long article in *Left News* (July 1941) chronicled the communists' defection and asked them why they had abandoned their analysis of the war as imperialist and their policy of revolutionary defeatism. Why moreover had the CPGB and the People's

Convention now decided to support the war? After all, the war was the same, the government was the same, its policy was the same. The *only* difference was that the USSR was now in it. The fact was that too much bitterness had been created on both sides. Kingsley Martin's scornful reviews of books by Pritt, Dobb and Pat Sloan (editor of *Russia Today*) gave some idea of how wide the gap remained.[50]

The right wing of the Labour Party evinced an astonishing degree of enthusiasm for Russia, bearing in mind their earlier ferocious condemnations. The *Daily Herald*, which had excelled virtually every other daily paper in the bitterness of its attitudes towards Russia after August 1939, now outstripped all others in the quality and intensity of its admiration. For six months after Russian entry into the war, virtually every day a banner headline carried news into Labour homes of the gigantic conflict; about half the editorials over this period were concerned with Russia or closely related subjects. 'Their tenacious resistance is a tremendous gift to the democracies', ran the editorial of June 30. The signing of the Anglo-Soviet treaty of July 1941 was seen as full recognition of the fact that neither country could hold out 'any hope of peace or security or decent life until Hitler and Hitlerism have been overthrown'.[51] At the 1941 TUC Conference, Citrine had only sweet words for the Soviet Union. He paid tribute to the 'Magnificent skill and unconquerable bravery of the Russian armies and people to whom the trade union movement pledges all possible help'.[52] The exigencies of war had forged friendship from the coldest of ashes.

Citrine felt it 'imperative to help Russia and particularly the Russian trade union movement in the ordeal through which their country is passing', and, undeterred by the failure of 1925, a joint committee between British and Soviet trade unionists was one form of assistance he decided upon.[53] Conference endorsed his idea, and in October he undertook a somewhat hazardous mission to Moscow to pursue negotiations. There he found that political freedom was still non-existent; the Polish trade unionists Alter and Erlich provided him with tales of police terror and the statistic that seven million people were still imprisoned. The committee was established on the premise that 'neither side should interfere in the internal affairs of each other', and was given a rather vague remit to help co-ordinate aid and propaganda against Hitler.[54] Citrine returned to write a highly sympathetic series of articles on Russian feats of production and sacrifice.

The Soviet Union scarcely deserved this astonishing reversal of public attitudes — after all, the only thing that had terminated her biased neutrality was invasion by her erstwhile collaborator — but popular enthusiasm is easy to understand. The immediate danger had been removed and the struggle was now shared. Andrew Rothstein argues that the working classes were never

Image repaired 67

really fooled by 'ruling-class propaganda' about the Soviet Union, and indeed a contemporary opinion poll indicates a substantial fund of goodwill towards Russia even during the Finnish War.[55] However, a more persuasive explanation is that public perceptions had shifted from the Soviet government to the Russian people. Churchill had set the tone himself in his broadcast of 22 June. After mentioning his lifelong opposition to Bolshevism he continued, 'But all this fades away, I see the Russian soldier guarding his native land.'[56] A few months after Soviet entry into the war Orwell noted a 'tremendous net increase in pro-Russian sentiment' but observed that it was not at all 'coupled with the faintest interest in the Russian political system'.[57] Russia was now perceived, in dramatic terms, as Britain's heroic ally, as a martyr on the cross of anti-fascism, as the avenging angel of socialism who would carry retribution into Germany.

Rather as in the dark days of the early 1930s Russia became a beam of hope, only more intensely so. The mass of hopeful information which had been produced during a time of intense economic crisis was now multiplied under conditions of military peril. An atmosphere crystallised in the country as a whole in which, one observer noted, 'criticism of Russia became tantamount to treason'.[58]

Inevitably interpretations of the events which had so recently been deplored were now transformed, particularly on the left. Michael Foot has neatly summed up the mood of the time:

Despite the crimes and blunders of the Soviet rulers and the chicanery of the Communist Parties in other lands, they [left-wing socialists] believed that communist revolutionary achievements would be vindicated. For them the Nazi-Soviet Pact and the Finnish War were appalling aberrations; unity between the Soviet people and other peoples in the war against fascism was a restoration of the proper historical process. And dominating this strong sentiment was a deep sense of relief about the war itself and Britain's chance of survival.[59]

The new image of the USSR was more diversified and more favourable than ever before. It centred around the Soviet war effort and at its heart stood the Russian soldier, presented as determined and heroic in defence of his country, but at the same time humane and civilised. On 23 February 1943 the *Daily Herald* featured a typical story with a picture of Russian soldiers captioned 'The men who beat Hitler'. The account alongside complimented their 'alertness and articulateness' and asserted that by nature they were 'kindly and not in the least bloodthirsty people'. The *N.S. and N.* even felt moved to describe the Red Army as the 'chief flower and symbol of a whole new society' and, moreover, a 'deeply cultivated body'![60]

Stalin now became universally popular as 'Uncle Joe', he was seen as a

68 *The Russia complex*

benevolent despot or, in Clive Bell's phrase, a 'sagacious autocrat'. He was still generally regarded as a dictator, ruthless when necessary, but these qualities, so offensive in peacetime, now seemed ideal qualifications for the job in hand. The efficiency and resilience of the Soviet economy received much publicity and was presented as a testimony to socialist planning. Articles, books and broadcasts abounded on Soviet agriculture, trade unions, welfare services and so on. The Soviet worker was boosted as the tireless and resourceful model that British workers should follow, and the left wing emphasised the comradeship and equality that characterised his relationships with his fellows. Criticism of the Soviet political system was muted and the new image was not affected by anything but the most minimal of 'counter'-information; even a reactionary Tory would shrink from criticising Britain's ally in a life and death struggle.

iv

The impact of the new image operated in several ways. There was concern within the Labour Party about the image itself. Members of the government were peppered with parliamentary questions on what were regarded as barriers to Anglo-Soviet understanding or slights against the honour of our great ally in the East. A few examples will illustrate the extent of this concern.

Reginald Sorenson, a left-wing Labour MP (though anything but a fervent Russophile),[62] complained in July 1941 that press pictures of the arrival of a Soviet military mission had been forbidden. This he saw as an absurd residue of yesterday's hatred and prejudice. The question of the Soviet national anthem generated slightly more heat. Left-wingers had been long convinced that the Controllers of the BBC were incorrigibly anti-socialist and anti-Russian. On 6 July 1941, just before the nine o'clock news, the BBC played all the Allied anthems, with the notable exception of the Internationale. In the House of Commons Sidney Silverman raised the matter: did this mean that the Soviet Union was not our ally?[63] The ommission persisted, however, even after 12 July when the Anglo-Soviet agreement was signed. Duff Cooper, the Minister of Information, finally resolved the question by removing the anthems altogether, explaining lugubriously that 'The increase in the number of National Anthems renders it impossible to do full justice to them in the time allotted'.[64]

Other proposals were made for scientific and cultural links; the Ministry of Information was criticised for providing inadequate facilities for the exchange of information[65] and on 24 February 1942 one MP obligingly invited the House to wish the Red Army many happy returns on the anniversary of its foundation.[66]

Naturally any hint of anti-Russian sentiment was pounced upon by the left and by the communists. Colonel Moore Brabazon, Minister of Aircraft Production and a pioneer pilot, said in a speech that he hoped the Germans and Russians would wipe each other out. He was taken to task by, among others, Jack Tanner (president of the AEU) at the Trades Union Conference for expressing such sentiments.[67] Protests from workers in aircraft factories eventually forced him to resign.[68]

The new image inevitably had considerable implications for Labour's foreign policy. It helped to bring the somewhat tattered ideal of a socialist foreign policy much closer to reality. Soviet foreign policy was now seen as a more logical reflection of internal socialist policies. The loud denunciations of Soviet 'imperialism' which had reverberated throughout the party in 1939 were now forgotten. *Tribune*'s diplomatic correspondent, for example, saw the Soviet Union as interested solely in peaceful national development and in peaceful foreign policy.[69]

The notion of direct working-class co-operation was once again popular; witness Citrine's Anglo-Soviet Trade Union Committee and Laski's hopes that the communist and socialist international would fuse now that West and East were united in war.[70] When British and Russian troops met in Iran in August 1941 the event was heralded by *Tribune* as the 'greatest, most significant thing that has happened to the workers of Great Britain and the USSR and the world'.[71]

Moreover with Russia, and after December 1941 the USA, co-operating in the containment and defeat of aggression, the notion of collective security again seemed to be excitingly viable — some echoes here of the wartime hopes of the old UDC and ILP. The Labour Party began to look with some confidence towards a post-war world in which peace would be assured by a continuation of the alliance of Britain, Russia and America.

A new strand of thinking was added by the left wing to the body of concepts we are calling 'socialist foreign policy'. It was earnestly hoped by Harold Laski that a close tripartite alliance would facilitate a mutually beneficial interchange of political ideas, with the West learning the secret of centralised planning from the East and the East learning the primacy of democratic freedom from the West.[72] Laski believed that, given security from external capitalist attack, democracy would at last be allowed to flower in the USSR and a more co-operative attitude would ensue. He argued that the duty of Western socialists was to assure the Soviet Union of their friendship in every way and to work for a post-war socialist revolution in the West. With some variations he held to this thesis throughout the war and into the post-war world.[73]

Gollancz reflected some of the confusions of the left wing, in which recent disillusion competed with renewed enthusiasm. He did not now believe that Soviet foreign policy had been any more or less reprehensible than the West's. The Soviet Union was still 'basically socialist' but its political system was the antithesis of socialism. Reflecting, perhaps, some of Koestler's arguments, he doubted whether this dictatorship would wither away and feared it would 'become sanctified as itself the final good'.[74] How, one might ask, could a country remain 'basically socialist' under a permanent tyranny? Gollancz compounded the uncertainties by asserting that, whatever its shortcomings, Soviet totalitarianism was 'immensely preferable' to the hopeless misery of the masses in Poland and the Balkans. G. D. H. Cole was deploying similar though more internally consistent arguments at this time. Russian entry into the war elicited from him a reaffirmation of faith in the Soviet Union which he expressed in his book *Europe, Russia and the Future*.[75] 'A country does not cease to be socialist,' he maintained, dismissing the recent past, 'because it follows for a time a radically mistaken policy.'[76] Cole's greatest fear was that the defeat of Hitler would witness a return to the old capitalist order. He envisaged, without a qualm, the possibility that the USSR would absorb Poland, Hungary and the Balkans. Whilst many social democrats would 'hold up their hands in holy horror' at this prospect, he declared that

I have never allowed my dislike of much that Stalin has done to blind me to the fact that the U.S.S.R. remains fundamentally Socialist or that the Soviet form of government may be the only one that is capable of sweeping clean the stables of Eastern and Southern Europe ....

and went even further:

I would much sooner see the Soviet Union, even with its policy unchanged, dominant over all Europe, including Britain, than see an attempt to restore the pre-war States to their futile and uncreative independence ... under capitalist domination.[77]

In a few years' time his stated preference would be put to the test.[78]

It was, however, hatred of the past rather than a preference for Stalinism that explains Cole's attitude. He looked for a post-war supranational political structure based upon three dovetailed economic zones in Western Europe, Central Europe and the USSR. The socialist task would be to destroy the barriers of nationalism and capitalism now, so that international socialism could inherit the post-war world.[79] Yet if this primary objective should be unattainable he was content, at this time, to visualise a Stalinist post-war Europe. Cole's arguments, always persuasive on the left of the Labour Party, were greatly reinforced by the creation of the new and generally accepted heroic 'technicoloured' image of the Soviet Union.

One further effect of this image can be discerned at this stage; it tended to make Britain's own role in the war seem woefully inadequate. A genuine feeling of guilt emerged in the Labour Party that its own country's war effort was incommensurate with that of Russia. The *Daily Herald*, for example, spoke of a large section of the party in expressing a sense of inadequacy and humility before the 'smoking altar' of Kiev.[80] It was this feeling of guilt which sought expiation in the Second Front campaign.

Notes

1 *LPCR 1940*, p. 123.
2 See Isaac Deutcher, *Stalin: a Political Biography*, pp. 454–60.
3 D. N. Pritt, *Autobiography of D. N. Pritt*, Vol. I, p. 260. Also H. Pelling, *History of the British Communist Party* (London, 1958), pp. 116–17.
4 See Herbert Morrison's analysis in a written answer, 368 H. C. Deb., 310–11, 23 January 1941. He described the constitution of the conference as ramshackle and 'unrepresentative'.
5 *Tribune*, 10 June 1941.
6 Reprinted in Gollancz, *Betrayal of the Left*, pp. v–x.
7 Critic's London Diary, *N. S. and N.*, 4 January 1941.
8 368 H. C. Deb., 185–90, 22 January and 310–11 23 January. For the interesting debate on the suppression see 463–528 , 28 January, Bevan, Strauss, Buchanan, Kirkwood, Acland, S. O. Davies and S. Silverman voted against.
9 *The Times*, 22 January 1941.
10 Newbury Labour Party was disaffiliated on 12 February — *The Times*, 13 February 1941.
11 *LPCR 1941*, pp. 184–5.
12 Morrison's decision was endorsed by Parliament by 297 to 11.
13 *LPCR 1941*, p. 110.
14 Michael Foot, *Aneurin Bevan: a Biography*, vol. I, 1897–1945, p. 333.
15 E. Llewellyn Woodward, *British Foreign Policy in the Second World War* Vol. I, pp. 478 and 486.
16 *Tribune*, 28 March 1941.
17 *N. S. and N.*, 17 May 1941.
18 365 H. C. Deb., 1314, 5 November 1940.
19 *N. S. and N.*, 31 May 1941.
20 Clement Attlee, *Granada Historical Record* interview, p. 24.
21 Woodward, p. 140.
22 W. S. Churchill, *The Second World War*, vol. II, p. 118.
23 Dalton, *Diaries*, 29 January 1941.
24 Woodward, p. 148.
25 Foot, vol. II, p. 38.
26 *N. S. and N.*, 5 July 1941.

72 The Russia complex

27 S. Orwell and I. Angus, *The Collected Essays, Journalism and Letters of George Orwell*, vol. II, pp. 183 and 461.
28 The choice of the word 'people' rather than 'government' might have had some significance.
29 *Daily Herald*, editorial, 23 June 1941.
30 Foot, vol. I, p. 339.
31 Dalton, *Diaries*, 22 June 1941.
32 *Tribune*, 18 July 1941.
33 Interview with the MP concerned.
34 372 H. C. Deb., 989, 24 June 1941.
35 See Douglas Hyde, *I Believed* (London, 1950), pp. 115–17.
36 *N. S. and N.*, 26 July 1941.
37 Interview with Michael Foot.
38 Douglas Hyde, p. 117.
39 Analysis of the contents of *The Listener* for 1941.
40 A few examples chosen at random: Jennie Lee, *Our Ally*, 1941; Dudley Collard, *The Soviet Bar*, 1942; Wright Miller, *How the Russians Live* (Fabian Socialist Society for Propaganda), 1942; K. Gibbard, *Soviet Russia — an Introduction* (RIIA), 1943; Ivor Montague, *Stalin*, 1942; Walter Duranty, *The Kremlin and the People*, 1941; H. Cole, *Joseph Stalin*, 1942.
41 For example, Sir Archibald Southby, 373 H. C. Deb., 2015, 29 July 1941.
42 Hewlett Johnson, p. 191. Communists avoided sending their collections to 'Establishment' funds like that founded by Mrs Churchill, preferring their 'own' funds.
43 Evidence found in the Cornelius manuscripts deposited in Swansea University Library by Mr Hywell Francis.
44 *LPCR 1942*, p. 10.
45 As Home Secretary, Morrison was in a position to know of these activities — Douglas Hyde, pp. 122–6.
46 Critic's London Diary, *N. S. and N.*, 26 July 1941. Frank Owen was editor of the *Evening Standard*.
47 *Tribune*, 26 September 1941.
48 Verbatim record of Conference, 30–31 May. *Left News*, July 1942, p. 2518.
44 For founder membership list see *Left News*, October 1941.
50 For Pritt and Dobb see *N. S. and N.*, 24 March 1942 and P. Sloan, 23 August 1942.
51 *Daily Herald*, 4 July 1941.
52 *TUCR 1941*, p. 245.
53 Letter from Lord Citrine to author.
54 *Ibid.*
55 Interview with Mr Rothstein and Tom Harrison, 'Public opinion about Russia', *Political Quarterly*, October 1941.
56 *The Listener*, 26 June 1941.
57 S. Orwell and I. Angus, vol. II, p. 206.
58 Douglas Hyde, p. 126.
59 Foot, vol. I, p. 335.
60 *N. S. and N.*, 10 October 1942.
61 In a letter to *N. S. and N.*, 7 March 1942.

62 Interview with Lord Sorensen. His question 373, *H. C. Deb.*, 436, 15 July 1941.
63 *Ibid.*, 161, 9 July 1941.
64 *Ibid.*, 583–4, 16 July 1941, and Coates, *A History of Anglo-Soviet Relations*, pp. 681–2. It would seem that to circumvent this embarrassing situation Cooper 'inspired' a request from his fellow Conservative, Major Lloyd, that the practice be discontinued. A. J. P. Taylor says the Internationale was firstly *included* before this happened (*English History*, p. 543). This conflicts with the Coates's account, which makes no mention of this.
65 376 *H. C. Deb.*, 115–22, 3 December 1941.
66 378 *H. C. Deb.*, 148–9, 24 February 1942.
67 Tanner's remarks reported in *The Times*, 4 November 1941.
68 Taylor, p. 528 n.
69 *Tribune*, 26 September 1941.
70 See H. J. Laski, 'Towards friendship with the Soviet Union', *Tribune*, 5 July 1941.
71 *Tribune*, 29 August 1941. The action was designed to pre-empt a possible pro-German regime in Iran.
72 See his article in *Tribune*, 5 July 1942.
73 See, for example, Laski's review of a study on the USSR by a group of Labour MPs called the Socialist Clarity Group, which took a similar line, *Tribune*, 13 April 1942.
74 *Left News*, July 1941.
75 Published by Gollancz, 1941. See also his *Great Britain in the Post-war World* (London, 1942), pp. 112–16.
76 Page 18; see the debate occasioned by this book in *Left News*, February–April 1942.
77 Cole, p. 15.
78 For Cole's post-war views, see his *The Intelligent Man's Guide to the Post-war World* (London, 1947).
79 Cole, p. 172. In an interview with the author, Margaret Cole revealed that, after the war, her husband's faith in the USSR outlived her own to the point where in public she had to affect a greater faith than she felt, in order to avoid embarrassment.
80 *Daily Herald*, 23 September 1942.

5 Help Russia! The Second Front campaign

> We are pledged to establish a Second Front, when are we going to keep our promise? [*Daily Herald*, 13 July 1942]

The Second Front campaign in the Labour Party was basically an agitation of the left, but it received some uncharacteristic echoes in other sections of the party. Aneurin Bevan was its spearhead. As early as 24 June 1941 he emphasised in the House of Commons the necessity of a land invasion to supplement British bombing attacks, and in *Tribune* he declared, 'now is our chance to strike'; an expeditionary force to the Continent was clearly envisaged, so why not now, when Hitler was fully engaged in the East?[1] This basic thesis was to inform appeals for a Second Front throughout the next two years. The *N.S. and N.* took rather longer to accept the Bevanite argument but, as the siege of Leningrad intensified, allowed itself to comment that a 'summer's immunity for the west from attack has been worth a victory to Hitler in terms of British complacency'.[2] It offered the first of the imaginative but rather bizarre suggestions which issued from the left in defence of Second Front arguments; to facilitate a British assault upon the Continent, women and children should be deported abroad and Britain turned into an island fortress to withstand invasion unhampered by civilian need.[3]

By the autumn Bevan's demands for a Second Front were strident, almost violent. If Churchill refused to attack in the West, he warned, the House of Commons would bring him down, and, failing this, forces would arise outside the House that would bring necessary changes about.[4] Bevan here outlined the strategy he was to follow: rousing public opinion to bring pressure to bear upon the government. Orwell, for one, doubted whether 'working men would do anything positive if the government were seen to let Russia down'.[5] The suspicion that the government was pulling its punches

Help Russia! 75

because of an anti-Soviet prejudice permeated left-wing thinking.[6] This suspicion, reinforced by the CPGB, manifested itself in the call for the removal of 'Munichite' and anti-Russian members of the government.

Another complaint the absence of a Second Front nourished was government administration of production. The need to produce more war materials was seen clearly by all sections of society. The *Daily Herald*, in tirelessly calling for a large increase in output, reflected the mood of the Labour Party. 'Is there nothing more that British ingenuity, enterprise and strength can do to aid the Russians?' the newspaper asked on 5 July and with rising intensity during the days before the Commons debate on production on 29 July. During the debate Emmanuel Shinwell criticised government complacency and asked why no substantial aid had already been given to Russia. Ernest Bevin, Minister of Labour and consequently one of the targets of this criticism, reproved Shinwell for raising the topic, pointing out that he had imputed motives to the government which could be misconstrued by friend and foe alike. This argument became the government's stock response to such criticisms.[7]

Labour Ministers in the coalition government were largely unsympathetic to left-wing demands for even more aid to Russia. They were wholly engaged with their own tasks and accepted, virtually without demur, the Prime Minister's handling of foreign policy, but in the NEC they could not escape left-wing criticism. Dalton's diary reveals a testy attitude towards Shinwell, whom he referred to throughout this period of the war as 'Shinbad'. Shinwell, rather than Bevan, proved the scourge of the party leadership at party meetings on the issue of aid to Russia; on one occasion he even moved the phlegmatic Attlee to jump to his feet and exclaim, 'That's a damned lie.'[8]

Yet the critics on the left were reflecting a widespread concern in the party and in the country that more should be done. On 9 September Lees-Smith told the House that the country was impatient for aid and that doubts existed regarding government intentions towards Russia.[9] On this occasion Attlee replied for the government, assuring the House that every member of the government was resolved to help Russia.[10] The left was unconvinced; during September demands for more aid intensified. On 14 October 1941 Shinwell put it to Churchill that in view of the public disquiet on this issue a debate should be held.[11] Churchill was clearly against the idea, which he thought would do more harm than good, yet he bowed to the pressure and on 23 October an important debate on 'British aid to Russia' was held in secret session.

A respected voice on foreign affairs, that of Philip Noel-Baker, spoke of the 'anger' and 'resentment' over the inadequacy of British aid; he felt that the government had failed to treat its ally's territory as its own, to regard the

Volga and the Don as *its* frontiers at this time of mutual peril. The war in the East had drawn away half Hitler's strength in France; now was the time to strike. But Noel-Baker rejected the notion of the Second Front — the campaign for which he identified with the communists — and advocated an aerial concentration on Hitler's oil supplies.[12] Josiah Wedgwood was less cautious. He was willing to risk a second Dunkirk if that would relieve the pressure on Russia.[13] Public opinion, he believed, was furious at government inaction. According to Bevan, the public believed the government was 'ratting' on the USSR by refraining from military action on the Continent.[14] Gallacher chimed in by demanding the expulsion of 'Munichite' Cabinet members and the inclusion of openly pro-Soviet MPs.[15]

Churchill must have been relieved at the comprehensive rebuttal of the Second Front thesis by Commander Stephen King-Hall.[16] The distinguished naval and military strategist explained that to draw thirty to forty divisions from the East to join the twenty already in France would require a force beyond British manpower capabilities. The volume of shipping required and the air cover needed would be absolutely prohibitive, given that Germany commanded the western coastline. He concluded prophetically, 'I doubt whether we should ever be able to put a foot ashore in the west until the German forces start to disintegrate.'[17]

In the last analysis the House had to be content with Eden's bland reaffirmation of the government's determination to do all that was possible, and more, to help Britain's sorely pressed ally.[18]

ii

In the winter of 1941 Russia's plight was sore indeed. Stalin's tortuous and damaging efforts to place a 'cordon sanitaire' between the USSR and Germany had counted for nothing. German divisions had punched a huge hole into Western Russia, taking millions of prisoners and killing many more. The ill equipped and unprepared Soviet armies stubbornly retreated, stripping the country of food and equipment, the achievements of a generation, as they went. As winter fell, German armies were on the outskirts of Leningrad and Moscow. Never was large-scale assistance from Britain more urgently required, yet the reasons that made help necessary also placed Churchill in an acute dilemma. If Russia was really on the point of collapse, then massive British aid might save her; but if Britain were seriously to denude herself of war resources in an unsuccessful attempt to save Russia, then Hitler would be able to march back over a prostrate USSR into a near prostrate Great Britain. Churchill had to compute the chances of Russian defeat against Britain's ultimate national safety, and the aid which Britain finally despatched was the product of this equation.

The left quarrelled with Churchill's computations. They believed his attitude, and those of his advisors, to be coloured by a profound 'anti-Soviet prejudice'.[19] Through an ideological short circuit, the left easily connected anti-Soviet proclivities with poor assessments of Soviet military capability and the consequent 'curtailment' of military and material aid.

The *Daily Herald* shared the left-wing concern that more should be done to assist the USSR, but it is interesting to note that Labour's official paper was careful to dissociate itself from the extravagances of left-wing arguments; on 25 October, for example, the paper rejected the proposition that the extent of British aid was restricted by any ideological or personal prejudice.

America's entry into the war in December 1941, and her stated determination to enter the European theatre, quickened the hopes of Second Front advocates that a landing would be made in the spring of 1942. They now argued that the accession of vast American material power made a land invasion a practical possibility, particularly now that German troops were holding their position only with difficulty deep inside Russia's frozen territory.

Churchill met some of the criticism of his conduct of the war by appointing one Minister in overall charge of production — a measure which had been vigorously urged by all Labour organs of opinion. But his position was not easy at this time. As Russian prestige grew, British fortunes in the war languished. Cripps returned from Moscow in January 1942 in what Orwell called a 'blaze of undeserved glory' for having 'got Russia in on our side'.[20] He made a very well received broadcast, emphasising Russia's need for war materials, and was boosted on the left as an alternative Prime Minister. Given the weakness of his position, Churchill attempted to buy Cripps with a government post; Cripps agreed to be bought, but exacted a full Cabinet post as his price.

The *New Statesman* talked on 28 February of a deep 'sense of humiliation' that Britain seemed to lack the moral and offensive spirit to emulate Russian military feats. The journal warned: 'The maintenance of an inactive army of over three million men to the passive defence of this island cannot be justified through yet another spring and summer.'

In January 1942 Shinwell was still a prominent advocate of the Second Front in the press[21] and still the *bête noir* of the leadership on this prickly problem, but increasingly Bevan's voice became the most persistent and ultimately the most respected on this issue. Bevan was aided by the fact that he was now editor of *Tribune*. Postgate had done a great deal to establish the journal as an economically viable and articulate voice of the left, but his relations with Bevan, which had never been happy, finally broke down in the autumn of 1941. Bevan took over.

The journal now became the voice of Bevan and his parliamentary supporters in their campaign against Churchill's leadership of the nation. Their attacks in 1942 focused upon the absence of a Second Front, and few issues of *Tribune* passed by without informative and sympathetic articles on Russia together with calls for a cross-Channel invasion. When German armies were massing to launch a spring attack upon the Red armies, *Tribune* typically declared that Britain's only course was to open a Second Front immediately, draw twenty to thirty divisions from the East and give the Red army a great victory. Any other course would seem like 'black treachery' to the Russians, an Anglo-American (by implication 'capitalist') attempt to dictate the peace when Germany and Russia had reached exhaustion point.[22]

A series of articles appeared in *Tribune* under the name of 'Thomas Rainboro', billed as a 'brilliant writer' and 'well known publicist'. He was in fact Frank Owen, former editor of the *Evening Standard*, a man well connected with some of the country's leading military men.[23] The articles attacked Churchill in language which even Bevan had shrunk from using. The most popular issue of the day, Owen observed, was the demand for the Second Front; despite support for the idea from Roosevelt, Sikorski, Chiang Kai-Shek, Cripps, De Gaulle and even Churchill himself, no such military operation had taken place. Instead we had only defeats to comfort us. Time was running out for Britain and for Russia. Owen posed the critical question, 'Have we time to afford Churchill's strategy?' The first stirrings of a 'Churchill must go' campaign were certainly present on the left at this stage of the war in the spring of 1942.

Whilst Bevan, Owen and company added their voices to those of Pollitt, Dutt and their political associates in calling for a Second Front, the rest of the party stirred uncomfortably. The *Daily Herald* sensed a 'deep uneasiness' in the nation over the inadequate provision of supplies to Russia, but held aloof from the Second Front agitations.[24] The united front presented by the Labour Ministers in the government was a strong disincentive to open criticism in the right and centre of the party. Labour Ministers were frequently put up to defend the government's record over Russia, perhaps deliberately, bearing in mind the location of the sharpest criticism. On 19 May, for instance, Attlee assured the House that whatever the risks, the convoys to Russia would get through with their vital supplies.[25] However, it was a fact that a gulf had opened up between a large section of the Labour Party and its government members over the Second Front issue. Widespread frustration was felt at Britain's apparent impotence whilst Russia once again began to take the full weight of Hitler's war machine. Some of this frustration was reflected in the Party Conference held at Westminster in May.

In his opening address the chairman, the trade unionist, W.H. Green, struck an openly critical note. 'Fronts, not stunts' were the only effective way to help Russia; he doubted whether the closest possible collaboration was taking place. Laski announced, to cheers, that the NEC would send a delegation to the Russian people to seek for the (somewhat convoluted) objective of 'a common basis that would enable their purpose and our purpose to march together in unbreakable union for all time'. Speaking for the NEC, Noel-Baker expressed confidence that the battle would 'soon' be joined by our forces against the enemy in Europe.[26]

The Anglo-Soviet pact of 11 June 1942 (signed in London), which envisaged at least twenty years' co-operation, was given an ecstatic reception by all elements of the Labour Party and by the country as a whole. The *Daily Herald's* view on 12 June was that 'the comradeship in arms is stronger in fact and feeling than any document can express', and on 13 June the editorial announced that 'a marriage has been solemnized between Britain and the Soviet Union'. Hannen Swaffer, the *Herald* columnist, argued that public opinion, made vocal at scores of meetings throughout the land, 'rendered possible the historic treaty'.[27] Certainly public opinion was overjoyed at this impressive show of diplomatic unity. Past differences were forgotten, the *New Statesman* now referring to previous doubts over the Baltic States as 'silly'.[28] A euphoric expectation took root that Britain and Russia would march together, through victory, towards a brighter future.

The section of the communique expressing 'full understanding' over 'the urgent task of creating a Second Front in 1942' was greeted with excitement. At last Russia's suffering would be alleviated and Hitler's power quickly crushed. No one could be blamed for interpreting these words as an unambiguous statement of intent by Britain (and, by implication, America) to breach the Continental coastline in the next few months. Churchill claims in his memoirs that this announcement was simply a ruse to maintain German forces in France; Molotov was given an *aide-memoire* in which Churchill stipulated that Britain could 'give no promise in the matter'.[29]

The euphoria of the Anglo-Soviet pact was somewhat punctured by the disastrous British reverses in Libya in the summer of 1942. Churchill was forced to defend his record against a motion of censure tabled by a leading Tory backbencher, Wardlaw Milne, and supported by assorted factions, including Bevan and his friends. Bevan was here concerned with a full-scale attack upon Churchill dealing with every aspect of his administration but focusing upon the absence of a Second Front. We should get at the enemy where he is, twenty-one miles away, argued Bevan, not 1,500 miles away in the Middle East. If the government was not ready to launch the attack, then why not? 'We cannot postpone it till next year, Stalin expects it; please do not misunderstand me, for heaven's sake, do not let us make the mistake of betraying those lion-hearted Russians. Speeches have been made, the Russians believe them and have broken the champagne bottles on them ... please do not speak with a twisted tongue on this matter.' Of Churchill Bevan said he fought 'debates like a war and the war like a debate. He wins debate after debate and loses battle after battle.'[30]

True to this analysis, Churchill won an overwhelming parliamentary victory of 476 to 25. He shrugged off Bevan's speech as a 'bitter diatribe',[31] but Maurice Webb in the *Daily Herald* was probably nearer the truth in judging Bevan's speech as 'the most considerable performance of any backbencher since the war began, if not in the present Parliament'.[32]

Certainly the Second Front campaign did not slow down following this debate. A delegation of several thousand women war workers appealed outside No. 10 Downing Street,[33] Maisky addressed over 300 MPs in the Commons,[34] 60,000 people attended a rally in Trafalgar Square[35]. According to a Gallup poll published on 27 July 60 per cent of the public favoured an invasion in 1942 whilst only 12 per cent did not.[36] Tom Driberg (according to Kingsley Martin, a 'fellow-traveller'),[37] an ardent Second Front advocate, successfully broke the electoral truce as an Independent for the Malden constituency. *The Times* gauged the mood of the country in judging that the effectiveness of the support given to Russia would be taken as the 'acid test of the ability and foresight with which the conduct of the war has been planned and developed'[38]. On 13 July the *Daily Herald* virtually joined the campaign; 'we are pledged to establish a Second Front, when are we going to keep our promise?'

iii

It was in this atmosphere that, suddenly, on 19 August, the campaigners for a Second Front were met with the fact of Dieppe. A joint force of British and Canadian troops had been firmly repulsed and suffered heavy losses.[39] It was inevitable that this failure should be built up into a success story. Britain's first foray on to the Continent since Dunkirk just had to have a few silver linings; the Second Front campaigners eagerly sought them and used them to upholster their arguments. *Tribune* felt that the raid had 'stirred the World' and proved that 'we could do much'.[40] The *New Statesman* columnist Tom Wintringham was sufficiently self-confident to propose his own strategy for the liberation of France; first a two-week raid on strategic targets combined with propaganda, then the siezure of air fields and the airborne landing of

Help Russia! 81

troops who would capture vehicles in the occupied country to launch their offensive!⁴¹ Upton Sinclair in *Tribune* went even further; he favoured the landing of one division in central France to stage an effort on the lines of Thermopylae.⁴²

The Second Fronters were, however, sufficiently well informed on military matters to know that October was definitely the last month when a cross-Channel landing could be undertaken. By late summer, with no sign of a Second Front being imminent, the left began to draw its own highly coloured conclusions. A revealing exchange in the *New Statesman* correspondence columns suggests the way left-wing minds were working at this time:

Sir
In this week's Leader you write, 'The Second Front can never be a purely military operation; it is whether we like it or not, part of a European war against facism. That may be one of the real reasons why it is postponed so long.'
Do you seriously believe this?
signed
John Maynard Keynes
Yes. — *Ed.*

Churchill returned from Moscow in September to make flattering references to Russia's 'rugged war chief' but no reference to Anglo-American plans to open a Second Front in 1942.⁴³ By August professional military opinion on both sides of the Atlantic had come out against such an enterprise. Churchill explained to Stalin that, given the small number of landing craft available, the force that could be transported across the Channel would be easily and damagingly disposed of by the twenty-two German divisions in France. Instead he offered 'Torch', the invasion of North Africa, in 1942, and the definite undertaking to open a Second Front on the Continent in 1943.⁴⁴ Stalin, however, was privately wholly unconvinced by the arguments against a Second Front in 1942, and insisted that the June communique had committed Britain to a course she was now refusing to take.⁴⁵

The British Labour Party shared some of Stalin's frustration. Arthur Greenwood told the House that fair support was essential; Anglo-Russian relations had been clouded for too many years by mutual suspicion 'created very largely by this [the British] side'.⁴⁶ For the left, an exasperated Bevan declared that the British people 'have more confidence in the sagacity of Voroshilov and Timoshenko than in that of Winston Churchill and they know that the Russian generals have declared that a Second Front is possible'".⁴⁷ As September passed and no Front materialised, anger on the left built up. On 25 September *Tribune* broke an unofficial Ministry of Information (i.e. imposed) silence on an interview in which Stalin had revealed that Churchill had not convinced him of the impracticability of a Second Front in 1942. A fortnight later Stalin made his discomfort public. At the time German armies had crushed Russian opposition in Krasmoda and Maikop, Novorossik and Elista and were fighting on the outskirts of Stalingrad. Never had German pressure been so intense and never the need for relief in the West more pressing.

On 23 October *Tribune* published a remarkable editorial. It took the form of an open letter to Stalin. It explained that highly placed anti-Soviet elements in Britain were trying to prevent co-operation. The masses, who were all for Stalin, lacked any real leadership; this leadership, Bevan's journal broadly hinted, should come from Stalin before it was too late. The editorial (despite its accompanying denial) can only be interpreted as an invitation to Stalin to make an open appeal to the British people over the heads of their government.

This article probably represents the high point of the Second Front campaign. The TUC had already shied away from too close an involvement. At the Trade Union Conference (7–11 September 1942) Jack Tanner of the AEU had tried to push through an amendment calling for the immediate opening of a Second Front, cleverly combining it with an expression of goodwill towards Russia so that opposition to the first part implied unpardonable rejection of the second. The heavy artillery of the TUC was called up to counter this strategy. Charles Dukes began by sourly observing that some elements in the TUC would claim a monopoly of friendship with the Soviet Union. Acceptance of the amendment would, he pointed out, imply that Congress had no faith in the direction of the war, particularly as regards the timing and location of a Second Front.[48] Arthur Deakin (TGWU) declared that the heart of the British trade union movement had been devoted to giving the Soviet Union the greatest possible support but he agreed with Dukes that the amendment would amount, at a critical time, to a virtual motion of censure upon the government. The big unions won the day with a vote of 3,584,000 against, but Tanner's resolution commanded 1,526,000 in its favour[49] and the wording of the final resolution reflected something of a compromise.

The ASTUC also provided a forum the Russians used to press their arguments for a Second Front in 1943. In June 1943 Citrine, Conley and Harrison visited Russia together with the secretary of the committee, Victor Feather. During this visit the British delegation was allowed to see virtually everything it chose. Citrine noted that wages had increased, that there were no signs of hunger, that most men worked a sixty-six-hour week and that industrial morale was extremely high. The Reuter and *Daily Herald* reporters, however, complained that censorship had become so bad that what was left of their stories ceased to make sense.[50] During the first session the Russians were told of Citrine's progress, or lack of it, in America, where he had recently tried to bring the USA into the committee but had succeeded only in forming a bilateral committee with an organisation representing only a portion of American trade unionists. They were reassured on the subject of current strikes in Britain, and were informed of the Labour Party's 'Help Russia' fund and of Britain's contribution to the war effort. It was the latter point that proved contentious, as it raised, inescapably, the issue of the Second Front. Citrine later told the TUC that when he was in the Urals virtually every question he was asked was 'When are you going to organise a Second Front?' At a speech in Stalinsk he felt moved to answer the question by defending Churchill. He pointed out that Britain was predominantly a naval power and argued that the essential supplies of material to Russia were as important as the Second Front. Nevertheless 'Russian trade unionists were very keen to induce us to demand that there should be a Second Front in Europe that year'.[51] Perhaps this concern helps explain the Russians' unusually cordial attitudes to their British guests, which moved the American ambassador, Clerk Kerr, to express surprise.

Certainly the British delegation found itself in a delicate situation. It had no competence to make policy decisions on this point. The TUC was still bound by the 1942 Blackpool resolution which eschewed direct pressure upon the government over the Second Front. Citrine had to tell the Russians at one of the ASTUC meetings that there was 'nobody in the world, certainly not in Soviet Russia, who was competent to advise the British Government on this subject'.[52] He asked them whether they would take independent action against their own government if Russian military advisors were opposed to it. This annoyed the Russians, who dismissed the Sicily landings as no substitute for a Second Front. Citrine pointed out that Britain too had made great sacrifices and had entered the war voluntarily. The Russians mentioned Munich, the British the Nazi-Soviet pact, tempers became somewhat frayed, and the committee was fortunate to survive this divisive exchange.[53]

As it was, the British delegation went to the 'limits of their authority' by agreeing to the desirability of a Second Front and hoping it would take place in the 'coming years'. Agreement was also absent on the Soviet proposal that the committee should be greatly widened to 'include all those organisations within the United Nations actively pursuing the fight against Hitler'. Such an extension, in Citrine's view, would amount in effect to a new International, and he believed the best way to unite the trade union world was through an open conference in which different points of view could be effectively reconciled.

The third meeting of the committee thus reflected the different conceptions of the committee's proper role held by each side. The British TUC viewed the committee as an advisory co-ordinating body, the Russians as a lever to be manipulated against the Churchill government and perhaps as a Trojan Horse for Russian entry into the world of Western trade unions.

Despite the efforts of the Russians in the ASTUC, much of the heat had been taken out of the second front campaign by the spring of 1943. The *Daily Herald* (11 November 1942) had dissociated itself from an agitation which might have 'disruptive consequences', whilst *Tribune* and the *N.S. and N.* shifted their emphasis elsewhere. The reason? Churchill was at last beginning to win battles as well as debates. El Alamein and the containment of the U-boats in the Atlantic, coupled with the relief of pressure in the east occasioned by the momentous victory at Stalingrad, slowed down the impetus of the campaign. Besides, Churchill could proudly point to the North African landings in 1942, soon to be followed by the successful invasion of Italy in the summer of 1943. Maybe these actions did not divert German resources from the Russian front as a major landing in France would have done, but they successfully diverted the attention of those elements in the Labour Party which had been inclined, largely through pro-Soviet sympathies, to advocate the latter strategy.

Ironically, it was the Second Fronters themselves who helped to postpone the cross-Channel invasion until 1944. On 11 November Churchill told Parliament that 'no amount of pressure by public opinion' would force him into an abortive Second Front, but there can be no doubt that by stimulating a widespread desire for action in 1942 the campaign helped the 'Torch' initiative. As A. J. P. Taylor points out, 'Churchill wanted a victory to still the discontent in England, Roosevelt wanted some action for the American army in 1942. North Africa was the only place where their wishes met.'[54] This campaign absorbed the resources which could have been used to open a Second Front in France in 1943.[55]

The Second Front campaign was yet further evidence of the dichotomy that was opening up in the Labour Party between the leadership and the rank and file of the party. Labour's coalition Ministers, the nucleus of the future Labour Cabinet, were wholly occupied by day-to-day administrative tasks. They worked in a context in which British power, interests and security were taken for granted. Instead of trying to change the established system they quite naturally worked within it. Foreign policy was the preserve of Churchill and Eden, on which Labour Ministers did not think to trespass. Hugh Dalton, while sustaining a lively interest in foreign affairs, offered no private criticisms in his diary of Churchill's conduct of the war, and on one occasion had even been known to remark to Eden, 'Why should you and I pretend to differ because we are nominally in different camps?'[56] Bevin later revealed, when the war was over, that on no occasion had Labour Ministers disagreed with Tory Ministers over major foreign policy issues.[57] The Second Front thesis was certainly not embraced by any Labour Minister; this role in the coalition government fell, paradoxically, to that highly individualistic Conservative Lord Beaverbrook.[58] There is some evidence to suggest that it was this very lack of enthusiasm which precipitated a challenge to the leadership in the autumn of 1942. At a time when the campaign was at its height, Laski openly admitted in an NEC meeting that he had no confidence in Attlee's leadership and wanted Bevin and Dalton to take over.[59] (Laski's revolt gained little support, but it is hardly surprising that Attlee came thoroughly to dislike this political academic.)[60]

A situation existed therefore in which the Labour leaders faced the realities of power under a charismatic Conservative Prime Minister whilst Labour Party activists and intellectuals continued to speculate and theorise as before when Labour had been in opposition. Thus the conflicting perspectives on foreign affairs which were to characterise the party's post war foreign policy can be seen to have been incipient in the middle years of the war.

iv

It has already been noted that the Labour left used sympathy for Russia through the Second Front campaign as a stick with which to beat the Conservatives, but by 1943 Russian prestige was a source of political capital used by others as well.

The CPGB was naturally exultant during these years and saw in this enthusiasm for Russia the seeds of a British revolution. 'To stand on the plinth of Nelson's Column,' wrote Douglas Hyde, at that time a member of the *Daily Worker*'s staff,

and look down on 50,000 faces, to see the hammer and sickle badge openly and proudly worn by almost everyone present, to hear great masses of people singing the 'Internationale' and 'Soviet Land' was to be carried away by a terrific emotion ... For years I had dreamed of this. Through the years when the mass of the people had been bitterly hostile to us ... Through the years when people had frequently publicly demanded that I take the hammer and sickle badge from my coat. This was a foretaste of the Soviet Britain of tomorrow.[61]

The CPGB did all it could to realise this objective. Rose Macauley complained in the correspondence columns of the *N.S. and N.* of the manipulation she had noted at meetings organised by the Russia Today Society. No critical questions were allowed, and the proceedings were conducted in an atmosphere of 'uncritical and pathological Soviet worship' which, she believed, could only harm the Soviet cause in Great Britain.[62] Within the Labour Party the CPGB certainly made some headway; Citrine believed that its case had been strenghthened by the feats of the Red Army, but trade union leaders were very careful not to shift their position on the key question of communist affiliation to the Labour Party. Communists, in fact, were making keen inroads into British trade unions at this time.[63]

The Labour Party itself, of course, was not loath to extract political mileage out of the Russian image, and past connections were heavily emphasised. The left in particular was eager to point out that the apparently superhuman Russian resistance proved that 'the USSR has discovered a method of inspiring and organising enthusiasm on its home front which other countries have yet to find'.[64]

Nor were individual politicians unwilling to exploit pro-Soviet feeling for their own ends. Orwell had already noted that 'all kinds of crooks' were doing so, but would he have included Dalton within this category?[65] Dalton gives a devastating insight into the mind of the practical politician in his diary entry for 12 December 1942. On that day he addressed the opening conference of the West Midland Regional Council of Labour, composed mostly of trade unionists and divisional Labour parties. In his address Dalton successfully tried out a new approach, of keeping 'Russia, Russian achievement and recent Russian pronouncements constantly prominent. In other words, in order to make my point, make it through a Russian word or act. While Russian stocks stand so high, especially in the Labour Party, I am sure that this is the best expository method.' It is also worth noting that two Labour politicians were able to return from the wings into the forefront of the political stage: Cripps, through his tenure as ambassador in Moscow, and Bevan as champion of the Second Front campaign. In striking contrast with his fellow barrister, D.N. Pritt, whose pro-Sovietism had virtually ended his chance of political office, Cripp's connections with Russia had plucked him from what threatened to be political obscurity in 1939 and placed him in a role which, despite his inadequacies, established his reputation and eligibility for the highest offices in the land. It is difficult to say whether Bevan's tactics over the Second Front were those of the opportunist. His was a personality that inspired definite judgements amongst those who knew him. To one of his friends and fellow MPs interviewed by the writer, Bevan was incapable of insincerity, utterly scrupulous in his pursuit of principle whatever the issue in question. To another of his colleagues he was a consummate actor, quite capable of picking up and embracing an issue if it could further his ambition of one day leading the Labour Party. The truth, one might guess, lies somewhere between the two judgements; like most highly successful politicians, he probably had the facility of frequently convincing himself that the requirements of his own career coincided with the dictates of principle.

Whatever his motives, Bevan used his championship of Russia to give full vent to his considerable power of oratory. By 1943 he was beginning to emerge as one of, if not the, leading figure on the left. His views figure prominently in the next chapter, which identifies the first glimmerings of suspicion that Soviet intentions in Eastern Europe were less than honourable.

Notes

1 370 *H.C. Deb.*, 10, 24 June 1941, and *Tribune*, 4 July 1941.
2 *N.S. and N.* 20 September 1941.
3 *Ibid.*, 27 September 1941.
4 *Tribune*, 1 October 1941.
5 Sonia Orwell and Ian Angus, *Collected Orwell*, Vol. II, p.175.
6 For example, see George Strauss's speech, 736 *H.C. Deb.*, 655, 12 November 1941.
7 Shinwell, 373 *H.C. Deb.*, 1339–46, and Bevin's reply, 1357–71, 29 July 1941.
8 Dalton, *Diaries*, 1 October 1941.
9 374 *H.C. Deb.*, 83, 9 September 1941.
10 Earlier Attlee had told the house that 'all aid had been given to Russia', 373 *H.C. Deb.*, 1978, 6 August 1941.
11 374 *H.C. Deb.*, 1239–40, 14 October 1941 (oral question).
12 *Ibid.*, 1943.
13 *Ibid.*, 1963.
14 *Ibid.*, 1971.
15 *Ibid.*, 1990–6.
16 *Ibid.*, 1962.
17 See also King Hall's correspondence in the *N.S. and N.*, 25 October 1941, and 8 November 1941.
18 374 *H.C. Deb.*, 2000–7, 30 September 1941.
19 Michael Foot, *Aneurin Bevan*, Vol. I, 1897–45, p. 338.
20 S. Orwell and I. Angus, vol. II, p. 240.
21 See Dalton, *Diaries*, 7 January 1942, and, for example, *Daily Herald*, 29 January 1942.
22 *Tribune*, 13 March 1942.
23 Foot, *Bevan*, vol. I, p. 365.
24 *Daily Herald*, 27 January 1942.
25 380 *H.C. Deb.*, 58, 19 May.
26 *LPCR 1942*, p. 96.
27 *Daily Herald*, 16 June 1942.
28 *N.S. and N.*, 20 June 1942.
29 W.S. Churchill, *The Second World War*, vol. IV, p. 305.
30 381 *H.C. Deb.*, 527–40, 2 July 1942.
31 *Ibid.*, 583–610.
32 *Daily Herald*, 3 July 1942.
33 *Ibid.*, 30 July 1942.
34 *Daily Herald*, 30 July 1942.
35 *N.S. and N.*, 1 August 1942.

36 W.P. and Zelda Coates, *A History of Anglo-Soviet Relations*, p. 274. 28 per cent answered 'Don't know'.
37 *N.S. and N.*, 4 July 1942. Driberg later became a Labour MP.
38 *The Times*, 31 July 1942.
39 Half the invading force were 'either killed or taken prisoner': A. J. P. Taylor, *English History, 1914–45*, p. 557.
40 *Tribune*, 28 August 1942.
41 *N.S. and N.*, 22 August 1942.
42 *Tribune*, 18 September 1942.
43 383 *H.C. Deb.*, 95, 8 September 1942.
44 Churchill, p. 430.
45 *Ibid.*, p. 441.
46 383 *H.C. Deb.*, 100, 8 September 1942.
47 *Ibid.*, 246, 9 September 1942.
48 *TUCR 1942*, pp. 254 and 258.
49 *Ibid.*, p. 261.
50 W. Citrine, *Two Careers*, p. 159.
51 *Ibid.*, p. 169.
52 *TUCR 1943*, p. 275.
53 Citrine, p. 167.
54 Taylor. p. 556.
55 See Arthur Bryant *The Turn of the Tide*, pp. 423–9.
56 Dalton, *Diaries*, 19 October 1942.
57 312 *H.C. Deb.*, 120, 20 August 1945.
58 Foot, p. 389, see also pp. 337–8.
59 Dalton, *Diaries*, 2 October 1942.
60 See Clement Attlee, *Granada Historical Record* interview, pp. 28 and 52.
61 Douglas Hyde, *I Believed*, p. 192.
62 *N.S. and N.*, 6 June 1942.
63 Citrine, p. 188. For Communist penetration of trade unions during the war see H. Pelling, *A History of the British Communist Party*, pp. 136–8.
64 Margaret Cole, in her introduction to N. Barou, *The Soviet Home Front*, (Fabian pamphlet, 1942).
65 S. Orwell and I. Angus, vol. III, p. 247.

6 Doubts renewed: the case of Poland

> Had the Soviet Government given any indication of their anxiety to help the Polish Army fighting in Warsaw, there would have been neither suspicion nor comment. Let us hope Mr Stalin will not withold any longer some expressions of sympathy for the men and women who are struggling against desperate odds. [Letter to *The Times*, 1 September 1944.]

i

By 1944 the heroic image of the USSR was sacrosanct; virtually all organs of opinion conspired willingly with the government to censor any criticism. *Animal Farm* was turned down by a series of publishers, and Orwell, who knew of three similar rejections, was angered when his mildly critical review of Laski's generously pro-Soviet *Faith, Reason and Civilisation* was turned down by the *Manchester Evening News*. Two years before, he had doubted whether public ehthusiasm for a new ally extended to admiration of her political system, but he perceived that 'socialism' *was* now identified with the USSR and that the two images were indistinguishable.[1] As in the heady days before the Nazi-Soviet pact, to be anti-Soviet was to appear anti-socialist, and public criticism of the USSR became as taboo in 1944 as praise had been in 1940. Raymond Blackburn, a Labour MP in 1945, suspected that a great many votes might have swung to Labour in 1945 'because of the triumph of Soviet arms and the belief that it proved the efficacy of a planned economy'.[2]

The protective enthusiasm of the Second Front campaign, along with constant tales of heroic sacrifice and endless hurrahs whipped up by virtually every section of the political spectrum, had helped to purge doubts about Soviet foreign policy intentions. By 1944 most Labour Party members were beginning to anticipate a post-war world in which the Soviet Union would play a constructive part. Citrine hoped that his joint committee would be the basis of a single world federation of trade unionists which would involve the

Americans as well. Laski hoped for a socialist international which would embrace social democratic and communist parties. It was widely believed that a massive leftward shift of opinion had taken place in Europe and that the USSR would benignly oversee the socialist developments in Eastern Europe. The ideals of the 1930s had reasserted themselves, and an immense investment of hope was being made in some form of post-war collective security organisation which would abolish the deadly uncertainties of the balance-of-power system. As in the first great conflict twenty years before, the Labour Party hoped it was fighting a war to end wars, and it was naturally assumed by rank-and-file members that the Soviet Union felt the same way. But those who studied Russian behaviour closely or who, as Ministers in the coalition, were privy to Foreign Office information, were less sanguine. Their doubts tended to centre upon Russian dealings with Poland. An ambivalent relationship was only to be expected — after all, only two years previously Stalin had assisted Hitler in virtually wiping Poland from the face of the earth. Even after Sikorski's government in exile had agreed with Stalin to co-operate against what had become the common foe, alarming stories of Poles being persecuted within the USSR continued to filter into England. In March 1943 the Labour Party's International Sub-committee considered a memorandum critical of the Russian execution of two well known Polish politicians. Trade unionists Dallas and Walker were in favour, but Laski, Noel-Baker, Morrison, Clay and Dalton helped to vote down the criticism.[3]

On 13 April 1943 German radio announced the discovery of mass graves in the Katyn forest, near Smolensk. It was here that ten thousand missing Polish officers had been interned. All of them, the Germans claimed, had been murdered in 1940 by the communists. Eloquent in detail and statistics, the German story appeared to provide proof of what the Poles had hitherto refused to believe. The London Polish accepted the German proposal of a Red Cross enquiry and were immediately accused by Moscow of collusion with the Nazis. Diplomatic relations were broken off and an organisation hostile to the London Poles called the Union of Polish Patriots in the USSR (UPP) was created in Moscow and soon began to take on the appearance of a potential puppet government. For once Goebbels was not lying; subsequent research has proved the truth of the allegations.[4] But at the time Allied unity was held to be paramount and comment was muted, being limited in the Labour press to criticisms of the London Polish for their precipitate and unilateral action. *Reynolds' News* put the blame on 'reactionary landowners with their eyes on a return to the feudal tradition and industrialists who did well out of the old Poland of cheap labour'.[5] The *N.S. and N.* was similarly critical, and *Tribune* accused the Poles of 'treachery'.[6] However, for *Tribune* Katyn may have been something of a watershed, for within a few months a remarkable change occured: it became the most prominent and outspoken critic of the Soviet Union. Bevan was concerned at Russia's prompt recognition of the right-wing Badoglio government in post-Mussolini Italy, her participation in the unjustifiably secret diplomacy of Teheran and her cultivation of the UPP. Prophetically, he feared that Stalin's attitude towards Eastern Europe had hardened and that social democracy would be destroyed after the war as 'Moscow communism' and 'Washington capitalism' fought over the body of Europe. Whilst other editors kept their doubts to themselves, Bevan was not the kind of political journalist to respect a silence. *Tribune* began to criticise Russia's 'national self-centered policy'. After the Teheran proposals, which meant, in effect, that Poland be shunted to the west at Germany's expense and to Soviet advantage, *Tribune* declared that 'the conduct of the Russian Government in the conflict with the Poles, gives ground for the worst misgivings'.[7] *Tribune*'s concern was shared by the *Socialist Commentary*[8] and by a body of Labour MPs with Bevan's friend Richard Stokes to the fore in the debate on the Teheran proposals in February 1944.

Other elements on the left of the party were concerned to discredit the Polish cause at this time. Powerful fire was directed against the exile government's production of anti-Soviet publications at British expense and the Polish Officers' Corps was accused of anti-semitism and even fascism; Tom Driberg spoke strongly in the two parliamentary debates which took place on these subjects in April.[9] Ironically, it was at this time that Polish forces were fighting so heroically at Monte Casino.

The *N.S. and N.* had no doubts that Russia was entitled to her broad corridor of land west of the Curzon line and needed it as security against future attack. A liberal, friendly policy was discerned on 22 January, but the Poles were urged to compromise in case the Russians recognised the UPP and thereby made Poland a 'dependency of Moscow'. In July the UPP was installed in Lublin as the Polish Committee of National Liberation (PCNL) to administer liberated Polish territory. How did the *N.S. and N.* react? Forgetting its previous analysis of the UPP as the puppet of Moscow, the journal described the new committee as 'widely representative and likely to become more so'. Churchill was urged to drop the government in exile, which was compared with the Vichy government, and to reach an agreement with Stalin and the Lublin Poles, who were compared with De Gaulle's Free French government.

Neither Churchill nor Eden had any intention of adopting such a course. Ever since Teheran, Eden had feared 'greatly for the Poles'; in a Foreign Office minute of 25 March he had written that Russia had vast aims which might include the domination of Eastern Europe and the Mediterranean and the communising of much that remained.[10] The creation of the PCNL naturally intensified these fears. At Churchill's request, Mikolajczyk, the Polish Prime Minister, hopefully travelled to Moscow in late July to attempt some accommodation with Stalin. A few days after his arrival the Warsaw uprising began. Anticipating imminent relief from the Red Army, the Polish Home Army, owing allegiance to the London government, rose against its German occupiers on 1 August.

ii

Much controversy still surrounds Stalin's role in this tragic episode. Critics claim that, realising the Polish forces might offer a political challenge, he deliberately halted the Red Army's advance and allowed the Germans to destroy a 35,000-strong resistance force and much of Warsaw in the process. There is evidence to suggest that the Red Army was genuinely stopped outside this strategic point on the Vistula by reinforced German forces, but other evidence suggests that, even if the Russian halt was not deliberate, it would have been had Stalin had any choice in the matter. He deliberately prevented Western aeroplanes from delivering aid by denying them airfield facilities east of Warsaw (Churchill considered halting convoy supplies in retaliation), he withheld Soviet supplies until it was too late, he sanctioned constant propaganda attacks dissociating the USSR from the rising, belittling the efforts of the Polish Home Army and condemning its leaders as 'criminals'. On 2 October the Polish forces surrendered. Hardly a building remained standing in Warsaw. Over 200,000 people had been killed. In a last broadcast from the city General Bor, the leader of the Home Army, invoked God's judgement on those who had betrayed Warsaw.[11]

Labour reactions were mixed. The press as a whole treated the subject with extreme caution, much to Orwell's disgust. On the far left, *Forward* and *Reynolds' News* made no mention of Warsaw throughout the eight weeks of the rising, whilst, on the right, the Beaverbrook-owned *Daily Express* greeted the surrender of General Bor with peans of editorial praise for the Soviet Union. Voluntary censorship in the press thus made information about events in the Polish capital a scarce commodity. At one point Churchill even enquired whether the Ministry of Information had imposed an official clampdown on news of the rising, and ordered that the facts be made known.[12]

The *Daily Worker* processed the official Soviet line for English consumption, vilifying the London Polish and accusing Bor of acting recklessly without consulting the Red Army; the communist daily neglected to mention that two days before the rising Moscow Radio carried a PCNL broadcast which said the 'hour of action' had arrived and exhorted the people of Warsaw to 'fight the Germans'. The *N.S. and N.* followed the *Daily Worker* version quite closely, similarly imputing disreputable political motives to the exile government and dismissing the deliberate halt accusation as an 'idiotic lie'. Unlike the *Daily Worker* however, the *N.S. and N.* accepted that requests for Western use of Soviet airfields had been refused, but was sure there must be sound military reasons. In fact wherever controversy arose the *N.S. and N.* accepted the Soviet explanation without cavil. Style of diplomacy rather than content of policy was the subject of its mild reproofs. Thus it was that five days after his surrender and denunciation by the USSR the journal could accuse General Bor of much anti-Soviet activity without offering a single shred of evidence to support the accusation.

The *Daily Herald* was circumspectly in support of the Warsaw Poles, supported the London Polish against the PCNL and urged Stalin to adopt a more flexible attitude. On 14 August W. N. Ewer described the deliberate halt rumour as the outcome of 'suspicion and hysteria' but has since told the author that it was widely suspected in journalistic circles that the halt had been deliberate; the atmosphere of the time was such that editors were not prepared to publish such rumours, however strongly they felt. Bevan was the single exception. At first *Tribune* suspected that both East and West were withholding aid in order to weaken resistance forces in Europe, but by the end of August this suspicion gave way to a hostile attitude towards the USSR. On 1 September it judged that the political handling of the Warsaw situation had 'done more harm to the good name of the Soviet Union than anything since June 1941'. *Tribune*'s criticism intensified throughout September and culminated in its reaction to the Soviet threat to court-martial General Bor. Whereas, before Warsaw, *Tribune* had questioned Soviet intentions, now it openly doubted them. Moscow, it seemed, was intent upon forcing the Lublin Poles on Poland, thus reducing Poland to a 'Vassal State'. The gulf between *Tribune* and the *N.S. and N.* on this issue was now unprecedented.

Of the Labour leadership, we know Dalton and Bevin accepted that German forces had inflicted a 'genuine and unexpected reverse' on the Red Army, but both were angry at Stalin's cynical procrastination over airfield use.[13] Dalton was well connected with the Polish socialists in the London government, and during the crisis Eden used his good offices to secure the dismissal of the embarrassingly outspoken Sosnkowski as commander-in-chief. The TUC and the Labour Party organisations acted on the issue of Warsaw. A joint delegation visited Eden on 29 August over the airfield issue and a letter was sent to the Soviet ambassador, Gusev.[14] Such sympathy for the plight of Warsaw tended, by association, to promote sympathy for the cause of the London Polish and to exacerbate the split in the left over Russian policy. Sections of the left sailed serenely through the Warsaw crisis, their faith in Russia virtually unaffected; one MP interviewed by the author had no recollection of the rising; 'we were winning and that was all that mattered', he explained. Interestingly, Ian Mikardo, one of the most pro-Soviet MPs post-war, told the author that he had many suspicions of Soviet conduct at that time. However, in the debate on the international situation on 28 September all Labour MPs (unlike a group of right-wing Tories) heeded the entreaties of Eden and Churchill to handle the Polish issue with extreme caution.

iii

The fate of Warsaw had receded from Labour memories by 12 December, when Winston Churchill spoke in the House on the subject of Poland.[15] He gave government sanction to the Curzon line in the east, compensated by large concessions in the west at the expense of Germany; the indigenous population to be deported. The Lublin Poles would, it was hoped, share the government of post-war Poland equally with the exile government in London — a position representing virtual acquiescence with the Soviet line on Poland.[16]

Behind this policy lay Churchill's October meeting in Moscow with Stalin and the Lublin Poles. There Churchill had exhorted Mikolajczyk to accept the Curzon line as the only alternative to virtual national extinction. Finally Mikolajczyk had agreed, but his government later demurred and he himself resigned, his government being replaced by a more intransigent group of emigres. The strength of the Prime Minister's diplomatic position was weakened by the 'zone of influence' agreement, confirmed at Moscow, which had conceded the Balkan area to Russia in exchange for the free hand Britain was soon to exercise in Greece.

Stalin scrupulously withheld criticism of Churchill's suppression of armed left-wing bands and, as a result, Churchill inhibited public expression of the opposition he privately felt towards Stalin's Polish policy. Russian dominance in Poland was the harsh price Churchill thought he had to pay for a working relationship with the Russian leader after the war.

These factors help to explain the extraordinary position Churchill took in the parliamentary division of opinion over Poland on 12 December 1944. His speech was delivered to the House in what one conservative MP called an 'ugly, apprehensive, cold silence'.[17] To bow to expedience was bad enough, but to be asked to feel enthusiasm for such unequal compromise was too much for the House to bear. The Conservative right wing was violently against the proposed settlement. The centre of both parties sadly accepted it as inevitable. Pethick Lawrence, speaking for the Labour Party, recorded dissatisfaction at the methods of Soviet diplomacy. The consent of all parties concerned should be the basis of such settlements, and the massive deportations envisaged would prove the dragon's teeth of future wars. Ironically, only from the extreme left did the Prime Minister receive enthusiastic support. J. D. Mack, an 'unrepentant Russophile' congratulated him for realising that in the final analysis Russia would, in any case, decide the future of Poland. After the war, he predicted, she would set an example of sympathy and understanding in her relations with her small neighbours, which some were 'too purblind to appreciate at the present time'.[18] The occasion is perhaps unique in British history: Churchill, traditional enemy of the left and of the Soviet Union, receiving enthusiastic support for his policies only from that section of the left characterised by the intensity of its admiration for the USSR.

The Labour press reflected opinion in the House. The *Daily Herald* complained that the fate of Poland was being settled by methods which were an affront to the Atlantic Charter.[19] Emrys Hughes in *Forward* believed that the territorial transfers would produce irredentist conflict in the future.[20] *Tribune* criticised the cynical deal over Poland but reacted sharply to the Tories' attacks, which it saw as 'directed against the alliance with Russia'. For what other reason did they attack Soviet policy in Eastern Europe yet accept the implicitly anti-Soviet actions by Britain in Greece?[21]

The left at this time had united in furiously condemning the 'scandal' of the use of 40,000 British troops to prosecute the monarchist government's suppression of the communist resistance group EAM-ELAS, which was making an armed bid for power. Churchill's fear was that a communist Greece would advance Soviet influence in the British-dominated eastern Mediterranean zone. His Cabinet colleague Ernest Bevin shared the same concern and robustly resisted a left-wing attack upon government policy over Greece at the December 1944 Labour Party Conference.

December also witnessed an historic event in trade union activities. On the 4th a meeting took place of the two bilateral committees with Soviet and American trade unions, to prepare a world conference of trade unionists. For the first time American and Russian trade unionists, each supporters of diametrically opposed economic systems, were sitting around the same table, and trade unionists the world over were presented with a glimpse of the international unity the closing weeks of the war would bring.

The World Trade Union Conference met in February 1945 to establish the World Federation of Trade Unions (WFTU). Reviewing the work of its embryo, the ASTUC, Citrine told the conference that the committee had established a 'friendship, a comradeship and an understanding that is not excelled by any kind of joint arrangements between any country and the Soviet Union'.[22] In retrospect he held to the view that the function of the committee was 'certainly not a political gesture' and had no doubt whatever that its activities aided Russia when she most needed help.[23]

Yet when the record of the committee is examined, the precise ways in which Russia was helped are difficult to identify. The committee certainly performed a useful task in helping to co-ordinate and distribute several hundred thousand pounds' worth of aid. It also enabled a useful exchange of information to take place, but apart from a measure of mutual enlightenment this can hardly be described as a positive function. Citrine also claimed that the committee 'certainly did not create problems for Anglo-Soviet relations'[24] but it can hardly be denied that one of the principal effects of the committee's deliberation was to bring into the open the rift between Britain and the Soviet Union over the Second Front which Churchill was doing his best to conceal. The 1943 TUC report on the joint committee was a record of noisy disagreement rather than constructive co-operation.

Another aspect which would hardly have improved Anglo-Soviet relations was the Russian attempt to encourage the TUC to put pressure on the Churchill government in the Russian interest. In the event this produced a possibly more favourable General Council policy on the Second Front issue and perhaps a tougher attitude to the post-war treatment of Germany. Citrine's conversations with the American trade unions were also disruptive, and on one occasion, in defending the Soviet trade unions against AFL attacks, he was forced into the uncomfortable position of having to give a virtual justification of trade union subservience to government control.[25]

On the other hand the tour of the Soviet delegation through Britain in 1942 was a great success, and the reciprocal British visits must have fostered many contacts, friendships[26] and feelings of unity. The committee also laid the foundations of the WFTU by providing a bridge between the organisationally separate communist trade unions and those of the rest of the world. By delicately bringing the two sides together through bilateral joint committees Citrine was able to engineer the formation of a tripartite committee which went on to lay the basis of the WFTU — in the light of history a remarkable achievement by a remarkable trade unionist.

iv

In February Poland re-emerged as the focus of Labour Party interest in Soviet foreign policy. Despite the entreaties of Churchill and Roosevelt on 5 January 1945, Stalin had accorded recognition to the PCNL as the provisional government of Poland. Churchill struggled hard at Yalta to free Poland from what threatened to be a puppet government, and returned with some confidence. It had been agreed that the provisional government, as it was now called, would be 'reorganised' to include representation from the London Poles, Poles in the USA and the home resistance movement. This new government would officiate until such time as 'free and unfettered' elections gave Poland a democratic government. With great panache, Churchill sold the Yalta agreement to the House as a triumph of Allied unity. Stalin's promises over Poland were presented confidently. 'I decline absolutely,' he declared, 'to embark here on a discussion about Soviet good faith.'[27]

The House, as a whole, warmly accepted the settlement. The fellow-travelling left, as in December, eagerly agreed with the Churchill analysis. D. N. Pritt ranked the Crimea conference amongst the 'most hopeful things that have happened in the world in the last twenty five years, or more'. Russia had no desire to absorb Poland, Pritt claimed. She wanted a free and independent Poland. However, he cited the absorbed Estonia, Latvia and Lithuania as countries to which Russia had given "freedom".[28] Tom Driberg strongly indicted the London Poles for their anti-Soviet beliefs, their lavish way of life, financed by the British taxpayer, and ended up by advocating withdrawal of recognition from this 'bogus emigré government'. The left, as a body, was more concerned with the future of Germany that with the fate of the Poles. Driberg quite seriously suggested that perhaps the best way of re-educating the German people would be by sending them to the USSR for a few years.[29]

The centres of both parties were pleased that the treatment of Germany would not be over-harsh and hopeful that an effective international security organisation would emerge from the projected conference in San Francisco. The Tory right wing, however, led by Mr Petherick, regarded it as shocking that the Prime Minister should regard the treatment of Poland as honest and fair. Petherick moved an amendment on Poland and spoke with great feeling on behalf of an ally who was being treated with less respect than a vanquished enemy. Twenty of his Conservative colleagues voted for the critical amendment, while eleven members of the government abstained. Of the Labour Party, only Richard Stokes, an outspoken critic of violations of the Atlantic Charter, cast his vote with the dissident Tories. The tiny ILP, however, also voted against the Polish settlement. In the debate McGovern had spoken strongly against Stalin, who he believed could never be trusted to carry out his promises over Poland.[30] In the *New Leader* one of its future editors made a fateful parallel; Churchill had followed Chamberlain to Munich, only a 'Russian Munich this time'.[31] *Forward* echoed the same sentiment.

Tribune seemed reasonably happy with the Yalta outcome on 16 February. Joint Allied consultation rather than unilateral action in separate spheres of influence would be the future watchword, and the agreement on Poland unequivocally pledged Pland's provisional government 'to the holding of free and unfettered elections as soon as possible on the basis of universal suffrage and the secret ballot'. The rhetoric of the Yalta communiqué, however, provided only temporary comfort to the grave doubts *Tribune* had long felt. On 23 February in an important two-page article entitled 'Revolution from above?' *Tribune* cast doubt on Russia's intention to extend 'socialism' into Eastern Europe (the retention of Horthy in Hungary and the monarchy in Rumania being signs to the contrary), and was opposed in any case to Russia's single-party totalitarian version of socialism.

Yet, in an obvious reference to the Petherick ammendment, *Tribune* placed an important limit to its criticism of Russia. 'Much as we may criticise the Soviet Government on certain features of her treatment of Poland, we do not and will not subscribe to an agitation aimed at re-establishing the diplomatic isolation of Russia.' The traditional ideological theme in Labour Party attitudes towards Russia had re-emerged here; the catalyst of Tory criticism seldom failed to improve Russia's image in the Labour Party. 'We know these people,' claimed *Reynolds' News* on 25 February. 'They will blow hopefully on any spark which might possibly blaze into discord between Russia and the west.' The Co-operative weekly was satisfied by the Soviet undertakings over Poland and indeed ceased to comment on Poland thereafter.

The *Daily Herald* too was impressed by the Soviet promises. Right into 1945 it had backed the legality of the London Poles, but had refused to criticise the USSR, which challenged this legality. Yalta seemed to solve its dilemma by assuming a democratic future for the government of Poland.[32] Michael Foot, an important contributor to the *Herald*, was less optimistic. The London Poles, he affirmed, were justifiably bitter at the settlement, and even now were dependent upon the goodwill of a government which had long vilified them. 'If we are not prepared,' he concluded, 'to ensure that the Lublin Government genuinely seeks the partnership of the other Poles and organises genuine elections, the Yalta Agreement will appear as one of the grossest fakes in history.'[33] The *N.S. and N.* applauded the statesmanlike decision over Poland as perhaps the best work of the conference.[34] No tears were shed over the fact that the London government had finally missed the tide. The 'little Tory cliques' which divided the House was lugubriously using 'talk of libertarian principles as a disguise for anti-Russian sentiments'. Churchill and Eden were to be congratulated for supporting Stalin's Polish policy.[35]

Finally on Yalta, two articles in *Reynolds' News* clearly revealed one of Labour's problems at this time: how to reconcile the traditional principles of socialist foreign policy as they had developed from Liberal radicalism with the threat to those principles posed by the Soviet Union. The author of both articles was H. N. Brailsford. The first appeared on 30 January 1944. While recognising the anti-Soviet elements within it, Brailsford thought it 'probable that the emigré government in London does represent the mass of the Polish nation'. He was opposed to the proposed annexations in the west and regarded the claims of the Soviet-backed Polish communists as quite fantastic, involving as they did the deportation of eight million people. 'No socialist and no democrat can back these claims,' he concluded.

The other was written over a year later, on 18 February 1945. Brailsford here welcomed as the greatest achievements of Yalta the very measures he had denounced so roundly twelve months before. Russia was justified in wanting a pro-Russian Poland, for the aristocratic, military and land-owning elements of the country were still appealing to reactionary elements in the West to open a new conflict with the Soviet Union. The deportations implicit in this settlement Brailsford now ignored, and he shed no tears about the 'democratic' government of January 1944 being abandoned by its Western allies in February 1945. Thus, to retain his confidence in the Soviet Union, he had had to abandon important principles. But the process had been so gradual, spread over some twelve months during a changing political situation, that Brailsford himself was probably unaware that it had taken place.

Despite Brailsford's confidence, the Yalta decisions were only the beginning of a new phase in the struggle for the soul of Poland. It transpired that Stalin's idea of a 'reorganised' Polish provisional government was identical with his earlier conception (which Churchill thought he had abandoned) of an 'enlarged' Lublin committee. This would entail merely the addition of a few outsiders. In the following weeks the Lublin Poles consolidated their position while Big Three relations worsened after a series of disagreements which included the issue of Polish representation at the San Francisco conference and the arrest in March of sixteen leaders of the Polish resistance who had been invited to Moscow for talks. On 5 July a new provisional government was set up which, despite their doubts, the Western allies recognised. Of its twenty one Cabinet posts, only seven of the least important went to non-Lublin Poles.

At Yalta Stalin had told Roosevelt that elections would take place a month after the liberation of Poland. They did not. Despite the lip service paid to the principle of free elections at Potsdam, elections did not take place until January 1947. (The communist-dominated government bloc won 327 seats to the 24 won by Mikolajczyk's peasant party. In October 1947 Mikolajczyk fled the country to save his life.)

Predictably, the *N.S. and N.* was quite happy with the Soviet interpretation of Yalta and accepted that the Soviet Union would demand friendship from her Eastern European neighbours,[36] but *Tribune*'s post-Yalta honeymoon was short-lived. It condemned the charges against the sixteen resistance leaders as 'fantastic' and judged that the arrests made Yalta 'null and void'.[37]

The contrasting perspectives of *Tribune* and the *N.S. and N.* which have run throughout this chapter were symptomatic of two schools of thought over Soviet intentions. The officially sponsored heroic ally image of the Soviet Union was particularly strong in that it centred around, not diplomats or statesmen, but the compelling and vivid focus of the 'stout-hearted Russian soldier'. Many in the Labour Party were happy to be intoxicated by this heady image, helping themselves along with the generous draughts of wishful thinking about Russia's good intentions. There were others, however, who refused to ignore the happenings in Poland or to dismiss their ominous similarities to Hitler's foreign policy style. The differing perspectives of Kingsley Martin and Aneurin Bevan over the issue of Poland epitomised these two Labour points of view.

In his analysis of domestic events Martin was prey to an 'obsessive misery', but he tended to look to Russia with a Panglossian optimism.[38] In a degenerating world he clung to the view that there flickered in Russia a light which, if protected and nurtured, could illuminate the world. His friend Maynard Keynes believed that on this subject he was a 'little too full perhaps of goodwill. When a doubt arises it is swallowed down if possible.'[39] Martin was in fact a rather woolly, slightly ingenuous, high-minded liberal, typical of a strong element in British left-wing dissent over foreign policy.

Bevan too was a temperamental rebel, dissatisfied with the basic structure of British society and similarly closely bound up emotionally and intellectually with the Soviet experiment. He was not, however, primarily a political journalist but an ambitious practising politician. Could this different career balance account for the different perceptions? Possibly — Michael Foot always believed Kingsley Martin to be a 'splendid gossip writer, rather than an acute political commentator, with a headline sense of news and a gift for making it readable'.[40] Just as a politician sometimes (perhaps unconsciously) allows what is politically advantageous to him to mould his political thinking, so a journalist tends to allow what is readable to dictate his copy. Martin was relatively inconsistent and credulous because he reflected in an uncanny way what his audience wanted to hear; but as people like to be told what they want to hear, he was a highly successful editor. Bevan was relatively consistent because he wished to use *Tribune* as a vehicle for the policies he favoured. Perhaps it was Bevan's political attennae which enabled him to read Stalin's *Realpolitic* so clearly; history's judgement certainly finds more often for Bevan than Martin. Yet Bevan was perhaps less successful as an editor because he was less interested in and less able to tell people what they wanted to hear. Perhaps, as with Crossman in later years at the *New Statesman*, and

McCleod at the *Spectator*, this is not an unusual fate for an editor who is more of a politician than a journalist.

Bertrand Russell once wrote that he 'would rather be mad with truth than sane with lies'. Kingsley Martin's biographer suggests that throughout the war he was trying to keep at least temporarily sane with lies.[41] Over the issue of Poland his peculiar brand of sincere dishonesty was reflected by substantial elements on the left. Bevan, his followers and a proportion of the centre and right of the party which the wartime embargo on criticism of the Soviet Union makes it difficult to identify, chose to struggle with the harshness of what was actually happening in Poland in the latter part of the war. Doubts born in 1939 had been renewed. The euphoria of peace would suspend them temporarily, but the second half of the decade was destined to see the worst of these fears more than justified.

Notes

1. S. Orwell and I. Angus, *Collected Orwell* Vol. III, p. 333.
2. R. Blackburn, *I am an Alchoholic*, (London 1959), p. 47.
3. Dalton, *Diaries*, 15 March 1943.
4. See, for example, Louis FitzGibbon, *The Kobyn Cover Up* (London 1972).
5. *Reynolds News*', 2 May 1943.
6. *NS and N*, 1 May 1943 and *Tribune*, 30 April 1943.
7. *Tribune*, 21 January 1944.
8. *Socialist Commentary*, April 1944.
9. See his PQ to Eden, 389 *H.C.Deb.*, 2010–11, 5 April 1944 and in debate, 2260–7 6 April 1944. See also 390 *H.C.Deb.*, 1159–1163 28 April 1944.
10. For full accounts of the rising see Jan M. Ciechanowski, *The Warsaw Rising of 1944* (London 1944), and for a wider treatment of the Polish issue E. J. Rozck, *Allied Wartime Diplomacy: A Pattern in Poland*, (London 1957).
11. Anthony Eden, *The Reckoning* (London 1965), p. 420.
12. S. Orwell and I. Angus, Vol. III, p. 261 and Churchill, p. 122.
13. Dalton, *Diaries*, 30 August and 6 September 1944.
14. *TUCR 1944*, pp. 120–121.
15. 406 *H.C.Deb.*, 1478–1488, 15 December 1944.
16. See Churchill, Vol. VI, pp. 197–212.
17. Mr Petherick 406 *H.C.Deb.*, 1540, 15 December 1944.
18. ibid., 1551.
19. *Daily Herald*, 20 December 1944.
20. *Forward*, 20 December 1944.
21. *Tribune*, 22 December 1944.
22. *TUCR 1945*, p. 264.
23. Letter from Lord Citrine to author.
24. ibid.
25. *TUCR 1945*, p. 368.
26. Citrine, pp. 110–124.

27 408 H.C.Deb., 1275–1280, 27 February 1945.
28 ibid., 1318–23.
29 ibid., 1336–44.
30 ibid., 1607–8.
31 F. A. Ridley in *New Leader*, 17 March 1945.
32 *Daily Herald*, 15 February 1945.
33 *Left News*, January 1945. See articles in same issue by Strauss (critical) and W. G. Cove (uncritical).
34 *NS and N*, 17 February 1945.
35 ibid., 3 March 1945.
36 ibid., 7 April 1945.
37 *Tribune*, 27 April 1945.
38 C. R. Rolph, *Kingsley*, p. 13.
39 ibid., pp. 172–3.
40 ibid., p. 291 f.n.
41 ibid., p. 252.

7 Triumphant Labour: a new dawn in Anglo-Soviet relations?

Revolutions do not change geography and revolutions do not change geographical need. [Ernest Bevin, *LPCR 1948*, p. 114]

If the Labour movement in Europe finds it necessary to introduce a greater degree of police supervision and drastic punishment for their opponents than we in this country should be prepared to tolerate, we must be prepared to understand their point of view. [Dennis Healey, *LPCR 1948*, p. 114]

i

Having rejected Churchill's overtures to continue the coalition government until the defeat of Japan, Labour broke away from the Conservative Party, which thereupon formed itself into a caretaker government until July, when polling took place. The election campaign was fought principally over domestic issues, but foreign policy was certainly not neglected by either party. Over the substance of foreign policy there was little argument; debate tended rather to centre round which party was the better equipped in terms of outlook, record and method to conduct this policy.

As both parties agreed that the successful continuance of the Big Three alliance was the *sine qua non* of a peaceful post-war world, so relations with Russia became an election issue. The Labour manifesto reminded the electorate 'that in the years leading up to the war, the Tories were so scared of Russia that they missed the chance to establish a partnership which might well have prevented the war'.[1]

Labour leaders like Cripps and Dalton exploited the mythology of Labour friendship with the Soviet Union. The atmosphere of the time is indicated by the fact that at the 1945 Blackpool Conference Bevin's assertion that 'left understands left' was widely interpreted as applying to the Soviet Union, whereas in reality he was talking about the French socialists. Ironically it was Labour who reaped the harvest of public pro-Sovietism which Churchill, against his natural political instincts, had done so much to cultivate during the war.

Critical comment upon Russia and her suspicious activities in Eastern Europe vanished from the pages of the Labour press. Even Bevan was 'terrified' that Orwell's *Animal Farm* might cause embarrassment if it came out before the election, and he asked Orwell to cease writing for *Tribune* until the election was over.[2] Such self-censorship had a beneficial effect upon Labour images of Russia: in trying to convince the electorate of the comradeship between their party and the USSR members of the British Labour Party, at the very least, succeeded in reinforcing such feelings within themselves, and the doubts sown by the Polish issue tended to be overlaid and diminished by these expedient sentiments.

In the event, Labour hardly needed the votes. Churchill's decision to take Attlee with him to Potsdam in case of a shock election result proved to be a far-sighted precaution. Labour romped home with 393 seats to the Conservatives' 213. The extent of the victory surpassed the expectations of all but the foolishly optimistic. The Labour Party had emerged from its political hibernation as a junior partner in a coalition government to become the party implementing socialism in post-war Britain. A history of barely fifty years had been crowned with unbelievable success. The British people had spoken clearly on their ballot papers in favour of socialism at home. Few Labour supporters doubted that the mandate extended naturally to a socialist foreign policy which comprised, as one of its key tenets, friendship and co-operation with the Soviet Union.

Only 135 of the new Labout MPs were trade unionists, and two-thirds had never been in Parliament before. The new members were noticeably middle-class — left-wing journalists and activists like Michael Foot, Geoffrey Bing, Benn Levy, J. P. W. Mallalieu; writers and lecturers like Barbara Castle, Maurice Edelman, Leslie Hale; lawyers like L. J. Solley and John Platts Mills. Many others had come straight from the services, and Hansard records that, in many cases, they retained their military rank well into the opening year of the new Parliament.

Many of these voices, like that of Konni Zilliacus, had been heard previously only at Labour Party Conferences and in the press. Now they were heard in the legislative chamber itself, and indeed for the first few months it was almost as if the noisy, protean politics of Conference had been transferred *en bloc* to Parliament. Upon first filing into their seats at Westminster the new members (to the embarrassment of the 'old guard') lustily sang the 'Red Flag'; clearly the mood of a large section of the new intake was buoyantly left-wing. Wisely the party leadership absorbed into the government the men best equipped to lead this volatile new membership astray. Bevan was Minister of Health, with a seat in the Cabinet; Cripps was President of the Board of Trade, also in the Cabinet, and Strachey, Shinwell and later Strauss were also given office. Consequently there was no immediate focus of backbench opinion in the PLP for several months after Labour's victory, and no well defined opinion groups emerged during this time. On the subject of a 'socialist foreign policy' there were as many ideas as there were Labour MPs. Nevertheless some themes can be discerned on this subject in general, and upon relations with Russia in particular.

Among many Labour MPs the assumption had long been held that all that was needed to implement a socialist foreign policy was the achievement of a Labour majority. The intervening war had only sharpened this expectation, firstly by demonstrating the ultimate sterility of traditional 'Tory' foreign policy, and secondly by clearing the decks for a constructive socialist approach which would establish an impetus for peace in British foreign policy and help create permanent machinery for its preservation.

The fundamental tenets of this socialist foreign policy were still held with passionate sincerity throughout a very large section of the Labour Party. To them the accepted analysis of international affairs was that the economic system of capitalism leads governments to pursue competitive foreign policies of territorial acquisition in their search for overseas markets. These policies were expressed through the media of balance-of-power policies, ruling (i.e. capitalist)-class-dominated Foreign Offices, and secret diplomacy. Eventually the system produced wars fought by the workers in the interests of big business; their labour and dignity abused in peacetime, the exploitation of the workers reached its apotheosis in wartime when they were killed in the interests of capitalist profits.

If foreign policies were the external expression of domestic economic systems, then it followed that the inception of socialism, provided it was true socialism, would automatically eliminate the policies produced by capitalism. A socialist government would co-operate with like-minded governments, particularly the USSR, towards the goal of collective security and would encourage socialist movements in other countries. Eventually national frontiers would exist only in the history books and a world federation of socialist States would peacefully dispense dignity and material plenty to the peoples of the world.

In 1945 some MPs conceived of the institutions of world government being created prior to socialism, which would develop at a later date; others looked for a coming together of States to form a federation once they had all turned socialist. The urgent desirability of a system of world government was a pervasive theme in the plethora of Labour maiden speeches.³ The United Nations was seen with passionate hope as the most likely embryo of a world government and as the best guarantee against another war.

The conflict against Hitler and Nazism, of course, had been regarded by the Labour Party as a fight for freedom, democracy and ultimately socialism, rather than as a war to advance capitalist economic systems or British national interests. Many MPs believed that Europe had been brought by the war to the brink of socialism. They confidently believed that Britain, where socialism had so dramatically 'happened', could, by the force of example and moral exhortation, exert her unrivalled moral authority to transform the leftward trends in Europe into the reality of socialism.⁴ Fred Peart, one of the new MPs, typically asked in a foreign affairs debate for a 'socialist foreign policy that will give a lead to all democratic forces throughout the world'.⁵ After the sacrifices of war, these socialists could not be expected to abandon their expectations lightly. Many of the new MPs moreover had undergone salutory experiences during their wartime service. Dennis Healey recalls:

Seeing the contrast between the Italian peasant who risked his life or the torture of his family to help an escaped British prisoner and the selfish cynicism of the collaborationist upper classes, we felt that victory would sweep away the old regimes and create the basis for lasting friendship with our Russian allies.⁶

This helps to explain why his contribution to the Blackpool Conference was a fiery clarion call to the Labour Party to unite with the forces of social revolution, socialist or communist, in post-war Europe. Laski, an enthusiast for a unified socialist international, liked the speech and recommended Major Healey for the post of Labour's International Secretary. He got the job.

It was only logical that this heightened socialist awareness within the PLP during these early months should identify the USA as a potentially aggressive force and as an ally to beware of. America, after all, was the pacemaker of world capitalism, a force which socialists believed to be dialectically opposed to the expanding power of socialism. W. G. Cove expressed in extreme terms what many of his fellow MPs on the left and centre felt when he wrote in September 1945; 'Socialism will perish in Britain if a Labour Government ties herself to America — for America, I repeat, has become aggressively imperialist.'⁷ Evidence for such a judgement was perceived in the abrupt termination of Lease-Lend in August 1945, widely interpreted on the left as an attempt to destroy the early flowering of British socialism.⁸ The conditions imposed by the Anglo-American loan agreement of December 1945 moved *Tribune* to declare it a 'savage bargain' and the *New Statesman* a 'devastating appeasement of American capitalism.⁹ But the most damning piece of evidence was Truman's decision in the autumn of 1945 to retain exclusive control of atomic weapon secrets until such time as effective international control mechanisms could be established.[10] In these early months Labour MPs made much play with the idea that American monopoly of nuclear technology was responsible for many of the difficulties experienced with the Russians around the conference table. Konni Zilliacus predicted that as long as America and Britain retained exclusive control over these secrets they would be responsible for stimulating an arms race with the USSR.[11]

The place Russia occupied in the socialist analysis of the post-war world was indeed central; good relations with the Soviet Union were the cornerstone of all conceptions of a socialist foreign policy. Russian military success had generally been interpreted as a testimonial to her centralised economic system. By her unsparing efforts in the war and her massive sacrifice in human life Russia had reassured many of those on Labour's left wing that the period between 1939 and 1941 had been one of tactical waiting rather than malevolent neutrality. The doubts which the Finnish war had raised, and which the fate of Poland had to some extent renewed, were subsumed in the first flush of socialism's victory in Britain. Among Labour's excited new MPs there was a feeling that a clean start with Russia was now possible; that Russia herself would be calmed and reassured by a government brimming with so much socialist fervour and international goodwill. Interest now focused squarely upon Soviet foreign policy intentions, and most Labour MPs felt there was little to worry about. Even Soviet encroachments in Eastern Europe could be comfortably explained away. Dr. S. W. Jeger explained that Russia was being forced to erect its own *cordon sanitaire* against American imperialist expansion.[12] *Tribune*, whilst sustaining many of its criticisms of Russia, could reassuringly explain Soviet expansion in Eastern Europe as an attempt to eliminate reactionary and therefore anti-Soviet elements which she had every reason to suppose the West supported.[13] As an earnest of good intent, *Tribune* suggested, Russian co-operation would be facilitated if Britain immediately gave India her independence and settled quickly over Greece and Trieste. The idea of a magnanimous gesture to disarm Russian suspicions was to become a popular prescription in the PLP in the post-war years.

Trade unionists in and out of Parliament could look with pride at the World Federation of Trade Unions, formed in February 1945 out of the embryo of Citrine's Anglo-Soviet Trade Union Committee. The union of Western and communist trade unions was regarded as a triumph, a symbol of comradeship and solidarity for the future. The WFTU represented $66^1/_2$ million workers in fifty-six countries. At the 1945 TUC conference at Blackpool, Ebby Edwards, with a rather unfortunate choice of words, was hopeful that the 'unity of the Russian and British workers will last for all time in solidified friendship'.[14] The criticisms of Russian trade unions by George Meany, fraternal delegate for the AFL (not a member of the WFTU) were met with cries of 'Shame' from the audience and prompted a defence of their role in Soviet society from Citrine.[15]

Much pro-Soviet sentiment was expressed in Parliament during the early months of the Labour government. Fred Lee, for example, claimed that the Labour benches were overflowing with MPs who would not entertain a policy that would result in the ostracism of the USSR.[16] Michael Foot, never obsequious to Russia, demanded that the government examine its own record over Greece and Spain before criticising the new Soviet-inspired regimes in Eastern Europe.[17] J. D. Mack even felt able to assert that Labour's election victory was to a large extent attributable to the example of socialist Russia during the war.[18] But by far the most persuasive advocate of friendship with Russia and apologist for her actions was Konni Zilliacus. His line of argument was often oblique but his speeches had a logic and lucidity that demanded serious attention.

In the 23 November 1945 debate on foreign affairs he asked that the self-determination clauses of the Atlantic Charter should not be interpreted in a way which allowed fascism to be restored in Eastern Europe. Communism, he maintained, was integrally bound up with the socialist working-class revolution in Europe and was in no sense a danger. Britain should at all costs avoid any identification of her foreign policy with counter-revolutionary influences. He ended his speech by looking forward to an economic union of the Western European democracies in 'conjunction' with the Soviet Union and in 'co-operation' with the USA; his subtle choice of words betrayed the direction of affiliation which he favoured. Zilliacus quickly became foremost among the group of Labour MPs who applauded developments in Eastern Europe and who urged the government to move economically and politically in the direction of the USSR.[19]

This policy, of course, was closely allied to the line advocated by the Communist Party, whose representation in Parliament, despite a poor showing in the general election, had been increased 100 per cent by the election of Philip Piratin for Mile End. In 1945 the CPGB had again sought co-operation with the Labour Party, but, despite the strength of pro-Soviet feeling, the National Executive Committee had given them short shrift. There was considerable opposition to this decision in the party, and at the Blackpool Conference a reference back calling for co-operation during the election with 'progressive parties' was defeated by a mere 1,314,000 votes to 1,219,000.[20] However, British communists must have been well satisfied that the voices of Gallacher and Piratin had been supplemented, in the defence and explanation of Russian foreign policy, by such a substantial reinforcement to the ranks of fellow-travellers in the PLP. Whilst the hard core of crypto-communists rarely exceeded twenty, in these early months their arguments fell on receptive ears and their influence in the PLP was consequently considerable.

It should not be assumed from the foregoing that the whole of the Labour Party adhered to a slavishly pro-Soviet 'thirties-style concept of a socialist foreign policy. Within the rank and file of the new MPs there were people who advocated a 'realistic' approach to foreign affairs. Patrick Gordon Walker, for example, called in his maiden speech for an end to US isolationism in order to counterbalance Soviet predominance in Europe.[21] Evan Durbin, the brilliant LSE don (destined to be tragically drowned in 1949) belonged to the same hard-headed school. In the debate on the United Nations in August 1945, for example, he urged his party to root out of its heart 'the last vestiges of pacifism' and to realise that peace could not be achieved unless it was defended.[22] Within the party rank and file these voices were in the minority, but within the Party leadership, the ex-coalition government Ministers, their sentiments were widely shared.

The dichotomy between the attitude towards the Soviet Union of the leadership and of the bulk of party activists in the country and in Parliament has already been referred to. During the war they had broadly shared Churchill's analysis of international affairs and accepted British diplomacy as the instrument for the advancement and protection of British interests. They also shared Churchill's private doubts about Stalin's methods and objectives. Attlee, for example, had no doubts that his intentions in Eastern Europe were expansionist and predatory. Upon returning from the San Francisco conference he pronounced the Russians to be 'perfectly bloody to deal with; they tell us nothing yet are setting up puppet governments all over Europe and as far west as they can'.[23] Furthermore Bevin certainly hoped for a bipartisan foreign policy after the war, and Attlee even saw fit to lavish praise upon those Conservatives who had assisted him at San Francisco, including one of Labour's pre-war *bête noires*, Lord Halifax.

In other words, by 1945 the leadership operated from 'realist' premises which were shared by only a minority of the rest of the party. Both sides looked out on to different Russias, different Europes, different worlds. Both envisaged different foreign policies to deal with the problems perceived. However, to compound the confusion, the leadership had delved into the lexicon of traditional 'idealist' foreign policy to inject the necessary rhetoric into the election campaign. The illusion that was fostered of a great new socialist dawn may have won votes, but it was to prove an albatross around the neck of the man given the responsibility of forming British foreign policy.

ii

Following Labour's victory the man considered by many, including himself, to be the next Foreign Secretary was Hugh Dalton. His qualifications for the job were incomparable—a junior Minister under Arthur Henderson in 1929, one of the leading party spokesmen on foreign affairs in the 'thirties, and one who advocated the non-pacifist line eventually adopted by the party: all this, as well as being a highly successful Minister in the coalition government. It has been suggested that Dalton's outlook on foreign affairs in 1945 was still strongly 'socialist'. This was only partly true.[24] He was certainly the principal architect of the Labour Party document *The International Post-war Settlement* but he prided himself upon its hard, realistic content, not upon its passages of an overtly socialist flavour, which were the work of Laski and others.[25] His diaries reflect the evolution of his attitude towards Russia in early and mid-1945.

He saw fit to record Churchill's view that the Soviet Union would respond only to pressure and that Stalin assessed his allies purely on the basis of their military strength, but he also gave space to Sir Gladwyn Jebb's enthusiastic comments upon Stalin's good nature, patience, humour and lack of dogmatism.[26] These two observed facets of Stalin's character — that he would exploit weakness but that he was a man with basically human qualities — were the keynotes of Dalton's attitude towards the Soviet Union. After a victory celebration at the Soviet embassy on 16 May he experienced a haunting doubt whether Anglo-Soviet relations were being well handled. He wondered whether we 'could not do more to break through this queer transparent wall which seems to separate us .... Recent indications are not very good .... I thought tonight, looking at these strong, tough, friendly yet curiously reserved Slavs, that we must face them with like qualities.' That night he told Attlee that he would like to be Foreign Secretary; 'I thought that probably I could come as near to understanding and dealing with these people as anybody. I was sure they had to be met with strength and understanding.'[27] Attlee's reply on this occasion was noncommital, but on the morrow of Labour's victory he told Dalton that the Foreign Office was his. A few hours later Dalton was told by his Prime Minister that because Bevin and Morrison were personally incompatible he had shifted Bevin from domestic affairs to the Foreign Office. Dalton was to be Chancellor of the Exchequer.[28]

By all accounts Bevin was himself surprised when he learnt that he was Attlee's choice as Foreign Secretary, but his close study of foreign affairs in the last years of the coalition,[29] his intervention over Greece in the 1944 Conference and his powerful speech on foreign affairs at the Blackpool

Conference suggest that he was not uninterested in the office. Bevin's power position within the party was certainly an asset to his new position; of Labour's coalition Ministers, his prestige was highest; he had been the hero of the electoral victory;[30] he could regularly mobilise the support of the majority of trade unionists, and he was one of the few Labour politicians equal to the task of resisting Churchill's pre-eminence in the sphere of foreign policy. His sway over the trade unions and the Party Conference was unique. He could command an immense emotional following and exploited it ruthlessly to overcome the threats to his foreign policy that were to come from the left wing of his party in forthcoming months. How is this support explained? Much of it lay, of course, in his dominant expertise in trade union and political affairs, but essentially his appeal was personal, stemming in part from Labour reaction to the personality of Ramsay MacDonald.

In retrospect it is easy for the historian to forget how traumatic an experience the betrayal of 1931 had been. MacDonald succeeded in totally discrediting the qualities which had helped him to power and Bevin, as the personal antithesis of Labour's first Prime Minister, was well equipped to emerge in MacDonald's wake as possibly the most powerful Labour politician ever. In appearance and speech MacDonald resembled a middle-class professional; Bevin was unashamedly a worker. MacDonald had been of proletarian stock but socially had aspired to equal his 'betters'; Bevin was proud of his roots and scorned the social toadying in which MacDonald had specialised. MacDonald had been an attractive man whom 'every duchess in London' might very well have wanted to kiss; one could not imagine them bestowing such favours upon Bevin's craggy features, nor indeed can one imagine him inviting such attentions, but herein lay a source of his strength. Being so irredeemably and unrepentantly inelegant in appearance and in speech, even the most humble and gauche could feel an identity with him.

Similarly, qualities which in others would have been disadvantages to overcome, in Bevin proved to be assets to exploit. His arrogance, for example; Michael Foot has written. 'The egotism was gargantuan, yet oddly inoffensive, almost endearing ... [it was] ... an expression of his confidence that his own class had the right and capacity to rule.'[31] Likewise his demagogic, bullying political style: Bevin's butchery of the revered Lansbury at the Party Conference of 1935 might have ended the career of some politicians, but for him it was a foundation of his later success, an element of the myth of omnipotence which his wartime success as a Minister helped further to propagate, and which rank-and-file trade unionists found irresistible.[32] Unlike MacDonald, Bevin was a genuine working-class hero, whose charisma was founded upon his apparent lack of it. In Cabinet he was the vital hyphen between the party leadership and the source of Labour support, the trade unions. If Attlee regarded the casting of Britain's post-war foreign policy as the major task facing his new government, he had certainly chosen the biggest man on his front bench to perform the task. And yet Bevin's record over Russia was a mixed one.

His role in the *Jolly George* affair (when, according to legend, Labour prevented the British government from giving aid to Poland againt the Bolsheviks) was an impeccable credential. But his attitude towards Russia hardened as the Bolshevik regime took its course towards authoritarianism. In 1927, for instance, he had joined Citrine in arranging the burial of the Anglo-Soviet Trade Union Council. Bevin had told the TUC on that occasion that the Russians recognised an 'alien and unscrupulous dictum: that the end justifies the means'.[33] Subsequently, throughout the 'thirties, he waged a bitterly vituperative battle against communist attempts to permeate British trade unions, particularly his own. The hero of the *Jolly George* was consequently equally well known as the scourge of communism within the unions.

Dalton had felt the Russians should be met with strength and understanding. In 1945 it seemed that Bevin was strong on the former quality and weak on the latter. He was a man of immense, pugnacious drive, breadth of vision and intellectual grasp. Always blunt, he could be abrasive, occasionally a bully; there was a danger that his robust political style might prove inappropriate when dealing with the deeply suspicious and hypersensitive Russians. This tendency, combined with his militant anti-communism, would give Labour party advocates of a pro-Soviet 'socialist' foreign policy a near-at-hand explanation should relations with the USSR deteriorate during the immediate post-war years.

The very least the latter group expected of him was a sharp break with the policies of the coalition. Churchill's call for continuity in foreign policy was regarded by *Tribune* as a snare; there was 'little chance that organised Labour would fall for such a proposterous suggestion'.[34] The first six months of the new government would reveal what Bevin's objectives in foreign policy were, and, perhaps more important, whether he proposed to approach these goals through policies which the rank and file of the party regarded as authentically socialist.

Drawing upon his experience in domestic and international trade union affairs, Bevin never failed to hit the note to which the great majority of trade unionists, not to mention other sections of the Labour Party, were receptive. As Foreign Secretary he seldom missed an opportunity to praise 'our great socialist ally, the Soviet Union'[35] or, as on 23 November 1945, to emphasise his commitment to a vision of world government. This last speech, delivered to the House of Commons, was a remarkable expression of internationalism (though not exclusively 'socialist' internationalism) and was received with great acclaim from all quarters. In his peroration Bevin declared that a directly elected world assembly would rescue countries from their national difficulties. He was 'willing to sit down with anybody, of any party, of any nation, to try to devise a franchise, or a constitution ... for a world assembly with a limited objective, the objective of peace'.³⁶ Few socialists could quarrel with his long-term objectives or with the manner and frequency with which they were articulated. The means by which he appeared to be working towards those goals was a different matter, and it was here that the question of 'continuity' arose.

iii

News of Labour's victory had inspired dismay in the senior ranks of the Foreign Office, who tended to identify Labour with a conciliatory policy towards Russia. One Deputy Under Secretary, Orme Sargent, had prophesied a communist avalanche over Europe, a weak foreign policy and the reduction of Britain to a second-class power.³¹ Some relief was felt when Bevin and not Dalton was chosen as Foreign Secretary, but nevertheless apprehension understandably remained.³⁸

In his memoirs Lord Strang records how he and his colleagues waited at Potsdam for their new socialist Foreign Secretary. Bevin dispelled his doubts in characteristic fashion. Upon their first meeting he took Strang by the arm and, whilst walking him up and down sang the 'Red Flag' to him in an undertone, ending his performance with a large wink.³⁹ At the Potsdam conference table Bevin provided further reassurance in his first dealings with Molotov.

The Soviet Union had not wasted the advantages which military occupation of Eastern Europe had given her. At Yalta the Declaration on Liberated Europe had expressed the resolve of the three governments collectively to assist the liberated satellite countries 'to solve by democratic means their pressing political and economic problems'. Britain and America had interpreted this formula to mean that the interim communist-inclined administrations set up by the Soviet government in Poland, Bulgaria, Rumania and Hungary would give way in due course to governments based upon free elections.

It was agreed that in all the liberated countries joint control councils would oversee the early stages of recovery. Germany had been divided into four zones of occupation under the overall authority of a Four Power Council Authority situated deep in the eastern Soviet zone. Such was the joint machinery which the allies had constructed to supervise the final taming of the aggressor and the resuscitation of Europe. At San Francisco machinery on a much grander scale had been constructed, the United Nations Organisation, to perpetuate peace through the continued unity of the wartime allies. With the removal of the unifying threat of Germany, the fears and national interests which had underlain the diplomacy of the wartime conferences moved to the centre of the stage. Even as early as the Potsdam conference in July 1945 the joint control machinery had become redundant.

Each side had acted according to individual interest, claiming a particular interpretation of the ambiguous Yalta accords as its justification. Britain and America worked to minimise Soviet influence in their own occupied areas. Among their motives was a fear that communism might spread in Western Europe; Italy's communist party, for instance, was powerful, and it was feared that the Soviet Union would encourage its activities, given half a chance. The techniques which had been pioneered in Poland were now being adapted to the rest of Eastern Europe. In Rumania, Bulgaria and Hungary the weak indigenous communist parties operated under the accommodating suzerainty of the occupying Red Army; in each case their members figured prominently in the administrations which had been formed. The Western representatives on the control councils were presented with a series of *faits accomplis* which they were powerless to prevent. In the name of anti-fascism not only right-wing elements but moderate and social democratic parties were coerced into impotence. Redistribution of property and social reforms were rapidly introduced but, as in the USSR, only at the expense of political freedom. In its zone of Germany the Soviet Union ruthlessly eliminated the last remnants of political life and placed in positions of power communists who had fled to Russia before the war. The Soviet occupation was assuming a character which greatly disturbed right and centre opinion in the Western democracies. Left-wing opinion in Europe, comprising the substantial Continental communist parties, was more receptive to Soviet claims that the political developments in Eastern Europe were the product of a healthy appetite for communism rather than force-feeding from the Red Army. At the Potsdam conference Bevin lost no time in demonstrating that the new left-wing government in Britain was under no such illusions and was not prepared passively to acquiesce in the forcible communisation of Eastern Europe.

Bevin alarmed Byrnes and Truman by the vehemence of his opposition to Soviet proposals.[40] He fought hard to reduce the reparations claimed by the Russians and urged the eastern rather than the western Neisse as the western frontier of Soviet-dominated Poland. He criticised the flouting of democratic procedures and the suppression of political liberties, and resisted Soviet attempts to achieve a foothold in the eastern Mediterranean. It has been suggested that Stalin, who would have preferred to have continued dealing with Churchill, sulked for two days upon Bevin's arrival, complaining of a cold.[41] Bevin's vigorous opposition to Soviet policies must have compounded his displeasure. But, whilst Bevin occasionally alarmed the Americans by his toughness, paradoxically his policy was more conciliatory than that which a Tory government would have pursued. For instance, Churchill wrote retrospectively that he had intended, if re-elected, to make the Polish frontier question a sticking point; he would have risked an open break with Stalin on this issue.[42] Bevin avoided such a showdown, and had not sought to organise opposition to Russia amongst the French and Americans. His private secretary discerned in his new master's handling of his brief a 'too pronounced slant towards Russia and against America'.[43] His conduct at Potsdam, however, could not really be described as a breach in continuity over foreign policy; his attitude towards Russia indicated a change in degree rather than substance from the policy of Churchill and Eden.

Reporting to the House of Commons on 22 August 1945, Bevin made customary obeisance towards the idea of Great Power unity but he firmly declared, in relation to the imminent elections in Eastern Europe, that Britain must aim resolutely to prevent the 'substitution of one form of totalitarianism for another'.[44] These new regimes were not representative of the majority of the people and Bevin would not grant them diplomatic recognition.

Following Potsdam, Russia had strengthened her position in Eastern Europe by signing bilateral economic agreements with the communist-biased governments. At the London conference of Foreign Ministers which began on 11 September Molotov infuriated Bevin with his obstructionist tactics. He strongly resisted Soviet attempts to move into the eastern Mediterranean, and, despite American suspicions that Britain was trying to use US power to bolster up a tottering Empire, Byrnes supported Bevin's line.[45] Towards the end of this futile conference tempers became frayed. Molotov observed tartly on 29 September that 'Eden was a gentleman, Bevin is not,'[46] a remark more suited to a tsarist Foreign Minister than a Bolshevik. The following day Molotov nearly walked out when Bevin likened his tactics to those of Hitler. Shortly afterwards the conference broke up.

The cautious conciliatory honeymoon of Potsdam was over for Bevin. Beneath the rhetoric of the conference table Stalin's design was clear: he was intent upon extending the wartime gains of Yalta through unilaterial diplomatic action. He intended to pick up as many of the pieces left after the earthquake of war as he could lay his hands upon. With the departure of France and Italy from the eastern Mediterranean only the UK stood between the USSR and the rich pickings in this zone and possibly North Africa as well.

It was logical that Moscow should direct its diplomatic and propaganda effort at the debilitated British Empire. Stalin must also have been well aware that the Americans would be loath to involve themselves too deeply in defending what were, after all, British imperial interests. Nevertheless the ranks of the Western democracies were beginning to close in the face of the Soviet expansion, and Bevin was keen to encourage this movement. His championship of the French claims for representation in all discussions had little to do with procedure; he knew where his best sources of support lay. The very first stirrings of an anti-Russian coalition can be discerned at the London conference, the unhappy conclusion of which left jagged edges of ill will between the USSR and the UK.

Bevin had to be restrained from declaring to Parliament that Russia's push for the Mediterranean had been the real issue upon which the conference had foundered.[47] His professional advisors were less successful during the 7 November debate upon foreign affairs, when Bevin told the House that the Soviet Union had tried to come across the 'throat of the British Commonwealth', an emotive phrase which marks, perhaps, Bevin's first shot in the Cold War.[48] It was also a phrase worthy of any Tory Foreign Secretary intent upon defending the crossroads of Empire in the Middle East. Sincere as Bevin's commitment might be to his visions of a reconstructed Europe and world government, he made it clear in this debate that he would not pay for their realisation in the coin of substantial economic, strategic or political British interests.[49]

iv

Bevin might have attracted more support for his attitude towards the Soviet Union's suspicious illiberalism in Eastern Europe had he not resolutely pursued continuity of coalition policy in other important areas like Greece, Spain and Indonesia. Despite the 'socialist' presentation of his policies, it soon became apparent, to the relief of the Opposition and the bewilderment of many of his own supporters, that on most issues and in most areas of the world he was assiduously advancing the policies of his Conservative predecessors. It is a peculiar feature of Labour Party thinking upon foreign affairs that particular causes attract particular groups of fervent advocates — Francis Noel-Baker over Spain, Richard Crossman over Palestine, Tom Driberg over Indonesia. Consequently, as Bevin's policies unfolded, pockets of disaffection were produced within the party which collectively tended to reduce the credibility of their most important aspect: his dealings with the USSR. How could he expect his left-wingers to understand his difficulties with the intractable Russians when in most other respects he appeared to be

Triumphant Labour 117

merely implementing and developing the policies of his 'anti-Soviet' predecessors?

Bevin also followed Churchill's policy over a subject of crucial importance to Labour, the pooling of atomic weapon secrets. Perhaps he did not, like Churchill, regard this knowledge as a 'sacred trust' but was cagily pragmatic over its safe keeping. To surrender nuclear weapons to the Military Committee of the new United Nations Organisation, he argued, would be to give soldiers the final word over their use. Better to wait upon the development of the world organisation before, as he rather vaguely put it, 'we can see clearly how matters stand'.[50] Even if they could agree on little else, Bevin's critics could unite in condemning his continuity of policy.

The anger of the left wing would certainly have gathered into accusations of betrayal had it known that behind the bipartisan appearance of Bevin's foreign policy was a bipartisan reality. In these early months he maintained secret contacts with Eden. Their mutual private secretary, Pierson Dixon, ensured that Eden was regularly briefed upon important policy areas and his advice was transmitted back to Bevin.[51] During the London conference of Foreign Ministers, for instance, on 14 September 1945, Eden advised Bevin to pursue a policy of 'absolute firmness against the Russians',[52] and on many other occasions Dixon ensured that the advice of his old master was relayed to his new one. Fortunately for Bevin, this revelation had to await the publication of Dixon's diaries. In the meantime the nascent split over foreign policy within the Labour Party was exacerbated rather than ameliorated by his handling of arguments within the party.

In some respects Bevin was a natural authoritarian to whom the processes of democratic discussion were irritating formalities. With party critics he frequently lost the patience which he sustained so massively in his dealings with Molotov. On some occasions he actually had to be persuaded by his colleagues to face his critics in party meetings.[53] Like all Ministers, Bevin had to discuss policy with a group of backbench specialists. Dalton shrewdly selected the members in his own group, but Bevin, the relatively inexperienced parliamentarian, had overlooked such a precaution, and in consequence his foreign affairs group was packed with his left-wing critics.[54] He did not allow this opposition to distract him from his policies but he paid a heavy price in exasperation: one Labour MP actually recalls him in tears when criticised at a party meeting.[55] When the group's chairman, Seymour Cocks, resigned, frustrated by the futility of his task, Bevin, more wisely, had him replaced by the right-wing J. B. Hynd.[56]

His dealings with Russia were frequently the most important item on his critics' agenda. According to one of his biographers, Bevin was well aware that the keenest critics he had inside his own party were 'those who watch eagerly and ceaselessly for any sign of his supposed prejudice against the Soviets'. Against those who urged a more conciliatory attitude towards Labour's 'most favoured nation' he replied that he would go half way but no more; he did not believe in appeasement to anyone.[57] The attitude of the Tories towards his handling of foreign affairs was a major element in fomenting divisions within the Labour Party. Churchill had expressed personal satisfaction that Bevin had been made Foreign Secretary. Initially generous in his remarks about Stalin, his erstwhile fellow statesman and drinking partner, within weeks of losing the restraints of office Churchill's attitude almost returned to their pre-war vehemence. He warned Bevin that communism was in the process of obtaining dictatorial powers in Eastern Europe. The knock of the secret police on the doors of innocent people was too frequent; now was the 'time for Britain to speak out'.[58] The rest of the Conservative Party echoed Churchill's sentiments and were delighted at Bevin's opposition to Soviet pressure in Eastern Europe and the Mediterranean.[59] At least one of his critics was convinced that during his first speech as Foreign Secretary, on 22 August, Bevin had been spurred on by Opposition cheers to the very precipice of indiscretion in his belligerent statements upon Russia.[60] Another of his critics put it differently: 'It is felt that when our policy meets with such hearty approval from the Opposition there must be something wrong with it. It is felt that if the Tories applaud it cannot be a Socialist Foreign Policy.'[61]

No doubt such statements caused the Tories to redouble their applause; they clearly enjoyed the situation. Brigadier Fitzroy Maclean, an expert on Soviet affairs on the Conservative back benches, took Labour's Russophiles to task, with some relish, in the November foreign affairs debate. He challenged the Labour Party election assertion that left could speak to left. Anglo-Soviet relations, he judged, were worse than at any time since 1941. He concluded that the leftist complexion of Labour MPs did not necessarily endear them to the Soviet leaders. 'Parlous Pinks and other left-wing diversionists', he added, inspired 'neither admiration nor respect in Moscow'.[62] In retrospect we can see that the brigadier was close to the truth. Bevin and his colleagues would probably have agreed, but not the bulk of Labour MPs. Between July and December 1945 a pattern had emerged in the discussion of foreign affairs in Parliament. When speaking on the subject of Russia in particular, Bevin spoke with the support of the Conservatives and of only part of his own party. The real 'opposition' was provided by the remainder. This opposition was as yet incohate, consisted of no precise groupings, and had no dominant spokesman. During the spring and summer of 1946 these characteristics were destined to develop.

Notes

1 *Labour Looks to the Future* (Labour Party, 1945), p. 50.
2 S. Orwell and I. Angus, *Collected Orwell*, vol. III, p. 454.
3 For example, in those of B. Strauss, P. Follick, J. Platts-Mills, J. McAdam, H. Vernon, H. Usbourne, K. Zilliacus and, most notably, in that of Raymond Blackburn.
4 See M. Foot, speech 414 *H. C. Deb.*, 2359–66, 26 October 1945, and B. T. Parkin, 415 *H. C. Deb.*, 1356–98, 7 November 1945.
5 416 *H. C. Deb.*, 687–91, 22 November 1845.
6 *The Observer*, 8 August 1973, p. 24.
7 W. G. Cove, *Left*, September 1945, pp. 491–2.
8 Dalton shared these fears to some degree; see Dalton, *High Tide and After: Memoirs, 1945–60* (London, 1962), p. 77.
9 *Tribune*, 14 December 1945, and *N. S. and N.*, 15 December 1945.
10 H. S. Truman, *1945, Year of Decision*, vol. I (Signet, 1945), pp. 585–6.
11 416 *H. C. Deb.*, 656, 22 November 1945. See also H. Hughes's speech, 415 *H. C. Deb.*, 1370, 7 November 1945.
12 415 *H. C. Deb.*, 643–70, 22 November 1945.
13 *Tribune*, 20 May 1945.
14 *TUCR 1945*, p. 292.
15 *Ibid.*, p. 364.
16 416 *H. C. Deb.*, 643–70, 22 November 1945.
17 414 *H. C. Deb.*, 2350–66, 26 October 1945.
18 416 *H. C. Deb.*, 614, 22 November 1945.
19 *Ibid.*, 824–8, 23 November 1945. This group of fellow-travellers included as its hard core W. Warbey, L. J. Solley, J. Platts-Mills, J. D. Mack, W. G. Cove, S. O. Davies, T. Braddock, S. Silverman, L. Hutchinson, G. Bing and D. N. Pritt (Independent Labour).
20 *LPCR 1945*, p. 82.
21 413 *H. C. Deb.*, 706–10, 22 August 1945.
22 415 *H. C. Deb.*, 1307–12, 7 November 1945.
23 Dalton, *Diaries*, 16 May 1945.
24 M. A. Fitzsimmons, *The Foreign Policy of the Labour Government, 1945–51*, p. 168. For discussion on this point, see Michael R. Gordon, *Conflict and Consensus in Labour's Foreign Policy, 1914–65*, p. 93.
25 Dalton, *Diaries*, 11 December 1944. He records that he had his way "on all essentials' and that now the Labour Party had a 'solid, sensible, realistic foundation on which to build'.
26 *Ibid.*, 23 February 1945. See also his entries for 14 March, 5 April and 10 April 1945.
27 *Ibid.*, 16 May 1945.
28 *Ibid.*, 27 July 1945. Morrison believed he had persuaded Attlee to put Bevin in the Foreign Office instead of the 'temperamental' Dalton — see his autobiography, p. 246.
29 F. Williams, *Ernest Bevin: Portrait of a Great Englishman*, p. 237.
30 R. B. McCallum and Alison Readman, *The British General Election of 1945*, (London, 1947), p. 199.

120   *The Russia complex*

31   Michael Foot, *Aneurin Bevan*, vol. II, 1945–60, p. 32.
32   On the question of personality and the formation of Labour Party foreign policy, see W. P. Maddox, *Foreign Relations in British Labour Politics*.
33   F. Williams, *Ernest Bevin*, p. 157.
34   *Tribune*, 8 March 1946. Laski wrote in *The Times*, 'I want to emphasise that the Labour Party is at no point committed to the doctrine of continuity in foreign policy,' 3 July 1943.
35   See, for example, 415 *H. C. Deb.*, 1337, 7 November 1945.
36   416 *H. C. Deb.*, 786, 23 November 1945.
37   Sir Pierson Dixon, *Double Diploma: the Life of Sir Pierson Dixon, Don and Diplomat*, p. 166.
38   *Ibid.*, p. 167. Dixon, Eden's personal secretary, made a strong personal plea for Bevin.
39   Lord Strang, *Home and Abroad* (London, 1956), p. 287.
40   Truman, vol. I, p. 240 n.
41   *Ibid.*, p. 443. Dixon suggests, however, that Stalin had been 'shaken' by news of the atomic bomb, p. 170.
42   W. S. Churchill, *History of the Second World War*, vol. IV, p. 672.
43   Dixon, p. 170.
44   413 *H. C. Deb.*, 283–300, 22 August 1945.
45   Herbert Feis, *From Trust to Terror: the Onset of the Cold War, 1945–50*, p. 123.
46   Dixon, p. 191.
47   *Ibid.*, pp. 185–6.
48   415 *H. C. Deb.*, 1342, 7 November 1945.
49   Williams writes that Bevin conceived it his duty to 'protect and advance' where possible Britain's national interests; *Ernest Bevin*, p. 253.
50   415 *H. C. Deb.*, 1295, 7 November 1945.
51   Dixon, pp. 179, 182, 195, and 197.
52   *Ibid.*, pp. 183–4.
53   Interview with Ernest Davies, Bevin's PPS.
54   Dalton, p. 23. Dalton observed that Bevin let the group pick itself, 'and in came all the pacifists and fellow-travellers, pro-Russians and anti-Americans, and every sort of freak harboured in our majority'.
55   Interview with the MP concerned.
56   R. Jackson, *Rebels and Whips* (London, 1968), p. 57.
57   Trevor Davies, *Ernest Bevin* (London, 1946), p. 213.
58   413 *H. C. Deb.*, 79–95, 20 August 1945.
59   Davies, p. 215.
60   *Ibid.*, p. 216.
61   419 *H. C. Deb.*, 132, 1 February 1946.
62   416 *H. C. Deb.*, 673–8, 22 November 1945.

8 Russia and the case for a socialist foreign policy: the left-wing rebels

> I was asked in this House whether I would safeguard British interests and I replied that I would safeguard them anywhere. [Ernest Bevin, *H.C. Deb.*, vol. 419, col. 1357, 21 February, 1946]
>
> Oh, Crossman! He was up to anything, I think. There is always that lunatic fringe. [Clement Attlee, *Granada Historical Record* interview (Panther, 1967), p. 32]

After the abortive London conference of September 1945 the outcome of the Moscow Foreign Ministers' conference in December was more hopeful, settling peace treaties with Italy, Japan and the satellite countries, establishing a UN commission on atomic weapons and producing the promise from the USSR that the governments of Bulgaria and Rumania would be broadened in exchange for Western recognition. Bevin was unconvinced. Byrnes appeared to have done a deal whereby America obtained a free hand in the Far East whilst returning the compliment to Stalin in Eastern Europe. Meanwhile Britain still bore the brunt of Soviet pressure in the eastern Mediterranean, particularly in Iran, jointly occupied since 1941 by British and Soviet troops. It was suspected that the USSR, whose request for oil concessions had been refused by the Iranian government, was behind the revolt in Azerbaijan, a province within its zone of occupation. Suspicion increased when the Soviets refused government forces access to the region. The issue arose during the first meeting of the General Assembly, in January 1946.

i

The Labour Party looked fervently to this meeting to provide the signs that progress towards the idea of world government was at last possible. The *Daily Herald*'s attitude towards this early attempt to make collective security a reality is fairly typical of the party as a whole. For the first few days of the Assembly, its pages were filled with expectant rhetoric. With Bevin's world government speech only a few weeks old, the editorial on 10 January 1946 expressed the hope that the conference would herald a 'genuine new era in the history of the world'. Support for the new organisation must be the principal objective of every nation. There was an early blemish, however. The Soviet delegation, led by Vyshinsky (more familiar to Labour Party members for his prosecuting role in the infamous Moscow trials), did not arrive until the twelfth day of the conference. 'Speaking for the friends of Russia', the *Herald* complained at the mystery with which the Russians had surrounded their absence.[1]

From the start the Soviets pursued a robust line in diplomacy. They accused the British, through their presence in Greece and Indonesia, of 'endangering the peace of the world'. Bevin's response was unequivocal. He hotly demanded that Vyshinsky 'absolve us or brand us guilty'. *The Daily Herald* approved his vigorous defence, pointing out, a little tortuously, that if the barriers of mistrust were to be broken down, then only free speaking on both sides would do it. It seemed that left could speak to left even if only at the top of their voices![2] In wholeheartedly supporting Bevin, Michael Foot, writing in the *Daily Herald* on 5 February 1946, described the Russian charges as 'fantastic' and attributed them to the communists' fear that social democracy had become a compelling ideological rival to their own creed.

In retrospect it seems probable that the Soviet fusillade over Greece and Indonesia was a ploy to distract attention from the sensitive question of her involvement in Iran. Possibly the Russians had calculated that time was on their side, that they had only to wait and allow the chemistry of revolution to work and Iran would fall into their hands; hence their policy of delay and procrastination over withdrawal. Bevin, however, was well aware of the importance to Britain of the Anglo-Iranian oilfields and was not going to allow Vyshinsky to outmanoeuvre him; he vigorously raised the question of Russia's failure to withdraw from Iran. Inevitably this tension over the Middle East robbed the first meeting of the UN General Assembly of any constructive achievement.

On 21 February Bevin presented the House with the unsatisfactory outcome. His speech reflected the difficulties of his position as a leader of a party with fierce pro-Soviet proclivities whilst being forced to adopt an implicitly anti-Soviet direction in foreign policy. His technique was to present an impression of fundamental good faith which the Russians were flagrantly refusing to reciprocate. He revealed, with some bitterness, that at Moscow in December 1945 his offer to extend the Anglo-Russian treaty from twenty to fifty years had been rejected (a proposal near to the heart of several Labour MPs). He denied the existence of a 'Western bloc', an allegation which the left were beginning to make. On the delicate subject of Iran, he confessed to doubts about the so-called Azerbaijan 'movement' whose legitimate aims Russia claimed to support but into which it allowed no press investigation. 'When a thing is not open to the light of the day,' he commented, 'that contributes to suspicion.' Bevin, however, was careful to nod in the direction of Russophile opinion. 'I cannot conceive of any circumstances,' he declared, 'in which Britain and the Soviet Union should go to war.' 'Those who make up the Soviet Union,' he insisted 'are members of the proletariat, and so am I. We are used to hard hitting, but our friendship remains.' He added, even more unconvincingly, that such disagreements were similar to those on the floor of the Labour Party Conference.[3]

Bevin's stout defence of British interests was greeted warmly by Harold Macmillan, the Conservative spokesman, who went on to praise him for continuing the best traditions of his predecessors, Churchill and Eden. Conservative praise gave added edge, as always, to left-wing complaint. M. Philips Price, a leftish Labour MP whose recent visit to the USSR had reassured him that the Soviet Union was not 'communising' Eastern Europe, believed that the Russian claim on Iranian oil was legitimate. He applauded Soviet efforts to liberalise Iran's reactionary capitalist government.[4] In his maiden speech the newly elected Emrys Hughes went further. He called for the withdrawal of all bases in the Mediterranean; in the nuclear age they served no purpose except that of provoking the USSR.[5]

Despite this opposition, reinforced predictably by the fellow-travelling element in the Labour Party, there is some indication from the Labour press that Soviet behaviour at the UN conference had caused substantial disillusion. The *Daily Herald* stated frankly, after the dust had settled, that the bitterness which characterised Anglo-Russian relations was of Soviet rather than British manufacture.[6] For its own part, the *Herald* chose to reveal that, several months earlier, it had offered space to *Izvestia* to explain Soviet activities in Eastern Europe on the understanding that the same right would be accorded to the *Herald*. The latter's article had been despatched on 19 October but still awaited publication.

The *N.S. and N.* did not believe that the USSR was intent upon making war, but it now perceived a more cynical impulse behind Soviet foreign policy; that of conciliating the USA whilst building up spheres of influence at British expense.[7]

Tribune warmly endorsed Bevin's behaviour as a 'great personal triumph'. If the Russians saw an inherently weak Labour government trying to hold together a disintegrating Empire, then Bevin's forceful diplomacy would be a useful corrective. Mutual respect, *Tribune* argued, was indispensable for genuine co-operation among equals; now was the time to stand firm.[8] On 22 February 1946 *Tribune* was wholly unconvinced by Soviet blandishments about 'revolutionary' developments in Eastern Europe; the agreement over the reconstitution of the Bulgarian government had never been implemented, the broadening of the Rumanian government had been a farce, pro-Western Yugoslavs like Subasic had been dropped, communist pressure upon Polish socialists was accelerating and in East Germany, by terror and trickery, the communists had achieved totalitarian control.

However, with one of those rapid shifts in opinion of which ideologically based journals seem capable, *Tribune* totally reversed its critical role over Russia in the space of a week. There was a very good reason: Churchill's Fulton speech.

ii

On 5 March 1946, at Fulton, Missouri, out of office but in American eyes still surrounded by the aura of wartime greatness, Churchill delivered a formal address in the President's home state in the presence of Truman himself. Churchill's most famous pre-war speeches had awakened the public to the dangers of an evil, expansionist philosophy. A year after the end of the war, the Fulton speech fitted the same mould. An Iron Curtain had descended across the Continent, no one knew the limits of Soviet Russia's objectives, said Churchill. The only way to check her expansion was by a firm united front between America and Britain.

At one stroke he had exploded the paper-thin illusion of Big Three unity. He had made devastatingly articulate those half-realised assumptions upon which British and American foreign policies already rested. A storm of indignation ensued. The speech had been curiously anticipated in the House of Commons on 5 March by the eccentric ILP MP John McGovern. He predicted that Churchill was about to make a sensational speech in the USA calling for closer union with the USA against the USSR.[9] The source of McGovern's information must remain a mystery, but its exclusive nature is witnessed by Eden's denial: clearly the Fulton speech was a surprise even to Churchill's closest foreign policy advisor.[10] McGovern's apparent telepathy was forgotten in the furore of complaint which the speech unleashed. *Tribune* declared, 'Nothing doing, Mr Churchill!' Could his fears over Poland be sincere when he had helped condemn her at Yalta? Whatever their objections to Soviet policy the British people did not want a military alliance against the Soviet Union as the price of their indpendence. Whilst we wanted the best possible relations with the USA, a military alliance was too close for comfort.[11]

Writing in *Forward*, Laski predicted that within such an alliance Wall Street would do all in its power to squeeze out a socialist government in

Britain. The *N.S. and N.* went even further: acceptance of Churchill's Fulton policy would make Britain the forty-ninth State, a dispensable aircraft carrier in the war that would inevitably ensue.[12]

There could be little argument about the facts upon which Churchill based his speech, and in retrospect his interpretation appears to be remarkably prescient, but how accurate was it in March 1946, and, given the traditional Russian fears, did it damage relations with Russia? Behind the expansionist tendencies of Soviet foreign policy there has been an even stronger theme of a search for security. Russian history is a catalogue of desperate fights against invasion from the east and from the west, and her foreign policy has always sought to secure her boundaries diplomatically and strategically from these potentially predatory neighbours. Communism reinforced both tendencies: expansionism through its proseletysing international aspect, and the search for security through its thesis of capitalist encirclement. This latter theme, an axiom of communist thinking, exercised a potent force in maintaining domestic cohesion and nourished the traditional Russian fear of external attack. The nightmare which faced the USSR at the close of the second world war was, therefore, an Anglo-American conspiracy to invade.

It is possible to argue, and persuasively, that this nightmare was of Russia's own making, and that Soviet policies in the Middle East and in Eastern Europe did much to make it a reality after the war, but this alone would not acquit Churchill of the accusation that his speech had the effect of exacerbating relations with Russia. To Russia his rhetoric must have appeared bloodcurdling, his accusations malevolent, and his virtual invocation of an atomic-armed Anlgo-American alliance against her alarming. Even if the patient is paranoid, there is every reason to dispell rather than give substance to his fantasies. History has appeared to prove Fulton right, but Fulton, to a degree, cheated history by being instrumental in its making. It was an ill timed speech; it is the Labour Party criticisms of Fulton, one suspects, that will more truly stand the test of time.

Some 120 Labour MPs from the left and centre voiced complaint in the form of a petition, demanding that the government publicly repudiate the speech.[13] A motion of censure was tabled against Churchill condemning it as detrimental to Anglo-Soviet-American relations.

However, the petition was ignored; the attempt at censure failed. The government had taken the line that Churchill's views represented only himself. Bevin is known to have been privately opposed to the tone and the timing of the speech, but he purposely withheld official dissociation from it. This was possibly a testy defiance of left-wing demands, but more likely Bevin, who would not at this stage have made such a speech himself, did not feel sufficiently opposed to its message to offer any public rebuke. Indeed, at this time he was incensed at Soviet intransigence in Iran. Instead of withdrawing on 2 March in accordance with the 1942 agreement, Russia was increasing her military presence. The Iranian government appealed to the Security Council. Throughout March tension mounted, but skilful Iranian diplomacy and Anglo-American pressure through the Security Council prevailed, and on 4 April the Russians agreed to withdraw. The crisis was over.

A few left-wing voices defended Soviet behaviour as defensive measures against Western aggression, but there was a large consensus of opinion in the Labour Party that Russia had broken all the rules; much of the protective goodwill engendered by the Fulton attack was dissipated. Writing in the *Daily Herald*, Michael Foot did not dispute Russia's right to a share in Middle Eastern oil, nor to a friendly government on her border, but he condemned her methods of 'direct,[15] flagrant and brutal intervention in the affairs of another country'. The Iranian crisis was something of a watershed in the *N.S. and N.* attitude towards Russia. After the first week the journal could find no excuse for Soviet behaviour; it was 'Soviet intransigence that is creating the anti-Soviet bloc which they have always feared'.[16]

In the second week the *N.S. and N.* concluded that Russia was simply seeking to extend her frontiers where she could, 'creating satellites around her borders and proclaiming herself the champion of workers and peasants throughout the world'.[17] By the third week it was comparing Stalin's tactics in Iran with those of Hitler in Czechoslovakia. The comparison, however, ended there; the objectives of the two men were held to be vastly different: 'the conception of a nation dominating the world by force is alien to a power which is based upon the dogmas of Marxiam socialism'.[18] The journal's advice to Bevin was to hold aloof from any anti-Soviet grouping, to be as conciliatory as possible, and to smooth the way for change in Soviet policy. *Tribune*'s analysis was similar, but not its recommended course of action. Bevin was criticised for being too passive over Iran; he should have countered the creed of communism with vigorous advocacy of the ideas of social democracy.

The tragedy of the Iranian crisis for members of the Labour Party was that it demonstrated ominously that the UN was not going to be the effective collective security organisation for which they had fervently hoped. During the crisis Stalin had publicly reaffirmed his faith in the UN, and in one sense the crisis appeared as a success for the organisation; the Security Council, after all, had finally been able to persuade the USSR to withdraw.[19] But by her breach of international law and her bullying tactics Russia had revealed that the spirit necessary to make the UN work effectively was lacking on her side. In Iran the corner-stone of Labour's 'socialist foreign policy', as formulated in the 'thirties, had been kicked away; yet it would take many months and several crises for the fact to be fully realised.

iii

The Labour Party had begun its tenure of power hopeful that a new chapter had been opened in Anglo-Soviet relations, but the vision of an imminent new world order had been disappointed. The frustrated idealism of the autumn and winter was translated by the spring of 1946 into a growing resentment against Bevin's foreign policy, marred as it was for the left and centre by British resistance to nationalist movements in Indonesia and Egypt, and Bevin's policy of supporting a right-wing Greek government against an indigenous communist bid for power. Over Palestine, Bevin was hopelessly compromised by his support for the Arab League — an instrument designed to resist Soviet pressure — and his policy came under furious fire from the strong pro-Zionist elements in the Labour Party.

In Europe and across the Atlantic the picture was even less cheerful. In Germany no progress had been made to implement the terms of Potsdam and the costs of British occupation were proving excessive.[20] In America the forces of socialism (to which many Labour Party members had looked with hope) had never seemed weaker and the power of Wall Street never stronger. The USA, with atomic secrets still intact, was extending its influence deep into the Pacific. Worse still, financially prostrate Britain was being forced to shelter under America's economic wing.

This was the depressing backcloth against which the decline in Anglo-Soviet relations was perceived by many MPs on the left and in the centre. Ironically, independence for India, presaged by Attlee's announcement on 15 March, failed to win Soviet co-operation in the way many left-wingers had prophesied in the past when urging a magnanimous gesture to disarm Soviet suspicions.

A ground-swell of opposition to Bevin developed in the PLP and among party workers; the issue of Foreign Office personnel was one of the early manifestations. It had long been an axiom of left-wing thinking that the social origins of professional diplomats could not fail to make them willing accomplices of bourgeois imperialism and anti-Soviet in outlook. After the war, when it seemed to the Labour left that a Labour government was not following an even remotely socialist foreign policy, this suspicion became more widely articulated, the implication being that Bevin was meekly accepting the advice of his officials.[21] Sir Richard Acland, William Warbey, Harold Laski, John Freeman and others, together with the left-wing press, elaborated these arguments in the months leading up to the Party Conference.

Bevin's robust defence of his Foreign Office staff routed his critics utterly and must have dispelled any remaining illusions that he was the gullible puppet of Foreign Office officials. It is significant that only four motions on this subject were put down for discussion at the 1947 Conference, compared with the twenty submitted in 1946.[22] In an interview with the author, Ernest Davies, PPS to FO Minister of State McNeil for several years, reinforced this point with his own judgement: 'he was never led by his staff; he used to listen and lead with imaginative suggestions. He had a brilliant mind — I know he used to ramble and reminisce, but his mind was working all the time.'

Bevin's rebuttal of other criticisms at the Bournemouth Conference was effective but less conclusive. Here he suffered attack after attack upon his policy relating to Greece, Indonesia and especially Spain, but the dominant source of complaint was directed against his handling of Anglo-Soviet relations. In his radically critical chairman's speech Harold Laski emphasised the affinities between the Labour Party and the Soviet Union, invoking once again the myth that the councils of action had thwarted Churchill's attempt in 1920 to break the Bolshevik revolution. He strove to justify the harshness of Soviet political methods by warning darkly that the forces of fascism in Europe were not dead, that the hooded men of counter-revolution were awaiting their chance to win back 'their ancient claim to live by exploitation'. Laski believed Russian suspicions of the West, which he allowed were excessive, were due in no small part to America's secrecy over atom bomb secrets and the attempts, since the Lillienthal report, to postpone international control for as long as possible.[23]

Many other speeches echoed Laski's dissatisfaction that Bevin had been unable to co-operate with the Soviet Union. The South Hendon DLP's motion regretted that the Labour Party had chosen to continue the 'traditional Conservative Party policy of power politics abroad'; this boiled down to a complaint by its mover, J. W. Kagan, that Bevin should find more in common with capitalist America than socialist Russia. The seconder of the motion, warned that "reactionary circles in this country are licking their lips at the prospect of wiping out the Soviet Union". He wanted Bevin to be given a mandate (i.e. virtually instructed) to reach agreement with the USSR at the forthcoming conference in Paris, adding sharply that when Bevin spoke in the House of Commons 'we want the applause to come from behind him and not from in front of him'. But it was the motion of the South West St Pancras DLP and the speech of its mover, E. Cook, that most clearly characterised rank-and-file unrest with Bevin's foreign policy. The motion called for a British foreign policy 'directed to ensure firm friendship with the progressive forces throughout the world and in particular with the USSR and that such a

A socialist foreign policy 129

policy should overide Imperial interest'. Cook suggested that the first part of his motion would be met by a reaffirmation of Labour's election pledge to cooperate with working-class struggles towards socialism all over the world. Relations with the USSR could be improved by more trade and cultural exchanges and by repudiating Churchill's proposal to align the Commonwealth with American monopoly capitalism against the USSR. It has already been observed that favourable attitudes towards the USSR were to some extent the mirror image of unfavourable attitudes towards the USA. Cook's view of America was typical of the Labour left in the immediate postwar months: 'America is a gigantic imperialism, absolutely wild chaotic and uncontrolled.... Great trusts and magnates rule America who hate us, fear us and loathe us. They are not the people to whom we should be tied.'[24]

Bevin began his reply in low key, explaining, as he often did, that foreign affairs was a bewildering area, fraught with danger, which needed to be handled with great care and foresight. He pounced on Laski's reference to the councils of action. 'Is there any man in this Conference,' he challenged, 'who historically did more to defend the Russian Revolution than I did?' Throughout the inter-war years, he claimed, he had defended the Soviet Union against attacks and in return the communists had tried to break up the Transport Union. His attempt to reach an understanding with the USSR was sincere. Those who said otherwise were making an untruthful and damaging statement: 'The greatest enemies of friendship are the Russian supporters in this country.'

As for trade, Cripps's offer to fly to Moscow to discuss such matters had not been taken up. As for cultural relations, Molotov's speeches were reported over here but not Bevin's in the USSR. As for the emergence of a Western bloc, there already existed a bloc in the East. Britain's task was to weld together Soviet socialism and American capitalism in order to keep the peace. On the subject of those notorious Tory cheers, Bevin philosophised that 'most of the greatest things in life are done at a time when you are a little unpopular, when at least you have got to think clearly where you are going'. Kagan's resolution he interpreted as a motion of censure upon himself. If Conference passed it he would travel to Paris in its shadow; not surprisingly it was withdrawn. The Cook resolution was overwhelmingly defeated.

Whatever the doubts of individual unions, Bevin's impregnable authority within the trade union movement, together with a typical Conference *tour de force*, enabled him to come away from Bournemouth with a massive vote of confidence. And yet, throughout the summer whilst the Paris peace conference dominated his attention, unease was fomenting within the Labour Party and outright revolt was not far away.

iv

From April to September the centre of diplomatic activity was Paris. Here an endless merry-go-round took place of identical suggestions, identical objections, increasing divisions between West and East. At one point Bevin's health broke down and he had to be replaced for a while by Attlee. Throughout May the Foreign Ministers had haggled over the subject of the European peace treaties. On the 4th Bevin reported disagreements over the accessibility of the Danube lands to Western trade, Italian reparations, the future of Trieste, and, most important of all, the question of Germany. The Potsdam stipulations relating to reparations and the treatment of Germany as a single economic unit had proved to be the major stumbling blocks. By July Britain was forced to divert £130 million to help feed the starving population of the British zone, and still machinery was being dismantled and despatched, together with raw materials, to the Soviet Union as reparations.

In the Eastern zone the Russians were imposing their by now characteristic political control, extracting massive reparation and refusing to allow movement of food and raw materials into the other zones. In May, whilst the Foreign Ministers met, General Clay called a halt to reparation payments from his zone and the British authorities followed suit shortly afterwards. Byrnes had gone to Paris with a draft treaty, along lines which Stalin had approved in Moscow the previous December, which he hoped would cut through the deadlock the terms of Potsdam had caused. The plan was to sign a treaty with a united Germany whereby four signatories would guarantee to keep the country disarmed. Bevin ended his report to Parliament on 4 June on an optimistic note; in Byrnes's plan he perceived the strong possibility of 'peace in Europe'. His optimism, however, failed to disarm the critics of his German policy.

Michael Foot proposed, quite sensibly in retrospect, that, as Potsdam had proved so unworkable, it should be torn up and another basis for the treatment of Germany created.[25] Other left-wing critics followed more predictable lines of argument. The Soviet accusation that the West was soft-pedalling denazification measures in its zones was echoed, the Soviet zone being held up as a model for British occupation. Julius Silverman pointed out that the Russians had made their zone a 'going concern'; as soon as the West could do likewise with its zones, he argued in Parliament, the USSR would talk of unity.[26] German unity was the issue in which the left was passionately interested, for the spectre haunting them was that of a divided Europe. *Tribune* (7 June) foresaw the danger of an armed polarisation in Europe, whilst the *New Statesman* feared that unilateral action over Germany by the West would divide not only Europe but the world into competing armed camps.

A socialist foreign policy 131

The left could hardly have been comforted in July when Molotov told the reconvened Foreign Ministers' conference that consideration of a treaty would be conditional upon a guarantee that ten billion dollars would be paid in reparations to the USSR. Its worst fears were fulfilled by subsequent developments. Molotov had also made counter-proposals to the American plan which Byrnes interpreted as a direct appeal for German allegiance.[27]

On 7 May, in Cabinet, Dalton and Bevan had resisted Bevin's assessment that the 'danger of Russia has become certainly as great as, and possibly even greater than, that of a revived Germany'.[28] They must have found the argument harder to resist in July when Bevin revealed to the Cabinet that a top secret Chiefs of Staff intelligence report showed that Russia was using East German factories and installations to produce submarines, aircraft and the German range of V weapons. Bevin followed up by arguing that the Russians were doing their best to weaken the Western sectors of Germany and dominate their own. To counter this policy, he had agreed to an American plan to fuse the economies of the British and American zones. He agreed that this would appear as 'ganging up' and as 'dividing Europe', but believed it would 'probably be quite salutary for the Russians to feel that we can if we wish, and that we mean business'.[29] By July, therefore, he had already decided to pursue the policy over Germany which the left most feared.

In August and September the American and British zone Governors set about forming bizonal agencies to deal with food, agriculture, transport, communications and finance. On 6 September Byrnes made a speech at Stuttgart in which he asserted that Germany should be given the opportunity to run her own affairs. Bevin endorsed this opinion, concluding that 'we must either have Potsdam observed as a whole ... or we must have a new agreement'.[30] The critical break over the treatment of Germany had been made.

As international relations between the former allies deteriorated in the summer of 1946, the official Labour Party organisation was proposing a goodwill mission to Moscow, thus exhibiting once more the perennial Labour faith in such gestures; the *Daily Herald* described it as a mission of 'high importance not only to us but to the world'.[31] Alice Bacon, Morgan Philips, Clay of the TGWU and the ubiquitous Laski set off on 28 July. After meeting several high dignatories and officials, including Shvernik, the President, the delegation was ushered into Stalin's presence on 7 August. Declarations of desire for sincere and lasting friendship were made on both sides. Stalin reminded them of Soviet help for the miners in 1926, the British delegation responded by reminding him of Labour support for the USSR in 1920. Apart from this piece of fraternal one-upmanship, little of substance was exchanged, and if the delegation's visit had any influence upon the direction of events in

Paris it was imperceptible. If, as seems likely, the decision to send the delegation had been a sop to Bevin's critics, its outcome failed to draw their sting. Throughout the summer months opposition groups began to form and coalesce.

After Bevin's brutal crushing of Lansbury at the 1935 Conference, pacificism had not been a potent force within the Labour Party, but it still remained as a potentially powerful element, and when Emrys Hughes was elected to Parliament in 1946 its voice was substantially strengthened. Pacificists were unhappy about the growing conflict in Anglo-Soviet relations because they feared it could sow the seeds of the ultimate catastrophe: a third world war. In consequence they tended to take refuge in utopian policies of world government and strongly resist the continuance of conscription in peace time. Hughes described this issue as the test of the Labour government.[32] Conscription was an issue which later attracted many of those who were pacifiist-inclined but not pure pacifists. Sorensen, for instance, who left his pure pacifism behind in the 'thirties, was still hostile to the continuance of conscription, and others of like mind, who detected its implications in Bevin's growing quarrel with the Soviet Union, were willing to lend their support in efforts to curb him.[33]

The fellow-travellers in the Labour Party numbered about a score, perhaps half of whom advocated a line indistinguishable from that of the Communist Party. After 1945 the hard core did not technically include D. N. Pritt, for he was now 'Independent Labour' but was closely connected with such MPs as John Platts-Mills, Lester Hutchinson, S. Solley and S. O. Davies. Their view was that the Soviet presence in Eastern Europe was laden with promise; socialist dictatorships, after all, were the essential prerequisite of a true socialist system.[34] As the *Labour Monthly* argued in April 1946, the Soviet Union was interested solely in reconstruction and higher living standards, and would collaborate with any friendly government. The only way to prevent war, argued the fellow-travellers, was through alliance with the USSR.

A rather more subtle version of this argument was advocated by Konni Zilliacus, certainly the most prolific and probably the most influential member of the fellow-travelling group. Though normally bracketed with the fellow travellers, he had parted bitterly from the communist line over Russia's invasion of Finland in 1939, and he always retained an independence of appraisal which probably explained the degree of respect with which his views were heard in Parliament, in the Labour Party and in the country. Zilliacus believed strongly, and rightly, that British commitments in 1946 were far too widespread and needed to be drastically reduced. He felt that no great decisions had been produced in foreign affairs by the change of government.

'We seem to be blindly impelled,' he told the House of Commons on 4 March, 'by the momentum of Imperial inertia.'[35]

He feared communism much less than the average Labour Party supporter, declaring on one occasion, 'I would trust communists more than I would some of the members opposite.'[36] He was convinced that Britain needed to come to terms with the forces of communism in Russia, and in Europe; he applauded the positive achievements of the post-war communist 'revolutions' in Eastern Europe. He felt in the spring of 1946 that Bevin had set his face against the 'unity of the working class and against the resistance movements which alone are capable of reconstructing Europe'. Rather, the forces of social revolution in Europe should be supported, even when communist-led, and a new and fundamental effort made to reach a settlement with the USSR; without such an agreement the UN would be a fiction.

Zilliacus was foremost amongst those fellow-travellers who believed the sacrifice of political liberties in Eastern Europe could be paid for in the coin of economic and social advance. For many such socialists the sight of old aristocracies being dispossessed and their lands distributed to the peasantry, all in a matter of months, was an overwhelming experience. Certainly, they argued, such changes had not been easy; 'firm political control' had been necessary. The remnants of the capitalist classes were not without influence and, as all socialists knew, their expected counter-revolutionary efforts had to be 'strongly resisted'. Such periods of disturbance were destined to be temporary; they would pass away with the achievement of a new economic base and the demise of the threat of capitalist intervention.

Many of those who applauded the events in Eastern Europe regarded with disdain those socialists whose liberal scruples and ignorance of political traditions in Eastern Europe led them to criticise these vital socialist advances. In retrospect it is clear that the fellow-travellers had little conception or experience of what was actually happening. To be in favour of firm political control or to accept the inevitably harsh transition to socialism was to be lulled into security by agreeable-sounding words with elastic meanings. How 'firm' should political control be? How 'harsh' the transition? A few imprisonments, some executions perhaps; but the systematic terrorisation of whole nations with permanent and comprehensive police surveillance assisted by informers, arbitrary arrest and execution? Were these justifiable means of achieving a new economic base? And how long should they last? Bevin was hotly opposed to the extension of totalitarian regimes and strove against the hard-core fellow-travellers to win the bulk of the PLP to his point of view. Advice rained in on him from other quarters.

v

The view of Seymour Cocks, the UDC veteran and chairman of the PLP Foreign Affairs Group which initially hounded Bevin, are interesting.[37] Cocks believed that communism and social democracy were based upon two totally different and irreconcilable cultural traditions and economic creeds. Far better than attempting to reconcile them, he suggested, would be the recognition by West and East of separate geographical zones of interest on each side of the Iron Curtain. On this basis, both blocs would co-exist quite peacefully and prosperously as long as mutual interference was avoided. Given the intense wartime sufferings of Russia, it was hardly surprising that she feared for her security; Western recognition of a 'Monroe doctrine' in the East would ensure this security. Cocks was advocating, therefore, a form of ideological *apartheid* in contrast to the integrative ideas so popular elsewhere on the left. McNeil described Cock's proposal as a 'council of despair',[38] yet ironically it was Cocks's solution which has stood the test of time, which has been virtually accepted by both blocs and which is now arguably one of the founding premises of *détente*. His scheme was too far-sighted; the West was not prepared to relinquish Eastern Europe without a struggle.

Maurice Edelman, at this time a young Labour MP, had his own pet scheme to break the deadlock in Europe; he urged that at the various points of Anglo-Soviet rivalry — Iran, the Balkans, the Adriatic — joint trading corporations should be established to transform friction into complementary effort. He envisaged that the home country would retain 51 per cent of the shares and that the Big Three should hold the balance under the aegis of the United Nations Economic and Social Committee.[39] Edelman believed that in this way the economic causes of war would be transformed into a stimulus to international trade, and, rather carried away, suggested that a constructive economic equilibrium would replace the dangerous balance-of-power system. The answer to his proposal was provided by a Moscow Radio broadcast a few days later which denounced his suggestion as a plan to 'enslave the Balkans'.[40]

Following the failure of the Paris conference, *Tribune* too produced its scheme for peace, a little reminiscent perhaps of Aneurin Bevan's style of thinking. *Tribune* believed that international conflict emanated from differing conceptions of justice and power. Britain should therefore call an international conference at which these concepts should be discussed as substabtive issues —a sort of international political theory seminar. Once the general principles of international behaviour on such subjects as atomic power, oil and international waterways had been agreed upon, then a major source of international disagreement would have been eliminated. *Tribune's* academic-sounding scheme remained a mere proposal.

Writing in the same edition, Laski still held to his wartime analysis of Soviet foreign policy that Russia was basically engaged in a search for security and represented a force for progress the potential for which the British Labour Party should attempt to realise. He wanted the Labour government to set its differences with Russia to one side, to soothe Soviet suspicions and conciliate their legitimate demands; a velvet glove, perhaps, inside a velvet glove.[41]

Kingsley Martin, in his biography, describes Laski as the leader of the left after the war. It could be argued that 1946 was, in a sense, 'Laski's year'. He completed a controversial tour of the USA, was involved in an expensive and well publicised libel case and was chairman of the Labour Party as well as being a vocal left-wing critic of Bevin's foreign policy. The American press dubbed him the 'Lenin of the British Reds'.[42] Robert Boothby complained in the House that Laski's 'lightest words, his bedtime musings are headline news for every paper in the US. He is regarded there as not only representing 100% of the Labour Government, but also about 80% of the country as a whole.'[43] On that occasion McNeil defended his friend, explaining that he had a gift for controversy,[44] but other members of the government were less impressed.

Attlee, who had been incensed by his interference over Potsdam, regarded Laski as a hopeless practical politician and as a bit of a nuisance ('a not very serious thorn, a slight irritation').[45] When asked if he had consulted him over the 1945 election, he replied emphatically, 'I wouldn't. God, no!'[46] It was true that despite undoubted intellectual gifts and voluminous knowledge of international affairs, Laski's vision was anything but clear; a man, perhaps, of much learning and little judgement. His attitudes towards communism as an ideology and the foreign policy of the Russian communists offers an interesting example. Laski was, strangely enough, the author of *The Secret Battalion*, the Labour Party pamphlet explaining why communist affiliation had been rejected. In this pamphlet he described the Soviet Communist Party as a 'conspiracy against the State', an organisation with 'no interest in political freedom'. No one knew better than he the callousness of Stalin's regime, the vast numbers who had been eliminated or imprisoned in the name of socialism, yet still he believed that these same leaders could be trusted in international relations, that they would co-operate genuinely with capitalist States. Laski never seemed to appreciate that if Stalin and his fellow members of the Politburo were not sincere communists, then they must be murderous political opportunists against whom it would surely be dangerous to drop one's guard. Alternatively, if they were sincere communists, geuine co-operation with the West would surely be prohibited by the terms of their ideology.

The most significant intellectual development of 1946, the germination of the Third Force ideas, was not, however, closely associated with Laski, but rather with his fellow intellectual G. D. H. Cole. In his book *Labour's Foreign Policy*, published in 1946, Cole had changed his views somewhat from 1942, but was still convinced that 'close friendship and collaboration between the British and Soviet People is an idispensable foundation for world well-being and the triumph of the socialist case". He now advocated a Western Europe based upon liberal socialism which he believed would pave the way to true cooperation with the Soviet Union. It was Britain's task vigorously to *lead* Europe towards this socialist goal; it was confidently assumed that Europe was ripe for such a conversion.[47] The germ of the Third Force argument is clearly visible in this analysis, but at this stage of its development it is more properly called the 'Third Alternative' argument. Not that Cole's ideas were unique; numerous articles and speeches in 1946 had been inching towards an independent socialist foreign policy directed towards Europe.[48] The Third Alternative concept was indeed incipient in a post-war world in which the two ideologically opposed super-powers seemed increasingly to dominate the foreign policies of every European State.

The first major elaboration of the idea occurred in the pages of the *New Statesman* in the form of a series of four articles during August and September 1946.[49] The articles represented a root-and-branch attack upon Bevin's conduct of foreign affairs. The first began with the sentence 'During Mr Bevin's first year at the Foreign Office we have witnessed a complete reversal of Labour's foreign policy'. The 'Munich analogy' was being wrongly applied; it was a mistake to confuse the conciliation of the USSR, a country engrossed in domestic reconstruction, with the appeasement of Nazi Germany. In any case Hitler and Mussolini had been given five years' grace before conciliation was abandoned, whereas Stalin had been condemned after only one year. It was true that the Soviet Union, in her efforts to achieve the ideal of a classless society, suspected enemies everywhere and in so doing often fostered emnity, but Bevin and Byrnes had done nothing to break through this vicious circle. The article concluded that the role of mediator was still possible for Bevin as long as he could exchange his 'angry inaccurate analysis' for cool reason.

The second dealt with Britain's growing dependence on American support. Bevin was believed to be relying upon America to defend the now indefensible British Empire; aid would be forthcoming only if Britain accepted subordination, on all main issues, to American interests. Given the difficulties of dealing with Russia, the dangers of relying upon the USA, the Cabinet should tailor its commitments to the cloth of diminished power and form an alliance with those States which desired to maintain their distance from the bipolar struggle. Britain's most willing allies in this venture would be the European social democratic parties, and Bevin should consequently support their struggles for power whenever possible. In the ideological struggle between communism and capitalism the European middle ground would be mopped up by one side or the other. He should move into this area and lead a campaign to create a positive 'third alternative', a Western Europe based upon social democracy. It is interesting to note that Soviet perfidy over Iran seemed to have been forgotten, and the picture presented of Soviet foreign and domestic policy was quite favourable. The image of America, following the Byrnes-led split over Germany, predictably reflected a highly critical attitude. However, a vital shift had taken place in the *New Statesman*'s attitude towards the Soviet Union, for the emphasis of the Third Alternative concept was upon neutrality; hopes of close co-operation with the USSR at least in the immediate future, had clearly been abandoned.

It seems probable that these articles were the work of Richard Crossman; for at least the next twelve months, he was to be the leader of the left through sheer force of intellect rather than personality. When he was appointed to the Anglo-American commission on Palestine it seemed as if he was being groomed for a junior post in the Foreign Office. However, when Crossman used the report as the basis for an attack on Bevin's Palestine policy he placed himself unequivocably in the dissenting camp. When Parliament reassembled in the autumn of 1946 it was he who led the left-wing revolt over foreign policy.

vi

The autumn revolt involved wider issues than just Bevin's handling of Anglo-Soviet relations. The story, however, is crucial to the analysis of the Labour Party's attitudes towards Russia and to the understanding of later conceptions of socialist foreign policy. 'Revolt' is perhaps too strong a word for what amounted to an abstention by some 100 Labour MPs, but it was certainly taken very seriously by the Party leadership and its repercussions had far-reaching effects, particularly during the ensuing twelve months. Effectively the revolt represented a reinforcement of those dissenting PLP groups described earlier — the pacificists, fellow-travellers and parliamentary left-wing intellectuals — by a significant element of the centre. Some indications of the depth of feeling had been evident in the 120 MPs who had urged censure of Churchill after his Fulton speech. But the autumn revolt represented a further stage in their discontent and their disillusion. The *N.S. and N.* editorial of 12 October defined the problem and outlined the course it would take.

There is a genuine and profound disagreement between the Government and a section of its supporters both on tactics and on principles, and it is almost certain that this disagreement will be expressed during the coming weeks on the floor of the House.

The journal was careful to make the point that the government's majority would not be put at risk.

On 29 October 1946 a letter was sent to Attlee marked 'Private and confidential'.[49] It was signed by twenty-one Labour MPs, including Crossman, Barbara Gould, Jennie Lee, J. Callaghan, Michael Foot, Harold Davies, Joe Reeves, J. P. W. Mallalieu and Woodrow Wyatt.[50] Of the other signatories, only W. G. Cove might have been identified with the fellow-travellers. The letter was a critique of government foreign policy, arguing that British social democracy could provide the 'genuine middle way between the extremes of American free enterprise economics and Russian totalitarian socio-political life'. The government, argued the signatories, was ignoring a unique opportunity; apparently affected by the 'anti-Red' view, it was following a course both politically and militarily so close to the USA that relations with the USSR were being seriously exacerbated. The letter went on to state the familiar socialist axiom of the 'thirties, that personal and political liberties would arrive 'once the degree of poverty and the fear of war have been overcome'. Whilst it attacked Soviet expansion, the government passed no censure upon the American atomic monopoly and acquisition of bases all over the world; only by 'vigorous pursuit of socialist policies at home and abroad' could Britain bridge the antagonisms between the USA and the Soviet Union.

Attlee's reply advised the signatories to talk to Hector McNeil, but rather precipitately, before seeing McNeil, they gave a copy of their letter to the press, and subsequently tabled a critical amendment (along the lines of their original letter) to the Address on the King's Speech.[51] To seek an amendment to this traditionally non-controversial statement was defiance indeed. The main instigators were Crossman, Foot, Hewitson, Levy, Silverman and Reeves, but they were now supported most notably by the fellow-travellers, Solley, S. O. Davies, Pritt, Platt-Mills, Hutchinson, Zilliacus and by others of similar mind, Warbey, Driberg, Orbach and Mikardo. Also supporting the amendment were several MPs soon to be closely associated with Richard Crossman in the 'Keep left' grouping, James Griffiths, George Wigg, Barbara Castle and Maurice Edelman. In all, fifty-eight MPs appended their names to the amendment. Five of them were PPSs, one of whom was also a member of the NEC.[52]

There was no doubt that the combined forces of the left, supported by

A socialist foreign policy 139

elements of the centre, had thrown down the gauntlet to the government. The *Times* reported that Attlee was surprised and angry at the amendment and that at the PLP meeting on 13 November the Prime Minister had 'severely rebuked' those supporters of the government who saw fit to move motions of censure whilst the Foreign Secretary himself was engaged in 'anxious negotiations in New York'.[53] The rebels, however, stood firm and withstood the pressure to withdraw the amendment.

The support of the fellow-travellers must have caused some embarrassment to Crossman and his co-signatories, for the former were seen by many as the leading element in the revolt.[54] This was not surprising in view of their vigorous parliamentary contributions in the autumn of 1946. On 18 October Zilliacus had supported the communist, Philip Piratin, in refuting allegations that democracy was being denied in the Polish elections;[55] on 23 October Zilliacus had again taken the field, supported by Pritt and Platts-Mills, in presenting a persuasive rationalisation of communist activities in Eastern Europe.[56] On 18 November the *New York Times* identified the 'well known Moscow sympathiser' Zilliacus as the motive force behind the opposition movement. At a party meeting on 13 November the real sponsors of the amendment had found it necessary to deny that they had been briefed by the CPGB or were affiliated in any way.[57]

Clearly this support, whilst swelling the size of the opposition movement, had the effect of blurring the Third Alternative policy advocated by Crossman and his associates. Michael Foot used his column in the *Daily Herald* on 15 November to help put the record straight, explaining that he was seeking a British-led upsurge of social democracy in Europe to counteract and to help reduce the polarising tendencies of American capitalism and Russian communism.

News of the amendment commanded headlines in the major dailies. The *Herald* criticised the heavy-handed methods of the rebels but saw some virtue in their Third Alternative proposals as long as they were set in the context of plans for world government along the lines proposed by Henry Usborne, MP.[58] Across the Atlantic, the *New York Times* concentrated upon the anti-American element in the revolt, and cited the *N.S. and N.* belief that America was now committed to anarchic capitalism abroad as well as at home.[59] The *Manchester Guardian* described the amendment, correctly, as 'the most serious public act of dissent from the policy of the Government which has so far been committed by Labour members'.[60] Worse was to come, for a further amendment was tabled on 15 November criticising the government's decision to continue conscription 'beyond the date when the present transitional scheme comes to an end'.[61] Whilst appealing mainly to the pacifist element within the Labour Party, this amendment was likely to attract the support of some of those opposed to the foreign policy that conscription was designed to underpin.

Attlee's irritation was understandable. With a parliamentary session behind it, the Labour government was beginning to get into its legislative stride. Faced daily with 'in' trays brimful with knotty administrative problems requiring urgent practical answers, Attlee was unlikely to relish a recrudescence of the factionalism which had so characterised the Labour Party in opposition, particularly when his Foreign Secretary was out of the country, for this meant that he would have to face the revolt himself. The scene was set for an intriguing parliamentary confrontation between the dissenters, led by the brilliant, iconoclastic debater Crossman and the colourless, laconic, occasionally authoritarian leader of his party.

In the debate upon the amendment on 18 November Crossman introduced the 'Third Alternative' thesis with an extremely able and persuasive speech. Foreign policy, he urged, echoing the case put forward by Attlee himself in 1937, should be an extension of the startling socialist experiment at home.[62] At the moment too many elements of 'Fultonism' were present in Britain's foreign policy, which was drifting into an Anglo-American grouping hostile to a country so recently her wartime ally and which, in any case, even now was far too weak to contemplate waging war. Military conversations with the USA and mutual standardisation of arms were disturbing symptoms of what amounted to a capitalist rather than socialist foreign policy. The formation of this Western bloc was destroying the centre and left parties in Europe by forcing them to choose between two extremes. Crossman urged a staunchly independent policy (even at some economic cost) which should be committed to the building of socialism and democracy wherever possible.[63] Behind its depth of analysis and elegance of exposition, his speech really amounted to a recommendation that Britain should not only slacken links with America and be more co-operative (and by implication conciliatory) with the USSR but also base her foreign policy upon a clarion call to social democrats in Europe. By any realistic standards this was a flimsy base, but perhaps one can understand why it was so earnestly advocated at this time on the left. In the wake of massively disruptive wartime experiences Europe was ripe for a movement to the left. Social democrats quite naturally were passionately concerned that it should move in the leftward direction which they favoured and they were beginning to realise that a possibly unique opportunity was slipping away.

The revolt stimulated sharp reactions, particularly from the Labour benches. W. Nally and George Brown (making his first speech on foreign affairs) rallied to Ernest Bevin's defence.[64] Captain Crookshank, for the Conservatives, gleefully rubbed salt in the wounds which the debate had exposed in the Labour Party. On Crossman's speech he commented, 'The voice is the voice of a university tutor but the words are those of a Politbureau member.' On the revolt as a whole he commented, 'In opening the door so wide to the doctrinaire socialists, I wonder if the Labour Party has not taken to its bosom a viper which will ultimately destroy it.'[65] Since November 1946 left-wing revolts against a Labour government have become a familiar parliamentary feature but at the time the size and nature of the split in the government's ranks was unprecedented, and Attlee's reply must have been awaited with great interest. He was characteristically straightforward. The amendment was misconceived, mistimed and based on misunderstanding. 'The fundamental misconception here,' he pointed out, 'is the nature and problems of international relations.' He went on to deliver a lecture to the left-wing intellectuals of his party on the realities of politics. He explained that foreign policy was not produced in a void, but was a function of dealings with other countries. Those countries were economic and geographic entities, each with its different outlook and needs. We could not expect them to automatically agree with us; 'compromise is the inevitable basis of any international relationship'. He then set about demolishing Crossman's critique.

America had the financial resources to help Britain in her weakened state, but it was absurd to call this economic assistance imperialism. Joint military arrangements with the USA did not signify an exclusive Anglo-American alliance but were an inevitable concomitant of the occupation of Germany. Continuance of conscription stemmed solely from obligations to the UN and (an unconvincing argument, this) was in no way directed against the Soviet Union. As for encouraging socialists abroad, 'Nothing could be more disastrous,' Attlee flatly declared, 'for co-operation in the world than that every nation, every great power should select their own particular party as its protégé.' In conclusion he insisted that Labour's foreign policy was based upon 'international co-operation for peace, social justice and freedom for all nations'. Bevin was the perfect instrument of such a policy, was no slave of abstract theory but a 'practical man trying to get things done'. It was grossly unfair that criticism of him came from people whose contributions to the Labour movement was 'dust in the balance' compared with his.[66]

Attlee asked that the amendment be withdrawn, and Crossman agreed to withdraw it. However, the ex-ILP-ers Campbell-Stephen and McGovern forced the issue to a vote. The government easily won by 350 to 0, but 122 of this majority was made up of Conservatices, Liberals and others. Some sixty or seventy Labour MPs publicly abstained by remaining in their seats whilst the division took place, but government whips calculated that, out of Labour's total strength of 387, the number of deliberate abstentions was nearer 100.[67]

Another setback was in store for the government when the amendment on conscription was debated. Victor Yates argued, in the by now familiar pacifist terms, that in the atomic age conscription was a pernicious waste of national energies. Tom Scollan added his own conspiracy theories; the socialist government had been 'got at' by the military chiefs through the National Defence Council, and the anti-Russian scare was a fiction propagated by the press. James Hudson questioned Attlee's assertion that conscription was purely a function of British commitments to the UN, bearing in mind that their scope was unknown.[68] Answering for the government, Hugh Dalton had to pay lip service to the transparent fiction that fear of the Soviet Union had nothing to do with conscription policies.[69] He repeated Attlee's UN argument, adding rather guardedly that the country had to pull its weight in the UN and could not expect to sponge off the American and Red armies. Fifty-five MPs voted in favour of this amendment. The group excluded most of the intellectual supporters of the earlier amendment and, with the exception of W. G. Cove and S. O. Davies, it excluded the fellow-travellers too, but it surprisingly included Nally, the defender of Bevin in the earlier debate.[70]

Thus ended what *The Times*'s lobby correspondent described as 'not a good day for the Government'. The *Daily Herald*'s reactions on 19 and 20 November had hardened; the result was clearly much more serious than it had bargained for. The *Manchester Guardian* rebuked the left for its illiberalism, anti-Americanism, feeble isolationism and lack of understanding of international affairs. It reported the jubilant propaganda capital being made out of the issue in Moscow.[71] *The Economist*, a lukewarm supporter of Bevin at this time, felt that the rebels had a right to question foreign policy and to propose socialist initiatives in Germany and Western Europe. However, there was no choice but to side with the USA. The weight of evidence was against the Soviet Union, which, by virtue of its policies in Poland, Persia, Turkey and Bulgaria, had given ample grounds for suspicion that it was planning deliberate aggression. On the other hand, it was 'inconceivable' that the US would deliberately initiate a policy which would lead to world war.[72] It is hard to tell how much support the rebels commanded within the Cabinet. Captain Crookshank had delightedly pointed out that both Bevan's wife and his PPS were among the dissidents, and inquired whether the Minister was a 'bit wobbly on this issue?'[73] It seems highly likely that Bevan was very sympathetic to the rebels, several of whom were his friends from previous battles. He had himself advocated similar ideas before accepting office and was destined to develop Third Force ideas after he resigned in 1951. However, Michael Foot insists that there was no liaison between Bevan and the rebels.[74] Dalton reveals that he felt a certain sympathy for the dissenting view, which he believed expressed the 'deep concern of a wide and sensible section of the

PLP ... about what Bevin seems to be doing and how he is doing it'; it should be borne in mind that Dalton's strong antipathy to Germany tended to dispose him favourably towards Russia as a counterbalance against future threats. But he was repelled by their 'besotted' tactics and the presentation of their ideas.[75] From the author's conversations with several Labour MPs it seems possible that Bevan, Cripps and Shinwell shared some common ground with the rebels.

There is no doubt that Bevin himself was furious that such a serious party division should have opened up whilst he was engaged in complex and demanding negotiations with the Russians in New York. His private secretary wrote in his diary on 18 November that 'the case of the 'Rebels' at home has been poisoning everything ... This is upsetting E.B, though he maintains a brave face.'[76] Some days later Dixon felt that the Russians had been encouraged to believe that a communised Europe was possible, and that America's faith in Britain had been shaken. The Americans, he believed, were beginning to look to alternative plans for investment abroad: the British Labour government was inevitably having to trim its sails.[77] Bevin himself maintained silence upon the revolt, but, as will be shown later, his crushing retaliatory blow would take several months to gestate.

The rebels did not escape immediate censure from other quarters. On 27 November the NEC considered the matter and sent out a letter of concern to the PLP.[78] Forty-four Labour MPs (mostly trade union-sponsored) signed a resolution demanding strong disciplinary action, but this was withdrawn when Crossman publicly admitted that the methods chosen by the rebels had been unwise.[79] Crossman and Edelman were both taken to task by their constituency parties, who asked them to explain their action in opposing the government.[80]

The revolt was over, but the government had been shaken by a demonstration which had made its huge majority seem suddenly vulnerable. Attlee must have viewed the new parliamentary session with trepidation, wondering whether Labour would be robbed of the fruits of its 1945 victory by internal divisions over foreign policy. Certainly more conflict was in store, but within twelve months the question of Soviet foreign policy intentions was destined to be settled for all but a minority of the erstwhile rebels.

Notes

1 *Daily Herald*, 23 January 1946.
2 *Ibid.*, 4 February 1946. *The Economist*, on 9 February suggested that Bevin's riposte had been too aggressive.
3 419 H.C. Deb., 1348–66, 21 February 1946.

4 Ibid., 1168–75.
5 Ibid., 1166–9.
6 Daily Herald, 22 February 1946.
7 NS and N, 16 February 1946.
8 Tribune, 8 February 1946.
9 420 H.C. Deb., 231, 5 March 1946.
10 Eden denied the rumours, saying he did 'not believe it for a single moment', ibid., 236.
11 Tribune, 8 March 1946.
12 Forward, 19 May 1946, and NS and N, 9 March 1946.
13 Sponsored by W. Warbey, Mrs Middleton, J. Diamond, E. Davies, R. Sorenson and Hector Hughes on 12 March 1946 (material made available to author by Professor Hugh Berrington).
14 Nicholas Henderson, one of Bevin's personal staff at this time, recalled this fact on an ITV programme on Thursday 19 September 1971. Truman and Byrnes adopted a similar 'no comment' approach to the speech, but privately Truman thought the speech (which he had read beforehand) would do 'nothing but good', Herbert Feis, From Trust to Terror, p. 78.
15 Daily Herald, 26 April 1946.
16 N.S. and N., 2 and 9 March 1946.
16 Ibid., 23 March 1946.
18 Ibid., 13 April 1946.
19 See H. Feis, pp. 80–7.
20 See speech by J. B. Hynd, the Minister in charge of the British occupation, 420 H.C. Deb., 1647–58, 18 March 1946.
21 See, for example. Laski's article in Left, December 1945, and N.S. and N., 2 February 1946 (in which the newly appointed ambassador to Moscow was described as the man 'least likely to get on with the Russians'). Also Harold Davies, 419 H.C. Deb., 1196–203, 20 February 1946.
22 The myth lived on, however. In 1948 Zilliacus wrote, "The Foreign Office, like the Mounties, has the reputation of always getting its men." Quoted in D. Caute, The Fellow Travellers, p. 273.
23 LPCR 1946, pp. 105–7. The Daily Herald described the speech as 'outstanding', 11 January 1946.
24 See LPCR 1946, pp. 151–2. Also speeches by R. M. Stewart, p. 161, and Zilliacus, p. 159. Tudor Watkins, MP for Brecon at this time, recalled, in an interview with the author, that his own views in 1945 had been that America was much more likely than the USSR to start a war.
25 Daily Herald, 18 March 1946. Foot believed, however, that most of the problems were due to Soviet intransigence, 423 H.C. Deb., 1928–38, 4 June 1946.
26 423 H.C. Deb., 1914–7, 4 June 1946.
27 Feis, p. 134.
28 Robert Stephens, 'What Stalin told Ernest Bevin', The Observer, 2 January 1977.
29 Stephen Amis, 'When Labour got wise to Stalin's tricks', Sunday Times, 2 January 1977.
30 427 H.C. Deb., 1487–522, 22 October 1946.
31 Daily Herald, 18 July 1946.
32 419 H.C. Deb., 1186–9, 20 February 1946.

A socialist foreign policy 145

33 LPCR 1946, p. 185. Victor Yates also spoke against conscription — p. 186. For the NEC Arthur Greenwood answered 'We are not conscriptionists at heart,' p. 187.
34 A point made by Lester Hutchinson, Left, August 1946.
35 420 H.C. Deb., 117–8, 4 March 1946.
36 426 H.C. Deb., 586, 29 July 1946.
37 Bevin had Cocks replaced by John Hynd after Cocks resigned in frustration. Robert J. Jackson, Rebels and Whips, p. 157.
38 Cocks, 423 H.C. Deb., 2046–53, McNeil, 423. See also Cocks's letter to N.S. and N., 4 May 1946, in which he thought the Big Three should meet to discuss his plan.
39 See his letter to N.S. and N., 6 July 1946.
40 Critics London Diary, N.S. and N., 20 July 1946.
41 Tribune, 30 August 1946.
42 N.S. and N., 9 February 1946.
43 418 H.C. Deb., 2110, 8 February 1946.
44 Ibid., 2112.
45 Clement Attlee, Granada Historical Record interview, p. 28.
46 Ibid., p. 52.
47 Gordon, Conflict and Consensus, p. 184.
48 See M. Foot and F. Brockway, Left, April 1946. Also Foot, Tribune, 7 July 1946.
49 N.S. and N., 31 August, 7, 21 and 28 September 1946.
50 Copy available in the LSE library.
51 Three MPs who signed the letter did not sign the amendment: B. A. Gould, J. Callaghan and Fred Messer.
52 See Daily Telegraph, 14 November 1946, for the initial forty-four signatories and 15 November 1946 for a further eleven. The Times, 16 November, reported that L. Hutchinson's signature brought the number up to fifty-eight. The PPSs were Wigg, Bruce, Mallalieu and John Haire, who was also on the NEC.
53 The Times, 14 November 1946.
54 See the Times editorial on this aspect of the revolt, 19 November 1946.
55 Zilliacus, 427 H.C. Deb., 1263–6 and Piratin, 1266–71.
56 Ibid., 1711–26, 1690–7 and 1542–53, respectively.
57 Manchester Guardian, 14 November 1946.
58 Usborne was a fervent advocate of advancing immediately towards world government.
59 New York Times, 18 November 1946.
60 Manchester Guardian, 14 November 1946.
61 Text of motion drawn from material on early day motions assembled by Professor Hugh Berrington and kindly made available to the author.
62 See Attlee, The Labour Party in Perspective, p. 226. Attlee wrote, 'The foreign policy of a government is the reflection of its internal policy.'
63 430 H.C. Deb., 526–30, 18 November 1946.
64 Nally, 549–55, Brown, 565–70. See also Brown's article in the Daily Herald, 18 November 1946, entitled 'Why I do not sign the Amendment'. Brown was PPS to the Minister of Labour at this time.
65 430 H.C. Deb., 5454, 18 November 1946.
66 430 H.C. Deb., 577–90, 18 November 1946.

67 *Daily Telegraph*, 22 November 1946. Some interesting abstentions were J. Freeman, D. Grenfell, H. Lever, Skeffington Lodge, J. Silkin, P. G. Walker, T. Fraser and K. Younger.

68 430 *H.C. Deb.*, 594–600, 600–6, 618–24, 18 November 1946, respectively.

69 *Ibid.*, 632–40.

70 Included were many of the pacifist-inclined MPs: Ayles, V. Yates, T. Scollan, V. Hudson and the 'Celtic fringe' pacifists, E. Roberts, G. Thomas, T. E. Watkins, D. J. Williams, M. Herbison and R. Richards.

71 *Manchester Guardian*, 19, 29 and 20 November 1946.

72 *The Economist*, 23 November 1946.

73 430 *H.C. Deb.*, 544–6, 18 November 1946.

74 Interview with the author. Bevan was naturally preoccupied with his own departmental duties, but generally agreed with the direction of Bevin's policies — Foot, *Bevan, 1945–60*, pp. 32–4.

75 Dalton, p. 168.

76 Dixon, p. 241.

77 *Ibid.*, p. 242.

78 *The Times*, 28 November 1946.

79 *Daily Herald*, 19 November 1946.

80 Jackson, *Rebels and Whips*, p. 57.

9 *Abandonment of an image*

> Bevin's opposition to Russia was not really ideological. He was just infuriated at their inflexibility; he used to rave about Molotov's unyielding 'Niet'. Bevin tried his damndest to get on with the Russians. [Ernest Davies, PPS to H. McNeil, 1946–50, in an interview with author]

The international situation at the close of the New York Foreign Ministers' conference on 12 December 1946 was not unhopeful. Molotov had recanted on some of the more obdurate policies which had stalemated the Paris conference, and peace treaties with the ex-German satellite countries had been successfully drafted, incorporating the principle of free navigation upon the Danube. Moreover Russia's advocacy of Yugoslav claims upon Italy did not prevent a satisfactory compromise from being achieved. The crippling demands of six weeks' concentrated diplomacy had not been unrewarded, and Bevin could be forgiven, in a broadcast on 21 December, for feeling that a new co-operative chapter had been opened in Russia's dealings with the rest of the world. Yet it was only three months later that President Truman was to enunciate the doctrine, so closely associated with his name, which virtually amounted to a crusade against communism. Beneath the accords of New York, strong undercurrents of disagreements were thus gaining strength; the early months of 1947 would see them made manifest.

Following the conference, hopes had been harboured in the West that the Russian-controlled regimes in the ex-satellite States would be inhibited, by the political clauses in the draft peace treaties, from continuing their flagrant violations of the democratic process. These clauses stated in each case that the governments of Bulgaria, Hungary and Rumania would take all the necessary measures to secure the 'fundamental human freedoms', including freedom of expression, of the press and publication, of religious worship, of political opinion and of public meeting.[1] In February 1947 Christopher Mayhew, then a junior Minister at the Foreign Office, informed the House that owing to the suppression of candidates, the pressurising of voters, and government control of the count, the Polish elections could not be regarded as fulfilling the Yalta agreement of free and unfettered elections; they were neither 'free nor fair' and it was 'useless to pursue the matter further in Moscow'.[2] In the wake of suspect communist electoral successes in Poland came news in February that Bela Kovacs, a leader of the Hungarian Smallholders' Party, had been arrested by the Russians and accused of counter-revolutionary conspiracy.[3] Unfavourable impressions were compounded at this time by the uncooperative attitude adopted by the USSR towards the UK. Bevin was keen to reinforce the goodwill born at New York by extending the 1942 Anglo-Soviet treaty from twenty to thirty years, but on 15 January a *Pravda* editorial placed the issue in doubt by perversely misinterpreting a section of the very December broadcast in which Bevin had spoken hopefully of future cooperation.

In this broadcast Bevin had answered the current left-wing accusations of partiality towards the USA at the expense of the USSR by declaring that Britain did not tie herself to anybody 'except in regard to her obligations under the Charter'. *Pravda* chose to interpret this statement as a denunciation of the Anglo-Soviet treaty and on 23 January dismissed the explanation contained in Bevin's explanatory note of the 18th. Eventually it took personal correspondence between Bevin and Stalin to resolve the difference of opinion with the Soviet leader, suggesting that before the treaty could be extended it ought to be updated and reworded in some respects.

Returning from a visit to Moscow, Field Marshal Montgomery was confident, in conversation with Dalton, that Bevin would get his extension.[4] On 29 January Mayhew reported that Stalin's 'conditions' were being considered but in the event the extension never materialised; consideration of the idea was overtaken by the open dissension towards which Soviet prevarications had contributed.[5] It is hard to see what the Soviet Union hoped to gain. The interpretation of Bevin's words was either absurdly paranoid or a calculated move to introduce difficulties into Anglo-Soviet relations. Whatever the motive, disappointment and bewilderment in the Labour Party were the result.[6]

Whatever its successes, the New York conference had left the intractable problem of Germany still dominating the stage of Europe. Despairing of agreement with the Russians and French, and fearing a Soviet attempt to woo Germany to communism, Bevin and Byrnes had concluded their plans for a bizonal fusing of economic policy.[7] Whereas Bevin and Byrnes looked towards a self-supporting, decentralised, pro-Western, unified Germany, Stalin sought a weak, centralised Germany sympathetic to the Soviet Union.[8] A pro-Soviet or communist Germany was unthinkable to Bevin and Byrnes, but a revived Western-oriented capitalist Germany would, in the Soviet view, rise up eventually to march destructively through the corridor of Eastern Europe in yet another attack upon the Soviet Union. Both sides paid lip service to the Potsdam ideal of treating Germany as an economic entity, but both sides had different conceptions of what this entity should be. Whilst struggling to undermine each other's position, both sides (with the exception of France in the early stages) arranged their zones to accord with their particular ideas of what a unified Germany should be like. Consequently, agreement became less likely as time went by, and the Four Power Council in Berlin became the focus of East–West disagreement. Ironically, the decisive break in relations arose not over the central problem of Germany but over the relatively peripheral issues of Greece and Turkey. Events within and on the borders of these countries, coupled with the UK's rapidly deteriorating financial position, were combining to produce a momentous change of direction in American foreign policy.

The situation in Greece had been catalysed into civil war following the September referendum in favour of the return of George II to the throne. The communists, supported by Yugoslavia, Albania and Bulgaria (and tacitly by the USSR) rapidly tightened their grip upon the north of the country, and even the presence of some 40,000 British troops in early 1947 did not prevent the effete Tsaldaris regime from being gravely threatened. Bevin saw yet another threat to the British position in the Middle East in the persistent Russian attempt to gain a foothold in the Dardenelles. Stalin had maintained at Potsdam that, as the Turks were too weak to ensure the security of the Straits, the Soviet Union should become, with Turkey, the joint regulator of transit. (As the Soviet Union was itself regarded as the principal threat to the security of the Straits in the first place, this argument seemed, to the increasingly apprehensive West, like a burglar offering to guard the house he was intending to rob.) Subsequently the Russians employed a series of increasingly threatening diplomatic manoeuvres to put pressure upon the Turkish government, fomenting, for example, separatist feeling amongst the Turkish border tribes, the Kurds and Armenians. The post-war Turkish army, despite accessions of British military equipment, could not be relied upon to put up any protracted resistance, and it was feared in London and Washington in the winter of 1946–47 that a sharp Russian thrust into Turkey could present the West with an irreversible *fait accompli*.

This was the situation in the eastern Mediterranean when, in February 1947, Hugh Dalton pursuaded the British Labour Cabinet that the extreme frailty of the UK's economic position made continued aid to Greece unrealistic.[9] On Monday 24 February President Truman received a note from the British ambassador explaining that as from 30 March 1947 the UK would have to withdraw all support from Greece.[10] This note jolted Washington into a series of rapid and major decisions. America had already deployed considerable diplomatic efforts in support of Greece and Turkey against the encroachments of communism, a policy underlined by naval visits to both countries in March and September 1946.[11] The influential 'Kennan memorandum', advocating a policy of 'containment' against the constant pressure of Russian communism, submitted in 1946, had put into words what many diplomats and officials, right up to Truman himself, were already thinking.[12] The fracture of the British 'thin red line' against communism brought the issue to a head. On 12 March Truman informed Congress that $400 million worth of economic aid would be provided for Greece and Turkey until June 1948. If the Kremlin had calculated that American isolationism would allow it to encroach with impunity upon the fading British Empire, it was proved disastrously mistaken. Paradoxically, it was partly to overcome the isolationist doubts in Congress that Truman framed his declaration into a dramatic global challenge against the spread of communism.

Bevin and the Foreign Office were naturally relieved at the American action in stepping smartly and unambiguously into the breach, but it should not be assumed that, on the eve of Truman's declaration, Anglo-Soviet relations had reached breaking point; far from it. Despite the difficulties over the Anglo-Soviet treaty, Bevin welcomed the opportunity to persevere with it, and his public utterances on Russia were anything but aggressively phrased.[13] It was still possible moreover for him to say in Cabinet at this time that the Germans were 'much more dangerous than the Russians'.[14] But the enunciation of the Truman doctrine, inevitably had the effect of inhibiting whatever further measures of collaboration he may have had in mind. It also stiffened Soviet attitudes towards the West. For example, on 25 March 1947 the Soviet Union vetoed a Security Council motion passing censure upon Albania for having wilfully neglected to remove the mines in the Adriatic which had damaged two British destroyers in October 1946, causing the loss of forty-four lives.[15] The Truman doctrine marked the retreat of the East and West behind the walls which Yalta had constructed. Apart from one major future initiative, the emphasis would now be on defensive preparations rather than attempts to co-operate.

ii

No doubt influenced by the recent foreign policy revolt, Harold Nicolson feared in January 1947 that the left or 'Red Flag' element in the Labour Party would gain strength as economic conditions in the UK deteriorated and as communism continued to spread world-wide. He feared that the 'patriotic' Labour leaders who relied upon American support would eventually be isolated and branded as warmongers.[16] When, a few weeks later, Nicolson applied to join the Labour Party, one of his reasons was that he felt that this would be the most effective way of fighting communism.[17] For once his analysis was wrong.

In reality what he called the 'Red Flag' element was losing strength as Russia's designs became clearer. Their support for Russia was not based so much upon genuine sympathy for Stalin's brand of Soviet communism as upon faulty images of what Stalinism meant. In the early months of 1947 government statements, newspaper reports and articles upon Russia and Russian foreign policy, covering such subjects as the further suppression of democracy, and in particular social democracy, in Eastern Europe,[18] the Soviet attitude over the Anglo-Soviet alliance,[19] Soviet attitudes over Germany,[20] the refusal to release fifteen Soviet wives to join their British husbands in the United Kingdom,[21] inevitably modified these images. Those in the Labour Party concerned to defend and explain Soviet-style democracies in Eastern Europe faced a particularly difficult task; in many cases they could not refute allegations of undemocratic conduct, they could only offer justification. These justifications tended to be based upon two premises; firstly that even the Soviet-style socialism now being implemented in Eastern Europe was preferable to a return to capitalism, and secondly that once the economic bases of society in Eastern Europe were reorganised on socialist lines it would be only a matter of time before their ameliorating effect upon harsh political regimes would begin to show through. By early 1947, however, these justifications were beginning to sound increasingly hollow. The emotive case of Poland was the most difficult to explain.

In the left-wing press Doreen Warriner, of the Fabian International Bureau, admitted that the Polish government had rigged the elections to prevent Mikolaczyck and the 'Western-orientated old gang' from gaining a majority, but she argued that in view of the government's success in economic reconstruction a change in government at this time would be disastrous.[22] In Parliament the Labour MP Mrs Leah Manning dwelt on the economic reforms initiated by the Polish government,[23] whilst Seymour Cocks somewhat feebly suggested that, in view of the recently improved relations between Britain and Russia and Eastern Europe, the government should turn a blind eye to the undemocratic excesses in Poland.[24] Other leftwingers, Tom Driberg and Geoffrey Bing, closer to the fellow-travelling position, sought to minimise the violations of democracy in Eastern Europe by pointing out the electoral corruption and manipulation that took place in Georgia, South Carolina (the home state of Secretary of State Byrnes) and, nearer home, in Northern Ireland.[25]

The task of justifying Soviet attitudes over Germany proved so difficult that only the communists and crypto-communists seriously attempted it. At the Moscow Foreign Ministers' conference in April Bevin was clearly seen to propose a constructive plan (*Supplementary Principles to Govern the Treatment of Germany*) designed to achieve the ideals of the Potsdam agreement. In their reply to this initiative it seemed that the Russians were being particularly obstructive, accusing the British, for instance, of employing five prominent Nazis in their zone of Germany. This charge was categorically refuted, but the Russians refused to withdraw it.[26] In May 1947 few Labour MP's could deny a Conservative MP's assessment of Soviet tactics: 'The charges are made. They are refuted. No attempt is made to justify them. And then they are repeated all over again.'[27]

One analysis of Soviet intentions which has stood the test of time well is that of Philips Price, an MP with foreign policy interests. He believed that there was no riddle about Soviet intentions in Eastern Europe. The Soviet Union obviously regarded pro-Soviet regimes in Eastern Europe as a *sine qua non* of its security. He suggested to Parliament in February that the UK should accept this as a fact of life — advice similar to that proffered earlier by Seymour Cocks.[28] Whatever the doubts about Soviet good faith, a large section of the Labour Party reacted with dismay at the announcement of the Truman doctrine, which they tended to see as an overreaction to a situation which was far from lost. The *Daily Herald*, staunch supporter of Bevin's foreign policy, saw no grounds for rejoicing at this development and was worried by the 'pessimism' in Truman's speech; it was felt that the President should have accompanied his 'blunt challenge to Soviet Russia' with a new initiative over the Dardenelles, and his loan to Greece with conditions that the Greek regime become more democratic. This was a time for Britain to use moral leadership to urge the USA to work for unity with the USSR.[29]

Michael Foot saw the Truman doctrine as the American flag following the American oil magnates. He advocated a solution popular amongst several Labour MPs: the internationalisation of Suez and the Dardenelles and the substitution of the UN for the US in the Middle East.[30] *Reynolds' News*, the Co-operative weekly, shared the analysis of the crypto-communists and fellow-travelling MPs on this issue; it regarded the doctrine as 'mischievous' and 'negative', an attempt by the US to open up the world as a vast colonial area for American imperialism.[21]

Tribune recognised that the 'two continental powers were now in the open' but claimed that Britain had a chance to pursue an independent balance-of-power policy. 'Both the USA and the Soviet Union may yet have to call in the old world to redress the balance of the new.'[32] The New Statesman saw the Truman doctrine as final evidence that UK dependence upon US aid was incompatible with adherence to the UN and the Anglo-Russian alliance.[33] Both journals believed that the UK should decrease dependence on the USA, possibly at some sacrifice, and should build around the recently signed Dunkirk treaty with France a bloc of non-aligned nations which would effectively hold the ring between the USA and Soviet Russia.

This was, of course, yet another form of the Third Alternative idea which had been at the heart of the foreign affairs revolt a few months previously, but now, as East and West threatened to pull apart, it appeared to become increasingly relevant. Perhaps stung by the Truman doctrine, the Labour left staged a revolt over the National Service Bill. This was a major revolt in which seventy-two Labour MPs defied a three-line whip and voted against the government on 1 April 1947, with twenty abstentions.[34] Foreign affairs, however, was only one strand in a complex issue on which Labour thinking was highly emotional. The Labour Party had never in its history advocated conscription in peacetime, and many MPs who revered the memory of George Lansbury dutifully voted for Rhys Davies's critical amendment. The speakers against conscription adduced economic and moral arguments against it rather than foreign policy reasons.[35] Rhys Davies was one of the few pacifists to touch on this subject, arguing that as Russian's conventional armed superiority was overwhelming it would in any situation be pointless to fight her. Zilliacus was the only speaker openly to eschew pacifist arguments and to centre his case squarely upon foreign policy issues.[36]

Crossman supported conscription as a means of maintaining any army after January 1949; until the UN was strong enough, Britain needed to maintain a degree of military strength at home.[37] However, this level need not be high because, as he boldly prophesied, there was no possibility of a war with Russia for seven or possibly fifteen years. He argued strongly that the term of conscription should be reduced from the proposed eighteen to twelve months.[38] Crossman went on to vote with the government on the second reading. Of those who voted against, only sixteen had also signed the November amendment to the address, revealing that a different section of the party was here expressing its disapproval. A fair number of fellow-travellers, however, marched through the 'no' lobby; of those who signed the Nenni telegram in April 1948, ten voted against and six abstained, whilst the rest voted with the government.

In the wake of the revolt the government was clearly nervous. Crossman had announced that he and some of his colleagues would argue against the length of service in the committee stage of the Bill. As all those MPs, except two, who were associated with the recently formed Keep Left group, had voted *for* the Bill, the government could expect its problems to increase rather than diminish.[39] According to one version, Attlee and some of his colleagues approached Crossman to do a deal.[40] Why Crossman, and not Rhys Davies, who had actually moved the amendment? The probable answer is that Crossman, as a non-pacifist, was likely to be less intransigent, and, following his role in the November amendment revolt, was the most prominent spokesman of the left. Crossman's demands were met; the period of conscription was reduced by a government amendment from eighteen to twelve months. The left had won a major victory, though, as events were to reveal, it was destined to be short-lived.[41] Another reason why Crossman was chosen was that he was the most prominent member of the Keep Left group.

Since January 1947 certain MPs who belonged to the editorial staff of the two intellectual weeklies, had been regularly meeting other like-minded MPs to discuss domestic and foreign policy issues.[42] In late April 1947, less than a month after the Truman Doctrine speech, Crossman, Foot and Mikardo published an important pamphlet *Keep Left*, with which twelve other MPs identified themselves.[43] The pamphlet suggested radical new directions for home and foreign affairs, ideas for the latter centring around a fairly sympathetic analysis of Soviet intentions. Molotov, the pamphlet argued, had demonstrated a more co-operative attitude in November 1946 at the New York conference, but the government had ignored the opportunity and had instead become increasingly dependent upon the USA. The Americans had now fully accepted the Fulton analysis, were seeking to use Britain and Germany as forward defences against Russia, and were pumping dollars into reactionary bulwarks against communism. This analysis of Russian aggressiveness was thoroughly wrong, argued *Keep Left*; 'Whatever we think of communism, the USSR has no similar economic motive for expansion.' Totalitarianism in Eastern Europe was certainly worth resisting, but with democratic socialism, not the methods of totalitarianism itself. Germany should be rehabilitated economicially into Western Europe, and Britain should end her disruptive policy of defending oil interests by announcing a phased withdrawal of armed forces from the Middle East. Britain, moreover, should reduce her political and economic dependence on the USA and should build a European regional security system under UN auspices.

With confidence arising from left-wing success over the National Service Bill, *Keep Left* arguments also extended into defence policy. In the atomic age the British Isles would be indefensible against the Soviet Union, and so, in view of manpower shortages at home, a substantial reduction in the UK's standing army of one million men was possible and highly desirable. *Keep Left* tended to minimise the Soviet threat, which, it believed, could better be answered with the message of democratic socialism than by the paraphernalia of war.

The publication of *Keep Left* in the wake of the Truman doctrine, and the left's tactical victory over the conscription Bill, created a stir within the Labour Party.[44]. The Labour left's confidence was high. Jennie Lee prophesied that the Labour movement was getting ready to 'lead its leaders'.[45] Before the Margate Party Conference assembled, however, a pamphlet entitled *Cards on the Table* was issued by the International Department of the Labour Party, written by its formidable young secretary Dennis Healey.

Since the war an interesting transformation had taken place in Healey's exceptional mind. At the Blackpool Conference this erstwhile member of the Communist Party had made his name with a fiercely left-wing speech. However, his job at Transport House, which involved explaining and defending Bevin's foreign policy within the party organisation at home and abroad, the reorganisation of international socialist links (through the International Socialist Conference) had brought him 'slap up against the unpleasant realities'.[46] In February 1947, for example, he had reported that, in Hungary, Russian influence depended upon the Communist Party, the communist-controlled political and military police, economic controls, petty persecution and a fair degree of physical terror. Social democrats were singled out for persecution and their parties infiltrated or taken over by communists.[47] Healey concluded that in a very short time after the war 'genuine socialism' in Eastern Europe was dead. Why should Transport House officials and NEC representatives perceive a different reality from those fellow-travellers who reported enthusiastically upon their visits? The answer to this question is extremely complex and relates, in part, as in any act of political perception, to the value structure of the observer; both types of visitor tended to see what they wanted to see. There are, however, some other possible explanations.

The fellow-travellers tended to be invited by the official communist 'establishments' in these countries and were often flattered by personal attention from their top political leaders. They also tended to be taken on conducted tours, visiting buildings and factories rather than meeting people, particularly members of non-communist political parties. The fellow-travelling element in the Labour Party moreover, accepted the need for a degree of harshness when socialism was being introduced, and were readier to accept that opposition was of the fascist or neo-fascist variety. The Transport House men, on the other hand, were making contact with the prime 'target' group of the communists — the social democrats. These people were quick to give their version of the police terror under which they suffered. Perhaps Healey and his colleagues gave less emphasis than they might have done to the impressive social reforms and economic reconstruction taking place in Eastern Europe, but by the same token the fellow-travellers often wilfully ignored the elimination of political freedom that was its cost.

By May 1947 Healey had abandoned any attempt to reconcile social democracy with communism in a new organisation. He had observed the manner of Soviet influence in Eastern Europe and decided that it should be resisted; *Cards on the Table* elaborated the theme. It pointed out that a power vacuum existed in Eastern Europe which Russia was threatening to fill and which Britain could neutralise only with the help of the USA. Healey endorsed the Truman doctrine. Britain's security and British social democracy could survive only if America could be persuaded to take on the responsibilities of power.

The pamphlet provided an intellectual justification of Bevin's foreign policy but was probably more outspoken than Bevin himself would have allowed himself to be at that time. The *Daily Herald* praised this 'Labour Party publication' and denied the *Daily Telegraph's* assertion that it was a 'socialist attack upon Russia',[48] but *Tribune* dismissed it as a 'painfully hypocritical' justification for power politics.[49] Clearly the stage was set at the Margate Conference for yet another set-piece conflict over foreign affairs between the able and articulate forces of the left — and Ernest Bevin.

iii

At the 1947 Conference Healey's pamphlet, which had been published — and this was unusual — without NEC approval, was attacked by left-wing members of the NEC, principally Laski,[50] and on the floor of the Conference by Crossman and Zilliacus.[51] Their complaints took the line that the document overthrew the foreign policy on which the Labour Party had been elected to power; it diminished the role of the UN and advocated an Anglo-American military alliance against the USSR. The Keep Left group itself, however, was completely routed at Margate by a speech from Ernest Bevin which ranks with his destruction of George Lansbury in 1935.

Bevin eshewed any systematic attempt to answer the highly logical arguments of *Keep Left* and relied largely on the emotive appeal of his own personality. He delved back nine months to find the weapon to destroy his enemies of the moment. Theatrically he accused them of stabbing him in the back whilst he was in New York, adding with a winning martyrdom. 'I grew up in the Trade Unions, you see, and I have never been used to this kind of thing.'[52] Bevin had raised his voice and the Keep Left group knew their carefully constructed arguments had been demolished. The left was despondent. Michael Foot was scathingly resentful of Bevin's blend of conference magic, particularly his attempts to 'portray all his critics as naive appeasers of Russia'.[53]

Following the debate, Crossman has revealed in a television interview, Bevin offered him his hand, saying, 'No hard feelings, Dick?' Crossman's reaction perhaps explains why, for all his brilliance, he lacked the personality to sustain his leadership of the left for any length of time. Like a spoilt child he answered shortly, 'Yes, there are,' and turned abruptly aside.[54] A year later Bevin confided to Harold Nicolson his regret that Dick Crossman, with all his ability, did not possess a more stable character.[55]

The confrontation of these two pamphlets was more than just a piece of conference haggling. The foreign policy sections of *Keep Left* represented the distilled ideas of the great radical analysts of international affairs, Angel, Brailsford, Morel, Lowes Dickenson and so on, who had provided the Labour Party with the intellectual bases of its inter-war foreign policy. Bevin's 'realistic' conduct of foreign policy had deviated substantially from these traditional guildlines. Now *Cards on the Table* provided the intellectual muscle to underpin Bevin's pragmatic practice. Healey's pamphlet was one of the first contributions from those intellectuals on the right of the party who virtually reshaped Labour's thinking during the 1950s.[56]

The issue of Russia arose elsewhere in the Conference, which provides something of a barometer of Labour Party thinking on this subject in mid-1947. Relations with Russia were inevitably a prominent theme of Zilliacus's composite motion and supporting speech, which advocated a United Europe of the left, under the regional provisions of the UN, led by a combination of Britain, France and, of course, the USSR.[57] Bevin answered Zilliacus's call for closer co-operation with the USSR by citing the example of Germany. At Potsdam, he recalled, Britain had agreed to pool Germany's resources before extracting reparations and setting up central agencies. In the event not one pound of food passed from the Russian to the Western zone. Bevin concluded with the words 'We are not the guilty ones.' Zilliacus's motion was easily defeated, only twelve hands went up in favour of it;[58] his arguments were too far removed from government policy to gain any mass support.

The friends of Russia were further rebuffed when Harold Clay (a member of Bevin's trade union) brushed aside the motion that the British Soviet Society be removed from the Labour Party's list of proscribed organisations;

he accused the society of being a communist-controlled front organisation.[59] In virtually the next breath, however, he saw fit to defend Russia against a critical motion which argued that, in view of the repressive Soviet regime and the restrictions of movement and expression placed upon the recent Labour Party delegation to Russia (August 1946), the report of the visit be deleted from the official report.[60] In rejecting this motion on behalf of the NEC, Clay (who had been a member of the delegation) argued that the visit had been worth while and claimed that there was 'no doubt about the friendship of this movement for Russia'.[61] Harold Davies, a left-wing MP, vehemently rejected the motion, which he compared to W. N. Ewer's damaging series of articles upon life in Russia.[62]

Conference agreed that Winston Churchill's United Europe Committee should be shunned by the Labour Party on the grounds that it proposed to exclude the Soviet Union from Europe, and a 'Cobdenite' resolution was endorsed on the importance of increased trade with the USSR. A speaker in support of the latter motion made the point that, in view of the impending American slump, the UK would be well advised to divert her trade towards the USSR, a country immune from slumps. Jack Tanner, another supporting speaker, noted with satisfaction that Harold Wilson, Minister for Overseas Trade, was shortly to visit Moscow for trade negotiations.[63]

Relations with America also received attention at the Conference. Zilliacus's call for co-operation with Russia had been accompanied by attacks upon Bevin's 'subservience to capitalist America', a theme which appeared especially apposite in the light of the Truman doctrine.[64] Michael Stewart, MP, saw danger in Britain's drift towards the USA and away from the USSR.[65] Another delegate felt that British policy in Greece appeared to fulfil by proxy American policies of encirclement. Tom Driberg went further, asserting that Britain was being manoeuvered into being an atomic aircraft carrier and an 'atomic target in a Wall Street war against world socialism'.[67] At the Margate Conference, however, well informed voices were now being raised in support of America, notably those of Aidan Crawley and Kenneth Younger. Younger expressed the view, soon to be fashionable after Marshall's famous June speech, that American foreign aid measures were 'acts of international socialism and not less because capitalist America had taken a lead'.[67]

In mid-1947 the right-wing elements of the party, particularly trade unionists, were still prepared to make declarations of friendship with the USSR, but they were alert, suspicious, and increasingly prepared to accept what many socialists would describe as the unwholesome embrace of the USA.[68] Soviet activities in Eastern Europe had had their effect. The fellow-travellers were still clamorous in their support of the Soviets, but now they

Abandonment of an image 159

were forced back upon justifications for undemocratic conduct rather than refutations of it. The left were much concerned about Bevin's increasing dependence upon the USA; the Truman doctrine had confirmed, for many, Kingsley Martin's view that America was 'an expansionist power on a scale never before known to history'.[69] The left argued strongly that this drift should be halted and a working relationship established with Russia, which, for ideological reasons, left-wingers believed had no serious expansionist designs. The *Keep Left* pamphlet represented a high-water mark for this point of view. However the centre of the party, including a growing proportion of those who had abstained in November 1946, were moving increasingly away from the left; following *Cards on the Table*, Bevin's excoriating treatment of the left at Margate, and more particularly, the ennunciation of the Marshall Plan, this movement gathered pace.

iv

Bevin left Moscow on 25 April with the words 'I am leaving with a feeling that Four Power unity is stronger than ever before'.[70] The truth was, of course, exactly the reverse. The 'Allies' had agreed only on financial trifles and German POWs, whereas deadlock had been reached over the important issues relating to Germany: reparations, demilitarisation, denazification, democratisation, economic unity, levels of industrial activity, the future constitution of Germany, and Secretary Byrnes's proposed Four Power pact against future German aggression. The question of occupied Austria had been a further stumbling block. W. N. Ewer, who covered the conference for the *Daily Herald*, believed that the most important issue, stemming from Russia's acute need for consumer goods, was the demand for reparations out of current production in the Western zones. When this claim made no headway, Ewer believed, the Russians shut up shop on all other issues.[71]

Bevin was not able to come home with his extended Anglo-Soviet pact. On 20 April *Pravda* had proposed that the terms of the treaty be widened to 'exclude participation of each of the contracting parties in all blocs or action aimed against the other party in whatever form such participation is disguised'. This wording, prepared with the Truman doctrine in mind, would clearly place unacceptable limitations on Bevin's freedom of diplomatic manoeuvre. When he reported on the Moscow negotiations to the House of Commons on 15 May, he said, however, that negotiations for an extension of the treaty were continuing.[72] *Izvestia* responded by accusing him of having 'sinned against the facts' in his report to Parliament; the Soviet newspaper went on to repeat some of the accusations which had caused the Moscow conference to founder.[73] When Bevin looked across Europe, still debilitated by war and further weakened by the cruel winter of 1947, he saw a Soviet Russia, her massive wartime armies still apparently intact, intent upon hegemony in Eastern Europe and, it seemed, casting avaricious eyes upon Germany. This was the stage upon which Secretary of State Marshall stood to make his speech on 5 June at Harvard, offering aid to the nations of Europe, including the Soviet Union, provided they could formulate a joint programme to administer it. This speech was far more than the kite-flying exercise it is sometimes described as; in fact it reflected a great deal of detailed preparatory work by the State Department.[74] Bevin's quickness off the mark, however, in welcoming the proposal and proposing immediate consultations in Paris, was essential in making Marshall's offer into a reality.

Pravda's editorial on 16 June condemned the plan as an extension of the Truman doctrine, as dollar imperialism, and as a plan for interference in the internal affairs of other countries.[75] Molotov, however, accepted the invitation of Bevin and Bidault to meet in Paris to discuss the proposal, and when Bevin informed the House of Commons of Molotov's acceptance the news was cheered.[76] Molotov had agreed only to talk, not to agree; it seemed that despite their country's sore need of virtually every commodity, the Soviet rulers were strongly resistant to the idea of opening up their closed society to accommodate Western economic co-operation. At the Paris talks, beginning on 27 June, Molotov maintained that a joint plan would be an invasion of sovereignty. He argued that each country should submit proposals individually, and he also objected to any German association with the aid programmes. Molotov's objections culminated — it seems upon Politburo instructions — in a formal Soviet withdrawal from the attempt to formulate a European response to Marshall's offer.[77] Apart from two quickly curbed attempts by Poland and Czechoslovakia, no Iron Curtain countries subsequently participated in the sixteen-nation Conference on European Economic Co-operation which began on 12 July in Paris.

The product of the conference's deliberations, the European Recovery Programme, was presented to Marshall on 22 September 1947. Over the next three years over $12,000 million were pumped into the ailing economies of Western Europe through the Organisation for European Economic Co-operation. Of this money the USSR and the Iron Curtain countries received not a cent.

Russia's motives are hard to fathom. Certainly her communist rulers were extremely reluctant to allow Western inspection of their country's economic needs, possibly out of a reluctance to reveal their true extent, possibly through a desire to preserve that insulation between Soviet society and the West upon which Politburo power to some extent rested. On the other hand, she may have genuinely feared the enslavement of "dollar imperialism", especially in

Eastern Europe. The economic resuscitation of this vital strategic area on anything but Soviet terms might weaken the bonds which the Soviet Union had so assiduously developed since the Red Army liberated it. Bevin and Marshall must have allowed themselves a sigh of relief, despite the seriously divisive effects of Russia's withdrawal. With Russia in the scheme, it would have been highly unlikely that Congress would have sanctioned the vast amounts of aid needed, particuarly if the self-proclaimed leader of the anti-capitalist crusade was to be a major recipient. Furthermore, if it was her aim to destroy the ERP and keep Europe weak, then Russia could have been far more disruptive within the scheme than outside it. Indeed, it seems that Stalin missed an important trick by withdrawing, for the pattern of the Soviet Union's subsequent reactions revealed that his objective was in fact to thwart European recovery. At every level — press, public statements, international organisations — Soviet propaganda directed a furiously intensified series of assaults upon the plan. The powerful communist parties in France and Italy were roused to take direct action. In France the communist-dominated General Confederation of Labour called for a general strike, and the Italian Communist Party similarly organised strikes and demonstrations. In September 1947 a secret conference took place in Poland involving the communist parties of Eastern Europe, France, Italy and the Soviet Union, the latter being represented by the Politburo's theoretician, Andre Zhdanov. The main aim of the conference was to co-ordinate communist opposition to the Marshall Plan and to create permanent machinery, the 'Cominform', to be based in Belgrade, for this purpose. The conference manifesto, published in *Pravda* on 8 October 1947, described the Truman—Marshall Plan as only a constituent part, the 'European subsection of the general plan for the policy of global expansion pursued by the USA in all parts of the world'.[78] The 'right-wing socialists' of Western Europe, including Attlee and Bevin, were singled out for denunciation as the catspaws of capitalist imperialism and as traitors to the working classes. At the same time the Soviet Union accelerated its consolidation of power in Eastern Europe, using methods which made her earlier behaviour seem scrupulous. Non-communist parties, particularly the social democrats, were relentlessly pressurised, whilst the role of communist parties, already pervasive, was made even more dominant.

The international labour organisations, in which Western representatives shared membership with Russians or East Europeans, now became forums of conflict, and these tentative exercises in international bridge building were destined soon to collapse. The organisation which had taken over the mantle of the Second International was the International Socialist Conference (ISC), a loose, rather informal organisation which had an information office based in London. The Western parties were in the majority and so could control the political stance of the ISC. Its Antwerp conference in December 1947 passed a resolution noting the Cominform's aim of destroying democratic socialism and affirming its determination to construct a democratic and socialist Europe.[79]

The WFTU was in a different situation. Citrine had been worried by the 'magical' rise in trade union membership from the Eastern bloc as it fell under Soviet control. The balance of voting power was steered into communist hands. In the Executive Bureau of the WFTU pro-Soviet trade unionists had a majority of five to four, and on the Executive Committee their majority was twenty-two to twelve; in the General Council the largest and most important body, they also held the whip hand.[80] The British had wanted Schevenels, the former Secretary General of the IFTU (formally wound up on 31 December 1945) to fulfil the same task for the WFTU, but Saillant, the Secretary General of the Confédération Général du Travail (CGT), had been elected instead. Citrine as president, however, restored some of the balance for the non-communist unions, and when he retired after a year in this position, Arthur Deakin of the TGWU (Bevin's trade union) took over.

The early months of the WFTU had been quite promising; the 1946 General Council report recorded 'good progress'. The TUC tended to be a little left of Bevin's foreign policy in 1946 and concurred with the WFTU's rather critical line on Greece; it also subscribed to the WFTU policy of severing diplomatic relations with Franco's Spain.[81] The TUC's relations with the WFTU, however, became increasingly difficult in 1947, and the Marshall Plan was the breaking point. In June 1947, the General Council of the WFTU, meeting in Prague, came out agianst the plan.[82] The Executive Bureau met in Paris in November and avoided discussion of the problem, but conflict was only a few months away.

In Parliament the issue of Soviet encroachment in Eastern Europe coincided with Marshall's Harvard speech. In June, during a foreign affairs debate, Anthony Eden summarised recent events in Eastern Europe. In Bulgaria Petkov, leader of the Agrarian Party, had been arrested and his party expelled from Parliament. In Rumania six prominent socialists had been arrested. In Austria the communists were seeking to extend their influence unconstitutionally, and in Hungary, and most recently, Kovacs, the Secretary General of the Smallholders' Party, had been arrested by the Soviet military authorities on an espionage charge.[83] Bevin, as usual, was in complete accord with Eden on the subject of Russia; he recalled that British protest in connection with the Hungarian affair had been dismissed by Molotov as 'interference'. 'I am convinced,' Bevin declared, 'that there is a determination to wipe out every opposition in these [Eastern European] countries.'[84] Russia's misdeeds were thrown into sharper relief by the altruism of Marshall's offer. After six weeks' futile striving for a settlement, Bevin confessed he had 'jumped' at Marshall's offer. He hinted that he was not going to let Russian prevarication frustrate progress on this issue.[85] The tone of the debate was predominantly critical of Russia. The trade unionist MP S. N. Evans delivered an attack upon Russia's foreign policy and internal regime which would certainly have been condemned six months earlier, but which now provoked virtually no criticism from the left and won plaudits from Bevin and from Conservative speakers.[86] John Haire, a member of the NEC, defended Russia's intervention in Hungary in terms of the land reform which had been introduced. His defence lacked conviction. D. N. Pritt's version of events in that country was assessed by one Tory MP as a 'bad case' argued on behalf of an 'extremely disreputable client'.[87] By withdrawing from the Marshall Plan this disreputable client lost most of its small remaining credit on the right of the Labour movement.

The *Daily Herald* saw this event as conclusive proof that Russia's policy was 'aimed calmly and deliberately at preventing European unity and creating that very division between East and West which the Russian leaders have so vehemently deplored'.[88] Many of those in the centre and also on the left, despairing of a benign interpretation of Soviet intentions, now moved towards a similar position. This movement was assisted by the improvement in the American image occasioned by Marshall's speech. The left was in a difficult position. Marshall's magnanimous offer to the Soviet Union and to Europe had seriously eroded the ideological precept that international capitalism was reactionary, acquistive and dedicated to the overthrow of socialism. On the other hand, Russia's withdrawal jolted their preconceptions of Russia as the peaceful, progressive champion of economic planning. In consequence the left wing of the PLP split along three major lines.

The fellow-travellers and near fellow-travellers, still numbering about twenty and still led principally by Zilliacus, interpreted Marshall Aid in traditionally ideological terms as a snare of dollar imperialism to be rejected in favour of closer economic and political co-operation with the Soviet Union.[89]

Key members of the Keep Left group began to move slowly but surely towards Bevin's position. Russia's rejection of Marshall Aid, her 'concerted' moves in Europe,[90] together with her 'extraordinary' propaganda attempts to encourage a European left-wing rising against right-wing leaders,[91] shifted *Tribune* and its related group of MPs and intellectuals increasingly away from Keep Left interpretations of Soviet intentions.[92]

The *N.S. and N.* together with its own related groups, came to occupy an unstable and vacillating position between the *Tribune* group and the fellow-travellers, still receptive to some of the latter's explanations but increasingly concerned by the drift of Soviet policy. The journal had initially greeted

Marshall's speech as a sensible, constructive, statesmanlike initiative with which the Soviet Union should co-operate.[93] Despite the vast improvement in the American image[94] the *N.S. and N.* was suspicious of political strings, and reluctant to put a British seal upon a plan which would harden divisions in Europe. But when Russia withdrew from the plan the journal advised Bevin and Bidault to go ahead and prepare their plan without Molotov.[95]

A fortnight later a *volte-face* took place when the *N.S. and N.* agreed that there was no 'justification for gambling on the Mashall offer', which, despite its apparent altruism, masked anti-Soviet motives. At a time when the American loan was down to its last dregs the *N.S. and N.* was disillusioned with American economic aid, which it believed had acted 'not as a stimulant but as a narcotic'.[86] Kingsley Martin had clearly been indulging in rethinking; Britain needed to cut her overseas commitments, to institute a siege economy, to encourage a distinctively Western European trade area which could develop new trade links with Eastern Europe and Russia. The *N.S. and N.* had withdrawn once more into the fastness of a non-aligned Third Force idea.[97]

Leonard Woolf was similarly engaged in developing this concept and in November 1947, in his Fabian pamphlet, *Foreign Policy and the Labour Party's Dilemma*, called for absolute impartiality between the USA and USSR, a British economy cut free from dependence on the USA and the development of 'political solidarity' between a non-aligned group of Western European countries. Woolf believed the UK should seek out and build upon the common ground between Russia and the USA and should be prepared to make every concession to the Soviet Union which 'can reasonably be asked of us'; he advised compromise, for example, on the Soviet claim for reparations out of current German production.[98]

Woolf's pamphlet, probably the most lucid exposition ever of the Third Force argument, was also in a sense its swan song.[99] The increasing polarisation of arguments and alignments following the Soviet rejection of the Marshall Plan had reached a stage where the Third Force thesis was virtually irrelevant; the chances of a socialist Europe receded as the defensive reaction to communism within Western European countries gathered pace. The inability of a non-aligned Western Europe to defend itself against the Soviet Union became more and more obvious as the prospect of a Soviet attack became more likely. Woolf's pamphlet is of unique interest, however, for the reactions it provoked within the Labour Party. The Fabian International Advisory Committee at this time was a microcosm of Labour attitudes towards foreign policy. On the extreme left were Doreen Warriner, Konni Zilliacus, Warbey and, to some extent, Harold Laski. 'Third Forcers' were represented by Crossman, H. N. Brailsford and Dorothy Woodman.[100]

Abandonment of an image 165

Maurice Edelman, Arnold Foster, Jim Griffiths and Gordon Walker represented a fairly central position, and Dennis Healey and W. N. Ewer were very definitely to the right of the spectrum.

In a dissenting foreward to Woolf's pamphlet Laski, who at this time accepted 'without question the high and benevolent purposes of the Russian Communist Party' and absolutely rejected that Soviet policy had any 'expansionist character',[101] felt that Britain should stear clear of capitalist policies of containment, rebuild political and economic ties with Eastern Europe, reach agreement over Germany, and end her opposition to left-wing forces in Greece.[102]

In a letter to his American legal friend, Felix Frankfurter, Laski was expressing grave doubts at this time. He felt that American attempts to mould Europe and Asia into a mirror image of itself would mean 'civil war in Europe, perhaps before the winter is over'. The third world war would be a direct result of this conflict. Laski was much depressed about the chances of reversing the trend; Bevin was too blindly anti-communist to perceive the opportunity for leadership which lay before him. Laski's perspective was, of course, strongly influenced by Marxian economic ideas and concepts of class. He saw the struggle for socialism in international terms. American policy was effectively buttressing the economic order which had produced fascism and which would always thwart the growth of socialism. It was logical for him to consider the USSR as a preferable ally in this global struggle.[103]

W. N. Ewer's powerfully argued and highly prescient comment, published at the end of Woolf's pamphlet, centred upon his assessment of the Soviet threat. In May 1947 Ewer had written a series of critical articles in the *Daily Herald* following his coverage of the Moscow conference. He had observed that communism under Stalin was essentially Russian rather than Marxist, was paradoxically 'perpetuating economic inequalities',[104] had negated the four freedoms and repudiated liberty, equality, and fraternity alike.[105] His analysis of Soviet foreign policy was in the same mould. He allowed that Soviet motives in Eastern Europe and the Middle East might be defensive but he also discerned strong ideological, pan-Slavic as well as traditional strategic and economic (i.e. imperialist) impulses.[106] The dilemma resolved itself in Ewer's eyes to a policy of "appeasement" (with which he identified Woolf's arguments) or 'resistance'. The former was dangerous and a hostage to the future, whereas the latter, which involved close co-operation with America, offered the best chances of success, provided it was made clear that Britain's stance was purely 'defensive'. Ewer endorsed Bevin's policies, though he agreed that they were open to criticism when they appeared to be overtly 'anti-Soviet'.

His final comments on Woolf's thesis are significant. He concluded that

166 *The Russia complex*

Woolf's prescriptions, including his advocacy of a Western group, would produce an unstable 'power vacuum' in Europe 'and in politics, as in physics, that is a certain cause of stormy disturbance'.[107] Soviet foreign policy, as in *Cards on the Table*, was once again the object of 'realist' observations about international relations.

v

Perhaps with the substantial criticism of the last TUC conference in mind, Bevin made a personal appearance at the Southport conference in 1947. In the rambling way Bevin always used when not speaking to a Foreign Office brief, he defended conscription, justified his foreign policy position, attacked Russia for her lack of co-operation over Germany and her prodigal use of the veto in the United Nations and concluded with a typical piece of self-righteousness: 'No one can accuse me of either saying a heated word or doing anything to provoke antagonisms during the period I have been in office.'[108] His veracity on the former point at least was very suspect, but this did not inhibit Dame Ann Loughlin (of the Tailors' and Garment Workers' Union and president of the TUC that year) from moving a resolution which warmly endorsed Bevin and went on to express very pro-American sentiments. This motion was carried by the same overwhelming margin that defeated an amendment attacking 'dollar diplomacy' and arguing for improved trade with Eastern Europe and the Soviet Union. Bevin emerged from Southport with his power base in the trade unions stronger than ever.

At the full party conference at Margate he had looked forward to the November Foreign Ministers' conference in London as 'almost the last chance' for economic unity in Germany and for a viable reconstruction of Europe. A small group of Labour MPs were more sanguine. In the autumn of 1947 Zilliacus visited Russia and Eastern Europe in the company of fellow MPs A. Allen, G. Bing, A. J. Campion, F. Lee, B. Parkin, G. Thomas and H. White. They met four Prime Ministers and many trade union leaders, and were greatly impressed by the reconstruction they saw taking place.[109] Stalin had received them personally and had been fulsome in his professions of friendship towards the UK; he had urged closer trade links with the Soviet Union and Eastern Europe. In Parliament Eden had some tart words to say about the group, which he accused of vilifying the Marshall Plan and supporting the Cominform. Eden also remained singularly unconvinced by Stalin's declarations of friendship; the whole group replied in a letter to the *N. N. S. and N.* that, on the contrary, Stalin had indeed been genuine and sincere.[110] Bevin's experience led him to share Eden's judgement.

Abandonment of an image 167

The conference opened on 25 November, its chances of success being assessed in the British press with a pessimism which proved more than justified. Molotov dispensed with virtually all attempts at serious negotiation and relied upon undiluted propaganda, accusing the West of rehabilitating top Nazis, of transforming Germany into a military base for the advancement of Anglo-American monopoly capitalism, of buying up German goods at artificially deflated rates and re-exporting them at excessive prices. Clearly, whilst the Marshall Plan had a chance of succeeding and 'Bizonia' threatened to become 'Trizonia', the Russians had no intention of negotiating a peace treaty and a new German constitution. Instead they retreated behind immovable verbal barricades. Even when Bevin contrived an informal *tête-à-tête* with Molotov on 3 December he remained equally intractable. Bevin told Harold Nicolson that on this occasion he reminded Molotov that he had defended Russia in the old days and meant her people no harm. Yet despite the fact that the Russians could not stand a war, they were risking one in which Britain would inevitably side with the USA, and that, said Bevin bluntly, 'would be the end of you and your revolution'. Molotov replied that all Russia was after was a 'unified Germany'. Bevin pointed out that even then Germany would become a long-term threat. Molotov agreed but repeated that he wanted a 'unified Germany'[111] It soon became clear that the conference was dead.

In his final statement Marshall unrepentantly reasserted Western views over Germany, exhuming the almost forgotten Western claim that the Oder–Neisse line be revised. At London the two sides ceased trying to draw their negotiating positions together and actually began to move apart. Both resolved to abandon diplomacy in favour of other means. For Bevin this entailed the formulation of a defensive system of alliances; for Stalin the cementing of the few remaining gaps in the Stettin–Trieste wall.

The year 1947 did not close without one hopeful sign: the signing of the Anglo-Soviet trade treaty on 28 December. The treaty had long been noisily advocated and impatiently awaited by all sections of the left. Despite Tory allegations that a bad bargain had been struck, the Cobdenite argument that the mixing of cultures and economies through mutual trade would lead to greater political understanding was never more hopefully applied than by the Labour left wing to this agreement. The government, however, was careful to deny that there was any political motive behind the agreement, which had been signed for purely economic reasons; Russia would supply timber and grain in exchange for steel rails, wood, rubber and manufactured goods.[112] In fact trade increased progressively as diplomatic relations worsened; in 1947 Britain imported £$6^1/_2$ million worth of Russian imports; in 1951, the second year of the Korean war, the figure was £53$^1/_2$ million. If indeed these trade contacts did have any ameliorating political effect it was lost in the vast divisions of the Cold War.

This chapter has covered 1947 with approximate chronological neatness. It was a year of doubt and crisis in which the different traditions in Labour Party foreign policy engaged in sharp and decisive conflict. These traditions were complex and closely interwoven, but, for the purposes of analysis at this stage, four can be discerned: pacifist, radical, Marxist and realist.

The Marxist tradition of sympathy with Soviet communism took something of a beating. Vigorous work by the fellow-travellers kept the tradition alive, but they were increasingly on the defensive; adherence to the tradition was severely tested by Soviet actions which tarnished its respectability.

Conscription was the issue over which the pacifist tradition came to the fore, and, aided by elements worried by Bevin's apparent anti-Sovietism, the pacifists were able to lead a major revolt against the government. The resultant compromise, a reduction in the term of National Service, represented a humiliating defeat for the government. However, when the dust had settled the pacifists had failed to prevent a Labour government from introducing peacetime conscription; even the concession achieved was destined to be revoked in December 1948.

The radical tradition, inherited from the Liberal Party and the UDC, was centred around *Tribune*, the *N.S. and N.* and their associated MPs and intellectuals. It expressed itself through the Third Force school of thought. At first sight a contradiction seems to be present: the radical tradition, if nothing else, was highly internationalist and bitterly opposed to balance-of-power politics, yet the Third Force idea was regional and advocated a third focus of power as a counter to the two super-powers. The emphasis in the Third Force thesis, however, was upon the power of ideas rather than the power of weapons and, far from betraying internationalism, the advocates of a Third Force were clutching at the last chance of making internationalism a reality. The UN had proved unworkable, riven by super-power division; the Third Force was not intended as a retreat into power politics but as a temporary *substitute* for the United Nations. Britain was to become the focus of a social democratic internationalism which would appeal to all non-aligned countries.

The credibility of the Third Force argument, however, rested upon the assumption that there was sufficient room for manoeuvre between the two super-powers, that there was, for example, no genuine threat of military attack from the Soviet Union against which American-supported precautions needed to be taken. After the Soviet rejection of the Marshall Plan and the formation of the Cominform this argument, though ably presented by Woolf

Abandonment of an image 169

and his supporters, began to lose ground rapidly; the virtual defection of the highly influential *Tribune* was one of the most important symptoms. The most effective of all was the realist tradition. This was the school of thought, developed notably by Bevin and Dalton, which finally succeeded in winning over the Labour Party in the late 1930s, which received reinforcement during the coalition years, and which dominated post-war Labour foreign policy in the person of Ernest Bevin. The tradition did not deny the major objectives of any of the others. The principal differences related to the best means of achieving these objectives, to the perception of the conditions necessary for their realisation, and to the measures needed when the conditions clearly did not exist. The elements of 'realism', therefore, included: a belief that in most circumstances people are moved by the threat of force rather than the appeal of ideas; that the ability to use or threaten force is a major foundation of foreign policy; that nation States tend to pursue their own interests; and that national security should not be seriously prejudiced in any pursuit of an international order.

Within the Cabinet there was no opposition to this hard-headed approach. Cripps's attempt to unseat Attlee in the summer of 1947, when the country faced a severe economic crisis, had nothing to do with foreign affairs. Dalton records a rumour around at this time that Cripps was interested in keeping the door open regarding co-operation with Russia rather than the USA.[113] However, Dalton, Cripps's choice as an alternative to Bevin for Foreign Secretary, was very close to Bevin's thinking, and Cripps's choice for Prime Minister was none other than Bevin himself.

Within the party the authority of Bevin's office together with his enormous personal following in the trade unions enabled him to quell opposition from the left during the first half of the year. During the second half his task was made easier by the direction of Soviet policies. The foreign policy of the Soviet Union itself conformed so closely to the principles of the realist school that, it is ironic to reflect, the best mentor of the Labour left in this subject was probably Stalin himself. Laski ruefully summed up the feeling of all socialist foreign policy advocates in the autumn of 1947: '... I have the feeling that I am already a ghost in a play that is over'.[114]

Notes

1 *State Papers 148*, 1947, Part II, pp. 314, 365 and 482. These treaties were ratified 10 February 1947. Italy and Finland had similar clauses in their peace treaties.
2 432 *H. C. Deb.*, 1375–6, 3 February 1947. On 18 December H. McNeil, the other Foreign Office junior Minister, had told MPs that these elections had involved

'wholesale falsification of the results by Government authorities', 431 *H. C. Deb.*, 1934.
3 Feis, *From Trust to Terror*, p. 173.
4 Dalton, *High Tide and After*, p. 201.
5 432 *H. C. Deb.*, 210 (written answer), 29 January 1947.
6 See, for example, *Daily Herald* editorials, 24 and 25 January 1947.
7 Molotov's speech of 10 July 1946 had done much to give birth to this fear; Feis, p. 133.
8 For a statement of Bevin's position, see 433 *H. C. Deb.*, 2296–300, 27 February 1947.
9 Dalton, pp. 206–9.
10 H. S. Truman, *Years of Trial and Hope*, vol. II, p. 122.
11 Feis, pp. 177 and 181.
12 George Kennan's memorandum was sent from Moscow to the State Department on 22 February 1946. A revised version of the memo was published anonymously in *Foreign Affairs*, June 1947, but was quickly associated with Kennan's name and thereafter with official American policy. See George F. Kennan, *Memoirs, 1925–50*, pp. 290–7 and 354–67.
13 See, for example, 433 *H. C. Deb.*, 2301, 27 February 1947.
14 Dalton, p. 189. This contrasts with his 7 May 1946 statement; see p. 131.
15 See *The Times*, 26 March 1947.
16 H. Nicolson, *Diaries and Letters*, vol. III, 1945–62 (London, 1968), p. 89.
17 *Ibid.*, p. 191.
18 See *Daily Herald*, 4 January 1947, and article by G. E. R. Geyde in *Tribune*, 3 January 1947.
19 *Daily Herald*, 25 January 1947.
20 See, for example, 437 *H. C. Deb.*, 1718–42, 15 May 1947.
21 *Daily Herald*, 10 April 1947.
22 *N. S. and N.*, 25 January 1947. See also D. Warriner, 'The real issues', *Political Quarterly*, January 1947.
23 433 *H. C. Deb.*, 2377, 27 February 1947.
24 432 *H. C. Deb.*, 1378, 3 February 1947.
25 *Ibid.*, 1377, and 433 *H. C. Deb.*, 2327–37, 27 February 1947.
26 See Feis, pp. 208–20.
27 Lord John Hope, 437 *H. C. Deb.*, 1903, 16 May 1947.
28 433 *H. C. Deb.*, 2345–51, 27 February 1947.
29 *Daily Herald*, 15 March 1947.
30 *Ibid.*, 14 March 1947.
31 *Reynolds' News*, 16 March 1947.
32 *Tribune*, 21 March 1947.
33 *N. S. and N.*, 22 March 1947.
34 Jackson, *Rebels and Whips*, puts the abstentions at twenty (p. 59). Gordon, *Conflict and Consensus*, sets the figure at seventy-six (p. 203).
35 These were: T. Scollan, S. Silverman, Hopkin Morris, Rhys Davies, Mrs F. Paton, Campbell-Stephen, Mrs B. A. Gould, S. Swingler, W. Wyatt, S. Cocks, and I. Mikardo.
36 435 *H. C. Deb.*, 1911, 31 March 1947.
37 Both *Tribune* and *N. S. and N.* supported conscription on the grounds that, to develop properly, the Third Force would need a military shield.

Abandonment of an image 171

38 435 H. C. Deb., 1868–78, 1 April 1947.
39 Mikardo and Millington were the two MPs.
40 Jackson, Rebels and Whips, p. 60.
41 See p. 199.
42 The whole group consisted of: D. Bruce, R. H. S. Crossman, G. Bing, M. Foot, H. Davies, L. Hale, F. Lee, B. Levy, R. W. G. Mackay, J. P. W. Mallalieu, I. Mikardo, E. R. Millington, S. Swingler, G. Wigg, and W. Wyatt.
43 The ideas were mostly Crossman's — interview with M. Foot.
44 See Daily Herald editorial, 2 May 1947.
45 Trubune, 9 May 1947.
46 B. Read and G. Williams, Dennis Healey and the Politics of Power, p. 26.
47 Reports filed with the minutes of the International Sub-committee of the NEC in Transport House.
48 Daily Herald, 22 May 1947.
49 Tribune, 23 May 1947.
50 Read and Williams, p. 61.
51 LPCR 1947, p. 106.
52 Ibid., p. 175.
53 Tribune, 6 June 1947.
54 ITV programme, Thursday 9 September 1971.
55 Nicolson, Diaries, vol. III, p. 145.
56 See S. Haseler, The Gaitskellites (London 1969), pp. 112–113.
57 LPCR 1947, p. 160.
58 Daily Herald, 30 May 1947.
59 LPCR 1947, p. 102.
60 Moved by F. M. Millar, St Pancras DLP, LPCR 1947, p. 103.
61 LPCR 1947, p. 102.
62 In the Daily Herald, 5 and 8 May 1947. See also Pritt and Ewer's debate on Life in Russia, 15 May. Rather like Clay, the Daily Herald was concerned to maintain a show of goodwill. Its reaction to the arrival of an official Soviet delegation on 10 April was very enthusiastic.
63 LPCR 1947, p. 172.
64 Ibid., p. 160.
65 Ibid., p. 174.
66 Ibid., p. 173.
67 Ibid., pp. 167 and 173.
68 On 23 May the Daily Herald asserted that 'Friendship can be achieved'.
69 N. S. and N., 7 June 1947.
70 Daily Herald, 26 April 1947.
71 Ibid., 25 April 1947, 'Why Moscow failed'.
72 437 H. C. Deb., 1740, 15 May 1947.
73 Reported in Daily Herald, 23 May 1947.
74 Marshall's speech had been foreshadowed by a somewhat enigmatic speech by Acheson on 8 May. Several State Department committees had been engaged throughout April and May in discussing the implications of economic aid to Europe — Feis, pp. 237–44. Also see Kennan, pp. 325–35.
75 Reported in Daily Herald, 17 June 1947.
76 439 H. C. Deb., 35–6, 23 June 1947.
77 M. Djilas, Conversations with Stalin, p. 128, and Feis, p. 249.

172 *The Russia complex*

78 Feis, p. 263.
79 *LPCR 1948*, p. 22, pp. 24–5, and pp. 222–31.
80 John P. Windmuller, *American Labor and the International Labor Movement 1940–53*, p. 140.
81 A critical resolution mustered 2,400,000 votes against a majority figure of 3,557000 — *TUCR 1946*, p. 139, and pp. 261–2.
82 Windmuller, p. 90.
83 438 *H. C. Deb.*, 2230–40, 19 June 1947.
84 *Ibid.*, 2336–43.
85 *Ibid.*, 2340–1.
86 *Ibid.*, 2339, 2330 and 2341.
87 Mr Richard Law, *ibid.*, 2330. See also speech of Major Cecil Poole, *ibid.*, 2278.
88 *Daily Herald*, 3 July 1947. For views of Czechoslovakia's enforced withdrawal see the editions of 8 and 12 July.
89 See unfavourable review of Zilliacus's book on foreign policy in *N. S. and N.*, 21 June 1947.
90 *Tribune*, 13 June 1947.
91 *Ibid.*, 20 June 1947.
92 With the exception of Ian Mikardo.
93 *N. S. and N.*, 14 June 1947.
94 See, for example, the editorial of 28 June.
95 *N. S. and N.*, 26 July 1947.
96 See Kingsley Martin's report of Gomulka's view of the Marshall Plan as an attempt to undermine the USSR with dollars and build up Germany as a bulwark against Bolshevism, *N. S. and N.*, 2 August 1947.
97 See *N. S. and N.*, 20 September 1947, for a redifinition of the idea.
98 Page 16.
99 See also G. D. H. Cole, *The Intelligent Man's Guide to the Post-war World*.
100 See N. Angell's agreement with this line in an article entitled 'Another great illusion', *N. S. and N.*, 6 December 1947, and Crossman's letter, 13 December, also supporting Woolf.
101 H. J. Laski, *The Webbs and Soviet Communism*, the Webb Memorial Lecture, 4 June 1947, p. 16.
102 Zilliacus, in a letter to *N. S. and N.*, 6 December 1947, expressed similar views more forcibly, declaring 'war against this whole phoney left school' (i.e. Third Force) in foreign policy. Woolf replied 13 December and Zilliacus responds again 27 December 1947.
103 Kingsley Martin, *Harold Laski* (London, 1952), p. 208.
104 *Daily Herald*, 5 May.
105 *Ibid.*, 8 May.
106 Woolf, p. 30.
107 *Ibid.*, p. 33.
108 *TUCR 1947*, p. 426.
109 See speech by G. Thomas, 443 *H. C. Deb.*, 160–74, 22 October 1947.
110 *N. S. and N.*, 1 November 1947.
111 Nicolson, pp. 115–6.
112 See H. Wilson's written reply to a letter from Sir Waldron Smithers, 451 *H. C. Deb.*, 82, 2 June 1948, and his statement, reported in *The Times*, 8 February 1949,

Abandonment of an image 173

that the rationale for the signing of the treaty was that 'It was to our economic advantage to do so'.

113 Dalton, *Diaries*, 25 July 1947. He added that Cripps was regarded in the USA as half communist.

114 K. Martin, *H. Laski*, p. 185 (in a letter to Frankfurter).

10 *The genesis of NATO, I. The coup in Czechoslovakia*

> I do not know whether Marx really educated anybody. What he did was to confuse me. [Ernest Bevin, *H. of C. Debs.*, vol. 454, col. 1300, 28 July 1948]

i

'You are playing a dangerous game,' Bevin told Molotov on 3 December 1947, 'and I cannot make out why.'[1] Following protracted futile wranglings in successive meetings with the Russians, this feeling of frustration and bewilderment was quite genuine among the Labour leadership; as Hector McNeil complained a few weeks later, 'What worries everyone is the inconsistencies between Generalissimo Stalin and Generalissimo Stalin.'[2] Attlee, broadcasting to the nation on 3 January 1948, spoke of a 'New Imperialism' which threatened 'the welfare and way of life of every other nation in Europe'.[3] A few days before the broadcast, King Michael of Rumania was finally toppled from his precarious perch by a communist-inspired *coup* supported by Soviet-trained troops.[4]

Whatever Soviet motives might prove to be, the Labour government was not prepared to give them the benefit of the doubt. 'We cannot go on as we have been going on,' Bevin had told the House when presenting the wreckage of the London conference to them.[5] Even at that time he was a considerable distance down the road towards the signing of a North Atlantic Pact. In June 1947, when discussing the Marshall Plan, Bevin and Bidault had discussed a defence pact involving the Benelux countries and Marshall had been informed of these developments during the London Foreign Ministers' conference. On 21 January 1948 he announced further developments in a major speech to Parliament. Not content with transforming Eastern Europe

174

into a series of police States, the Soviet Union, he declared, had shown by her attempts to wreck the Marshall Plan that she had ambitions in Western Europe as well.[6] In response Western Europe must draw 'closely together'; the time was 'ripe for a consolidation of Western Europe'. Bevin was unveiling his concept of 'Western union'.

This would involve mutual defence treaties initially between Britain, France and the Benelux countries, but ultimately it would look to Western Europe 'as a unit'. Bevin was careful not to present this initiative as an anti-Soviet one; he placed much greater emphasis upon the economic aspects of Western union, stressing that it would not be an 'exclusive' grouping and insisting that it would be in accord with the regional provisions of the United Nations charter.[7]

In the same speech he announced that, despairing of four-power cooperation, he and his Western colleagues would arrange meetings in London between France, Britain, America and the Benelux countries to discuss the future of Germany under a bizonal or hopefully a trizonal basis. In the Control Council on 11 February Sokolovsky condemned these developments as the 'progressive inclusion of Western Germany in a military and political Western bloc'.[8] Under a fortnight later the Russians put the finishing touches to their bloc in the East by inspiring the communist *coup* in Czechoslovakia.

Since the war Czechoslovakia had successfully walked the tightrope between East and West through the medium of a hybrid coalition government, comprising a communist Prime Minister and Minister of the Interior (Gottwald and Nosek) with Jan Masaryk, son of the founder of the republic, as Foreign Minister, and the distinguished statesman Eduard Benes as President. However, as the temperature between East and West rose, the viability of the coalition diminished. The Czech communists were worried in February that the forthcoming general election would lessen their power and, as a precautionary measure, Nosek busied himself with weeding out non-communists from the Prague police force. When Nosek ignored a majority Cabinet directive to desist, a number of non-communist Ministers proffered their resignations. The communists thereupon mobilised their supporters in factories and in the streets; on 22 February Nosek began arresting political opponents. Faced with armed communist groups on the outskirts of the city, the presence in Prague of a Russian Deputy Foreign Minister (Zorin), a communist-organised national strike, and by a collapse of support among social democrat members of the Cabinet, Benes accepted the proffered Ministerial resignations and appointed a communist-dominated government on 29 February. On 10 March the body of Jan Masaryk was found on the pavement outside the Foreign Office building. The communists claimed that he had commited suicide.

At the very least these events clarified some of the confusion in Western diplomatic circles; there was little doubt any more that Stalin was determined to consolidate his hold upon Eastern Europe. In January it became clear that Western Europe, reinforced by the expectation of Marshall Aid, was moving towards an integrated political position which would entail the establishment of a unified Western Germany. Czechoslovak frontiers bordered on those of Russia in the east and Germany in the west; given her traditional pro-Western cultural and political traditions, Czecholovakia was a weak point in the Stettin–Trieste line, a potential drawbridge whereby Western influences might enter Eastern Europe and possibly the Soviet Union herself. Stalin had pulled the drawbridge up.

Czechoslovakia, of course, had enormous symbolic importance in the West, and the resultant storm of diplomatic protest was sharpened by residual feelings of guilt.[9] It is hardly surprising that, following the *coup*, analogies with Munich multiplied and became a highly important element in the political psychology of the day. The obvious implication of the analogy, that Stalin had crushed Czechoslovakia as Hitler had ten years before, was, however, far from the truth. Despite the benevolent support of the USSR and the incipient threat of the Red Army, the *coup* in Czechoslovakia was engineered from within and by a communist party which commanded a substantial degree of public support — Gottwald had, after all, been able to call a national strike. The NEC's fiercely condemnatory statement of 3 March saying that Czechoslovakia had 'fallen victim to aggression from without aided by treachery from within' was therefore guilty of the same fallacy.[10] Such a judgement was, however, symptomatic of the high state of tension which the *coup* engendered. On 29 February Dalton wrote in his diary, 'Forty-eight hours ago I saw World War Three starting in six months or less.' He went on to anticipate one of the less palatable features of NATO: 'We should have to drag ourselves back behind the USA ... we should have to line up with all the worst reactionaries and the Catholic Church! Ugh!'[11]

Thoughts of war reverberated around the Foreign Office and Defence Ministry. On 8 March Alexander, the Defence Minister, declared that 'the Navy is prepared' and could go to sea in ten days.[12] The *coup* certainly catalysed Western attempts to draw together, helping the European Recovery Programme to its presidential signature on 3 April and, very probably, restraining the Congressional financial scalpel upon the amounts to be granted to the Western governments.[13] Bevin announced the details of ERP to the House on 4 May together with an explanation of the machinery of Western union which had been formally constituted by the five-power Brussels treaty signed on 17 March.[14] He again emphasised the 'equal' importance of economic and social aspects of the treaty, but few could have been deceived by this piece of window dressing; Western union was primarily a defence against the Soviet threat. Bevin, yet again, was striving to present 'realist' policies in a way which conformed with the idealistic traditions in Labour foreign policy.

He also announced that a 'wider circle' was needed; he spoke favourably of the proposal by St Laurent, Canadian Foreign Minister, of a world-wide system of regional defence arrangements based (more window dressing) on Article 51 of the United Nations charter.[15] Thus two complementary processes, both originating on opposite sides of the Atlantic, were well under way in the spring of 1948. The economic initiative to resuscitate Western Europe which had begun with Marshall's Harvard speech in June 1947 had travelled across the Atlantic to a full conclusion in the form of ERP in April 1948. At the same time Bevin's plans for the defence of Europe had proceeded via the Anglo-French Dunkirk treaty, through the unifying stimulus of Marshall's initiative, to the Brussels treaty of March 1948, and was now making its own transatlantic journey to America and Canada. In fact as Bevin spoke to the House of Commons on 4 May a draft Atlantic Treaty was already being discussed in the State Department and in the National Security Council. On 19 May the historic Vandenberg resolution proposing direct American involvement in the defence of Western Europe was introduced into the Senate.[16]

Meanwhile, within the international labour organisations, further splintering was taking place. In March 1948 an ISC conference expelled Eastern European socialist parties which were deemed to have been absorbed into the communists' orbit and went on to pass resolutions welcoming ERP. At the 1948 Labour Party Conference, Zilliacus attacked this policy. He pointed out that Labour was cutting itself adrift from the greater part of the working class in Europe, which was led by communist or left-wing (i.e. pro-communist) socialists. He caused some indignant responses by describing those socialists in France and Italy who supported the Marshall Plan as 'MacDonaldite socialists'.[17] Despite these protests the die had been cast. In April another conference of Western European socialist parties was held on the subject of European unity and in June an ISC conference passed a resolution envisaging a reintegration of Germany into Europe to restore the 'balance of forces' in Europe. The Vienna conference also pronounced anathema upon 'the dictatorship' in Eastern Europe. The basis of the Western social democratic international had thus been founded.[18] The case of the WFTU was rather different, as it was the communists who held the voting strength within the organisation. In February the Western unions had asked for a meeting to discuss the Marshall Plan. The secretariat was evasive and suggested a later date, in April. Deakin responded by saying, 'If the WFTU is to be regarded merely as a body dealing with those questions acceptable to the USSR we know where we are.'[19] Victor Tewson, frequently a member of British delegations to the WFTU, wrote in the February edition of *Labour* (the TUC journal), 'If the silence of the British trade union movement is regarded as a sign of weakness a great mistake has been made.' The TUC in fact was very definite at this time; it convened a special meeting in March with non-communist countries to devise ways of assisting the ERP. Present at this meeting, which was very similar in spirit to the Vienna meeting of the ISC, were the AFL (together with the CIO for the first time at an international conference)[20] and the German trade unions. The conference was successful in establishing an ERP Advisory Conference and Committee — here again was the germ of an alternative Western organisation.

When the WFTU Executive Bureau met in April, Carey of the CIO declared the organisation to be 'deader than a doornail'. However, after concessions had been made by the communists, he observed a little lugubriously that it had been 'brought back to life'.[21] Neither side was yet ready to abandon the WFTU; the Western trade unions were reluctant to appear as wreckers and the communists were naturally interested in keeping intact a useful vehicle for their political arguments and influence. An attempt was even made to resucitate the Anglo-Soviet Trade Union Committee, which had not met since October 1944, but the initiative failed.[22]

ii

Under the pressure of Soviet provocations, Bevin's foreign policy received still more fervent support from the Conservatives and from the right and centre of his own party. In the debates in Parliament their support rather than the criticism of opponents was the distinctive feature.[23]

During the Labour Party Conference on 20 May a National Union of Mineworkers' resolution was moved by Will Lawther, expressing firm support for Bevin's foreign policy from 'his fellow trade unionists'. The resolution was massively endorsed by over four million votes and a critical amendment inspired by Zilliacus attracted only 224,000.[24] The number of dissenters over foreign policy reduced considerably as events seemed to prove Bevin's analysis of Russian intentions. The defection of *Tribune* from the ranks of Bevin's opponents was more important than it seemed on the surface; only three MP's were associated with its editorial policy, and one of those, Ian Mikardo, sustained his opposition to Bevin even after Czechoslovakia. *Tribune*, however, was the second major printed voice of the left and carried weight in all sections of the party. The ex-editor, Aneurin Bevan, was still associated with the journal via his wife, Jennie Lee, MP, who sat on the editorial board; Michael Foot, its editor and a *Daily Herald* columnist, was already in 1948 a highly respected voice on the left and considered widely to be a 'heavyweight' on foreign affairs.[25] Even before the breakdown of the London conference *Tribune* had been advocating the policies which Bevin expressed in his 'Western union' speech.[26] On 19 December, following the breakdown, a sense of relief can almost be detected in the *Tribune* editorial. Now the course was clear. Russian policy was reinterpreted; Stalin had ignored a great chance to co-operate after the war by assuming on ideological grounds that conflict with the West was inevitable. Marshall's offer had briefly raised hopes of co-operation, but Russia had instructed Eastern European States to hold back and had ordered the communist parties of the West to smash the American initiative. The best way of dealing with the Soviet Union would now be from a position of strength; it was Britain's task to build it. *Tribune*'s perception of the Czechoslovak *coup* was typified in its headline 'Murder in Prague'.[27]

In his *Daily Herald* column Foot, on 27 February, had no doubt that during the most 'tragic week since the end of the war ... a welter of lies and distortions has been involved to disguise a brutal attack upon free speech and government'. The *Daily Herald* itself now discerned a 'familiar pattern' in Eastern Europe; communists professed unity and friendship with socialists whom they joined in coalition governments; they then set about seizing control of internal security and public information agencies; then a campaign of hostility and vilification would ensue against the other members of the coalition, particularly the social democrats, and, choosing their moment, the communists would seize power, accusing their erstwhile colleagues of conspiracies and plots with foreign capitalists. The *Daily Herald* agreed with Foot that the task was now to build up strength in Western Europe and to deter further Soviet incursions.[28] The example of *Tribune* and the *Daily Herald* suggests that within the Labour Party a process of reinterpretation of Soviet foreign policy was taking place through a readjusted, almost hostile, image of the Soviet Union. The predictions of war which followed the Czechoslovak *coup* revealed that a new element, fear of a sudden Soviet attack, had been added to the Labour Party perception of Russia, at least on the right and centre.

iii

In January a letter from Keep Left MPs[29] to the editor of the *Daily Herald* may have given the impression that the Third Force argument was alive and well, but other signs indicated that its collapse was imminent. On 4 May Ben Levy left the camp. A member of Keep Left, he had also signed the amendment to the King's Speech in November 1946, in the hope that Bevin would attempt to develop a socialist European grouping independent of the USA and USSR. He felt that Bevin had ignored that option and now it no longer existed — Bevin's duty now was to 'save the world from war and devastation'.[30] Bevin's decision to rely upon the USA was the right one; Czechoslovakia had proved the ruthless, reactionary nature of communism and furthermore it was now clear that reliance upon Marshall Aid would not prejudice the future of British socialism. These were widely shared thoughts, and elements of them are found in the minds of others who still paid lip service to the Third Force concept. Another signatory of the *Daily Herald* letter was Michael Foot, but his fervent advocacy of defence against the Soviet Union made his continued support of the Third Force unconvincing. Crossman sustained his advocacy into the January foreign affairs debate but his support too lost credibility through his new attitudes towards the USA. He was forced to admit that, along with many others, his 'own views about America' had 'changed a great deal in the last six months'.[31] The Third Force idea was clearly losing its sharpness. Bevin's concept of Western union confused the issue still further, because some elements on the left chose to see in this ambiguously packaged idea signs of their very own Third Force. The *N.S. and N.* chose to interpret Western union in this fashion on 21 February. Marshall Aid, which the journal had previously condemned as a 'narcotic', was now seen as the stimulus Western union needed. To complete the *volte-face* the journal not only argued that America should defend Western Europe but proposed that the cost of 'containment' should be borne solely by her.

The Czechoslovak *coup* threw the *N.S. and N.* into an even greater disarray; on 6 March it described the *coup* as not in any sense Russian aggression; on the 13th Kingsley Martin accepted that Masaryk had commited suicide; on the 20th the editorial criticised Russia severely for provoking the very anti-Soviet coalition in the West it had sought to prevent; on the 27th it judged that 'the *majority* of the Czech workers have repudiated the Western form of democratic socialism and substituted totalitarian socialism'.[32] On the same day, clearly unnerved by the 'war fever' that gripped the country, the journal retreated once more into the Third Force concept of an economic and social union of Western Europe which 'does not identify itself with the policy of either of the great antagonists but maintains its struggle for freedom'. As always in a crisis the *New Statesman* seemed to have lost its head.

A slight variation upon the theme of a European socialist Third Force was provided by the notion of a United Socialist States of Europe (USSE); this envisaged a popular European-wide campaign to produce a federation of socialist States in Europe. The idea entered on to the Labour Party stage at the

Margate Conference on 20 May through a resolution moved by Fenner Brockway, the ILP-er who joined the Labour Party in January 1947.[33] The ILP had long championed the notion of a USSE, before and during the war, but the campaign reached a crescendo in the shadow world of the ILP when, following the Truman doctrine, it predicted that World War Three was not only inevitable but imminent; the only salvation of the world lay in the creation of a USSE independent of either 'Wall Street or the Kremlin'.[34]

On 21 and 22 June 1947 a conference involving like-minded socialists from thirteen countries met to co-ordinate the call for a USSE. As the Cold War progressed the ILP proceeded to advocate its plan with a fervour in inverse proportion to its chances of success. In support of his resolution Brockway argued that Britain could not wait for all Europe to go socialist but should lay down a plan for a socialist Europe, drawn up in collaboration with other Western European socialists, which would provide them, and the UK, with a 'winning' political idea.[35] For the NEC Dalton accepted the philosophy of the USSE but disagreed with Brockway. We must, he said, wait until all the native socialists movements of Western Europe had achieved their success. Dalton had earlier made clear the leadership's determination to deal only with governments, not oppositions. 'You should begin,' he said, with a sideswipe of left-wing propagandists, 'not with conclaves of chatterboxes but with functional advances by governments who have the power to make their decisions operative.'[36] The conference endorsed the idealism of the USSE, but Dalton had made it clear that the realism of the party leadership was not being compromised.

Fear that a third world war was imminent was also a feature of pacifist thinking during these months. Why pacifistic socialists should have been so ready to predict a holocaust is not entirely clear — perhaps because their antennae were particularly sensitive to danger or perhaps because their utopian schemes for the reform of the world were better presented in a crisis atmosphere. In January Emrys Hughes had predicted atomic war by 1952 and had advised that, as a first step towards saving the world, Bevin and Molotov should be replaced as Foreign Ministers.[37] Following Bevin's Western union speech, Hughes condemned what he held to be Western preparations for war on the USSR. He demonstrated his tendency to favour the Soviet case by arguing that American war preparations had done much to justify Soviet suspicions;[38] furthermore his newspaper, *Forward*, remained inexplicably silent on the subject of the Czech *coup*. The other major pacifist spokesman, Rhys Davies, was less inclined to extend indulgence to the Soviet Union, which he recognised as a tyranny led by a dictator.[39] However, he equalled Hughes in his forebodings of war and in his passionate opposition to anything likely to conduce to it.

The fellow-travellers' banner was held principally by Zilliacus during the spring of 1948. In a speech which Tom Driberg described as his 'best yet'[40] during the January debate, he criticised Western union as a return to power politics; Fulton was now a reality. Zilliacus altered his position slightly on the subject of the Marshall Plan, which he admitted was a generous offer that Russia had been mistaken in rejecting, but he was opposed to the overall anti-communist policy of which the plan was only a part; this policy, he shrewdly observed, would also thwart the forces of social change in Asia and Europe.[41] The Co-operative *Reynolds' News* pursued similar arguments, welcoming events in Rumania and the progress of revolution in Eastern Europe, where the paper believed 'great and wonderful things are being attempted by and on behalf of the common people'.[42] On 24 January *Reynolds' News* spoke for most of the Labour Party's fellow-travellers and even for the Communist Party in calling for an end to dollar dependence, a major settlement with the USSR and a new attitude towards Eastern Europe, but like the pacifist weekly *Forward*, the *News* maintained silence upon Czechoslovakia. Zilliacus exercised no such restraint; he described it as a 'bloodless semi-revolution carried out in constitutional forms'.[42] Platts-Mills saw it as a 'great victory for the workers'.[44] On 17 April the same MP featured in the *Daily Herald* headline 'Platts-Mills sends telegram'. This was the famous 'Nenni telegram', signed by thirty-seven MPs, expressing support for Pietro Nenni, the Italian socialist whose party was fighting the crucial Italian elections in alliance with the powerful Italian Communist Party. In the delicately balanced situation in Italy it was thought that the communists might seize control, and the British Labour Party was consequently opposed to Nenni's political position. Even the *N.S. and N.* parted company with Nenni; in its opinion collaboration with communists in government was a risk which 'no socialist can now accept'.[44] Michael Foot and Jennie Lee felt strongly enough to put down a motion repudiating Nenni.[45]

The Italian press gave prominence to this action by a large group of Labour MPs in defiance of government policy. The group was surprisingly large for an action which bore the fellow-travellers' hallmark, but the mystery was resolved two days later when sixteen MPs disassociated themselves from the telegram — some claiming that their signatures had been secured under a misunderstanding.[46]

To the NEC this was the final straw. The country was facing great dangers from the threat of foreign aggression and, from their view point, a minority had been consistently sympathising with the source of that aggression. As in 1940 over the explusion of D. N. Pritt, the NEC decided to act firmly. Signs of irritation had long been present. In the January debate, J. J. Lawson had expressed a typical view in stating to 'the world' that Zilliacus spoke only for an 'insignificant proportion of the voters in this country'.[47] In the same debate Attlee accused the apologists of Eastern European regimes of denying human rights.

With the Nenni telegram the party leadership decided the limits of toleration had been reached. On 21 April Morgan Phillips wrote to Platts-Mills on behalf of the NEC, listing the charges against him. Apart from sponsoring the Nenni Telegram they included, for example, his membership of the proscribed British-Soviet Friendship Society.[49] Platts-Mills's reply on 24 April failed to satisfy the NEC, which thereupon took the drastic step of expelling him.[50]

At the 1948 Annual Conference an attempt was made to suspend standing orders to enable Platts-Mills to speak as Cripps had done in 1938, but Morgan Phillips argued against the proposal. Conference endorsed his arguments, but only by 2,560,000 votes to 1,400,300; a strong element in the party instinctively recoils from harsh discipline. The *Daily Herald* was not so squeamish. The editor had no regrets about the expulsion of a man who had 'supported the Italian communists at a critical time in the history of Italy and the West'.[51] In retrospect the leadership may seem to have been unduly heavy-handed — the fellow-traveller element, after all, was an insignificant one which in no way threatened the government's majority on foreign affairs — but the atmosphere of the time was tense, and initiatives like the Nenni telegram attracted press attention abroad and detracted from the unanimous anti-communist stance which the government sought to present to the world.

Government action was also taken against communist infiltration in the civil service. Here again the signs had long been apparent. Laski, a member of the NEC and if anything one of the voices most favourable to the communist case, insisted that, following the creation of the Cominform, and the CPGB's clear allegiance to it, communists should not be allowed to damage Britain in the way they were disrupting France.[52] The *Daily Herald* was even more vehement in ridiculing the CPGB's three-year plan for Britain as a scheme designed to sabotage Britain industrially, and drastically weaken her ability to resist the Soviet Union. In February Morrison drew from Czechoslovakia the lesson that British trade unionists must exercise increased vigilance against 'anti-democratic conspirators who would use industrial power to undermine the democratic State'.[54] During the Commons debate on the Defence White Paper, Alexander bitterly attacked the communist amendment to reduce Britain's armed forces by half a million men as a specious attempt to reduce her defences against enemies 'without and within'.[54]

On 15 March Attlee informed the House that no communists (nor, for good measure, 'fascists') would henceforward be allowed to work in the civil service, on the ground that their political ideas might involve 'acceptance by the individual of a loyalty which in certain circumstances can be inimical to the State'.[55] The *Daily Herald* affirmed that the order would receive the unfailing support of the Labour Party, but this confidence proved premature, for forty-five Labour MPs placed their names on a motion objecting to the measure.[56] Only five of the signatories, however, felt strongly enough to carry their arguments into the division lobbies.[57] The *Daily Worker* had no doubt that this measure by the Attlee government meant that a 'police State' in Britain was imminent; the communist daily did not say whether this police State would be more or less draconian than those recently created in Eastern Europe.[58]

iv

Following the Czechoslovak *coup*, Sir Pierson Dixon, formerly Bevin's private secretary but now His Majesty's ambassador in Prague, wrote in his diary that the PLP had swung round decisively against international communism.[59] Whilst this was an over-simplification — the process was a long and gradual one rather than a sudden change of heart occasioned by the *coup* — Labour Party feeling against Russia naturally hardened substantially during the spring of 1948. Images of Russia were also responsible for the domestic measures taken by the Labour government against communism at home. The Anglo-Soviet trade agreement of December 1947 had raised some expectation that Russia would be more likely to co-operate in the political field, but the events in Rumania and, much more important, in Czechoslovakia massively outweighed any possible improvement in the Soviet image; there were, moreover, other factors at work, not so important in terms of international relations but nevertheless extremely detrimental.

In 13 January Dimitrov, the communist Bulgarian leader and hero of the Reichstag fire trial, threatened nine dissenting deputies in the Bulgarian Assembly with the same fate as Petkov. (Petkov was hanged in September 1947 for 'conspiracy against the State'. A British note of complaint at the time described it as 'judicial murder'.)

[60] The symbolic importance of Dimitrov has been referred to in an earlier chapter;[61] the effect of his desertion from Western standards of political conduct in the view of Laski made 'most decent people sick at heart'.[62]

A further issue centred around the Soviet wives who in the spring of 1948 were still apart from their husbands. On 25 February Bevin deplored an attitude that was 'entirely incomprehensible to us',[63] but he was unwilling to take any action or to indulge in the retaliatory measures which left-wing MPs Hugh Delargy and Woodrow Wyatt (also at that time a left-winger) were urging upon him.[64] Replying to a debate on the subject on 9 March, Hector

The genesis of NATO I 185

McNeil gave some idea of the damage this issue had done to Labour Party images of Russia: 'The Soviet administration must understand that this single action has cost them more possible friends than any political activity in which they have indulged.'[65]

Two other points deserve a mention. In February the USA published the damning Soviet–German secret treaties of 1939, and in March the Geneva conference on 'Freedom of Information and the Press' condemned Soviet press censorship.[66] A more important factor, touched on frequently during the second half of this study, was the greatly improved image of the USA.

It has already been noted than an improvement in the image of one of the super-powers tended to take place at the expense of the other. As the American image improved the Soviet one suffered by comparison. However, in the spring of 1948 an extra dimension was added to Labour images of America; the USA was now regarded as a source not just of economic sustenance but of military protection against the very real threat of attack now perceived from the USSR. It was a symptom of the highly charged atmosphere that Arthur Koestler could write in *Tribune*, 'There will either be a Pax Americana or there will be no Pax,' without unleashing a storm of criticism in the correspondence columns. Moreover those left-wing critics who tried to equate Soviet shortcomings with those found in the USA were having a hard time of it; as Koestler wrote in the same article, it is foolish to equate an 'imperfect democracy' with an 'imperfect totalitarian regime'.[66]

As already noted, the party leadership had become very outspoken in its attacks upon Russia. Bevin, his alliance policy decided upon and safely under way, was now bluntly condemnatory. Attlee added to his New York remarks a second series of criticisms which stimulated some defensive responses from Sidney Silverman, Emrys Hughes[67] and Ian Mikardo,[68] but over the party as a whole this hard line from the leadership probably had the effect of compounding the manifold doubts that already existed.

The disenchanted Keep Left element associated with *Tribune* now shared the Bevinite image. An interesting exchange took place between Michael Foot and George Bernard Shaw revealing the huge gulf which had been opened up between the *Tribune*–Webb–Shaw attitudes of the 1930s and the *Tribune* of 1948. Under normal circumstances Shaw's eccentricities would have occasioned little comment but, given the atmosphere of the time, Foot could not allow his claim that Stalin was 'the greatest statesman on earth'[69] to pass uncontested. Did Shaw really think, he asked, that with 'rigid censorship, forced labour, secret police, and show trials' the atmosphere in the Kremlin, Belgrade and Prague was anything other than sheer terror?[70] His judgement now doubly distorted by the harsh rebuff which he felt he had received, Shaw replied that Foot was calling for war with Russia 'like Bevin and Mosley rolled into one'.[71] In defending 'the Fabian sage' Sidney Silverman revealed that the 'thirties image was not completely destroyed on the left: 'Russia and the Russians have been totally transformed, morally, spiritually, industrially, socially and politically in a generation.'[72]

The fellow-traveller image survived virtually intact throughout this period, the only important deviation being provided by Zilliacus's criticism of Russian withdrawal from the Marshall Plan; as in 1939 over Finland, he refused to go the whole way with the communists.

The *N.S. and N.*, important as a mouthpiece of the Third Force school of thought, was relatively generous in its interpretation of the Soviet role in Czechoslovakia. But its vacillations concealed an increasingly critical assessment of the narrow and provocative nature of Russian foreign policy, and its gradual acceptance of the Marshall Plan as an essential and acceptable aid to European recovery revealed that its attitude towards America was becoming far less critical. An article appearing on 24 January deserves special attention. Entitled 'The Russia Complex' (and written by Richard Crossman), it analysed with great perception the problems inherent in Labour Party perceptions of Russia.

The article explained that despite their domestic conflict with communism at home, some socialists still felt in 1948 an attachment to the Soviet Union 'all the stronger because it is remote, strange and slightly terrifying'. It was not only the intellectuals but 'countless working-class socialists who wanted to think well of the USSR and give it the benefit of the doubt whenever they can'. The Soviet Union was an integral part of the Labour movement's past. In the days when Labour had been excluded from national affairs, socialists had transferred some of their patriotism to Russia 'because patriotism seemed to be a Conservative monopoly'. Russia had been a vision of Utopia at the time when the Labour Party needed a vision. But the time had now come when Labour had to overcome this emotional attachment. Socialists must cease to judge political friends on the basis of their friendship towards Russia, must change the 'yardstick' by which 'left' distinguishes from 'right', and must 'break down the fixation of Russia as a Utopia'. Social democracy was now strong enough to change the world by itself; it no longer needed the 'myth of Soviet Russia' to 'compensate for its sense of frustration'.

Even before the Czechoslovak *coup*, therefore, Crossman had been calling for the abandonment of the political role which the image of Russia had played in British socialism. The ostensible reason was that British socialism had 'grown up' and no longer needed this image, but there can be little doubt that the major, unspoken reason was that since the war this utopian image, once widely shared, had been almost totally eroded for all but an increasingly diminishing section of the Labour Party. At least some of the inconsistencies noted in the N.S. and N. editorial policy can be explained in terms of its efforts to overcome its own 'Russia complex'; its degree of success during the subsequent highly eventful year is one of the themes developed in the next chapter.

Notes

1 Nicolson, Vol. 3, *1945–63*, pp. 115–16.
2 446 H.C. Deb., 502–18, 22 January 1948.
3 *Daily Herald*, 5 January 1948.
4 Britain sent a note of complaint on 2 February, see 447 H.C. Deb., 1444, 16 February 1948 (written answer).
5 445 H.C. Deb., 1874–87, 18 December 1947.
6 Molotov had virtually admitted this to Bidault in Paris, Bevin revealed, 446 H.C. Deb., 389–92, 21 January 1948.
7 *Ibid.*, 398.
8 Lucius Clay, *Decision in Germany* (London, 1950), pp. 350–1.
9 On 26 February 1948 Britain, America and France sent a note of protest to the USSR, *The Times*, 27 February 1948.
10 *LPCR 1948*, p. 23.
11 See also Dalton's thoughts on the Czech *coup*, *LPCR 1948*, p. 118.
12 *Daily Herald*, 9 March 1948.
13 Feis, p. 305.
14 450, H.C. Deb., 1105, 4 May 1948.
15 *Ibid.*, 1110.
16 Feis, p. 310.
17 *LPCR 1948*, p. 116.
18 *Ibid.*, pp. 24 and 224.
19 *Daily Herald*, 9 February 1948.
20 Windmuller, p. 130.
21 Ibid., p. 135.
22 *TUCR 1948*, p. 199.
23 See, for example, J. J. Lawson, 446 H.C. Deb., 447, and F. Bellenger, 450 H.C. Deb., 1173.
24 *LPCR 1948*, p. 200.
25 Judgement based on interviews with MPs.
26 *Tribune*, 12 December 1948.
27 *Ibid.*, 27 February 1948.
28 *Daily Herald*, 24 February 1948.
29 They were D. Bruce, D. Crossman, M. Foot, R. W. G. MacKay, I. Mikardo and W. Wyatt, *Daily Herald*, 22 January 1948.
30 450 H.C. Deb., 1136, 4 May 1948.
31 446 H.C. Deb., 561–9, 21 January 1948.
32 Author's emphasis.
33 See *New Leader*, 18 January 1947. Fenner Brockway delayed joining the Labour Party until after the death of James Maxton, the much-loved ILP leader — interview with Brockway.

34 Headline of *New Leader*, 18 October 1947.
35 *LPCR 1948*, pp. 172–3.
36 *Ibid.*, p. 177.
37 *Forward*, 17 January 1948.
38 *Ibid.*, 31 January 1948.
39 450 *H.C. Deb.*, 1358–62, 5 May 1948, see also *LPCR 1948*, p. 159.
40 *Reynolds' News*, 24 January 1948.
41 See Zilliacus's speech, *LPCR 1948*, p. 185, letter to *Tribune*, 28 May,and speech 450 *H.C. Deb.*, 1327, 5 May 1948.
42 *Reynolds' News*, 18 January 1948.
43 Caute, *The Fellow Travellers*, p. 283.
44 Jackson, *Rebels and Whips*, p. 203.
45 *Manchester Guardian*, 20 April 1948.
46 The twenty-two definites were: G. Austin, P. Barstow, T. Braddock, G. Cove, S. O. Davies, W. Dobbie, E. Hughes, L. Hutchinson, H. Lever, J. D. Mack, M. Orbach, G. Royle, J. Silverman, S. S. Silverman, G. Solley, Vernon, W. Warbey, K. Zilliacus, J. Platts-Mills, S. Swingler, G. Bing, H. Davies (last three also members of Keep Left).
47 446 *H.C. Deb.*, 447, 21 January 1948.
48 *Ibid.*, 621. On 27 February the NEC took the unusual step of refuting the fellow-traveller accusation that the Marshall Plan was a 'Sinister plot' to prepare an attack on the USSR — *Daily Herald*, 28 February 1948.
49 For a list of proscribed organisations at this time, see appendix section, *LPCR 1949*, p. 223.
50 Jackson, p. 202.
51 *Daily Herald*, 29 April 1948.
52 *Forward*, 3 January 1948.
53 *Daily Herald*, 27 February 1948.
54 *Ibid.*, 2 March 1948.
55 448 *H.C. Deb.*, 1703–8, 15 March 1948.
56 The EDM was signed on 17 March 1948. The signatories included the following: Mikardo, Warbey, E. Hughes, Edelman, Solley, Platts-Mills. A mixture, in fact, of Keep Left, fellow-travellers and pacifists. Crossman and Foot did not sign. On 18 March Ernest Thurtle moved an amendment to this EDM endorsing the government's action. It was eventually signed by twenty-four MPs mostly from the right of the party. They included: R. Gunter, A. Crawley, J. Mann, Thomas Reid and Ivor Thomas.
57 *The Times*, 14 April 1955, article by W. L. Guttsman on Labour rebellions.
58 *Daily Worker*, 16 March 1948.
59 Dixon, p. 254.
60 *Daily Herald*, 14 January 1948. Bevin refers to the event, 446 *H.C. Deb.*, 389, 21 January 1948.
61 See p. 000.
62 *Forward*, 24 January 1948. The article was entitled 'Dimitrov's retreat from Reichstag'.
63 447 *H.C. Deb.*, 1936, 25 February 1948.
64 *Ibid.*, 1198, 9 March 1948. Also written reply to Wyatt, *ibid.*, 143, 16 February 1948.
65 *Ibid.*, 1204, 9 March 1948.

66 *Daily Herald*, 31 March 1948.
67 *Tribune*, 18 June 1948.
68 *Forward*, 11 June 1948.
69 See *Daily Herald* editorial, 4 May 1948.
70 *Ibid.*, 13 May 1948.
71 *Tribune*, 4 June 1948.
72 *Ibid.*

11 *The Genesis of NATO, II. The Berlin blockade and its aftermath*

> In retrospect nothing that the Labour Government has done in foreign affairs seems more reasonable, necessary and obvious than helping to organise NATO to protect Britain and Western Europe from Russian military aggression. Likewise, nothing it did represented a greater divergence from traditional socialist principles of foreign policy. [Richard Rose, 'The relation of socialist principles to British Labour foreign policy, 1945–51' (unpublished Ph.D. thesis, Bodleian Library), Oxford, 1961, p. 307]

i

On 24 June 1948 the Soviet Union closed all road and rail links with West Berlin from West Germany, precipitating a crisis which, except for Cuba in 1961, came closer to causing war with the West than any other post-war crisis. The uneasy peace which had developed into the Cold War had finally reached a temperature where it threatened to transform itself into a world-wide, possibly atomic, war. Berlin looked to be the flashpoint.

The struggle for Europe in these early days of the Cold War was rather like a game of chess. Communist ploys in France and Italy[1] had been successfully countered by the summer of 1948, and in Greece[2] they were making no headway, but the really important struggle revolved around the centre of the board — Germany. The Western position was dangerously weak in that deep in Soviet territory it had a pawn, Berlin, which was extremely difficult to defend. This pawn was crucial. Whoever held it would prevent his opponent from fully controlling Eastern Germany and, it was believed, control of Berlin also held the key to control of Western Germany. The West believed that if the Soviets gained Berlin they would eventually have the whole of Germany, control of Germany would lead to control of Europe, and with communist successes multiplying in China they might well achieve their stated ambition of claiming the whole world for communism. General Lucius Clay, the American commander in Berlin, had seen the situation in these terms as early as 10 April, when he informed the Pentagon that 'We have lost Czechoslovakia ... We retreat from Berlin. When Berlin falls — West Germany will be next. If we mean to hold Europe against communism, we must not budge from Berlin ... I believe the future of democracy requires us to stay.'[3] Bevin was of the same opinion. On 4 May, when the Soviets were just beginning to apply pressure upon Berlin from the west, he stated, 'We are in Berlin as of right. It is our intention to stay there.'[4] On 20 March 1948 the Four Power Control Council set up at Potsdam to supervise Germany's transition to peace broke down when the Soviet delegation walked out; it never met again. The Soviet Union, keen to frustrate Western plans to create a unified West German government, almost immediately began to interfere with Western access to Berlin, access which the West claimed was guaranteed by prior agreements.[5] The Russians had other reasons for coveting the former capital. It was a symbol of Western presence in the Soviet zone, a revealing window for the West in the fabric of the Iron Curtain and, perhaps most important, a window into the West for East Germany. To close this window would help to insulate Eastern Europe from the West; it would also be a lesson to any satellite country, for instance Yugoslavia, which might be contemplating a unilateral slackening of the relationship with Moscow.[6]

The Western attitude towards Germany had altered rapidly as a result of Soviet behaviour. Following the war, the emphasis had been upon denazification, occupation, the extraction of reparation and the prevention of Germany from ever reaching a position of strength from which she could again threaten the security of Europe. Now (with France beginning to fall into line) the emphasis was upon restoring Germany economically and politically, and bestowing upon her an increasing degree of self-government. Behind this new policy lay two motives: the first was to deny Soviet attempts to control a unified Germany; the second, to errect a resuscitated West Germany as a bulwark against the USSR. On 2 June the London conference concluded with recommendations that Germany should be fully integrated into plans for European recovery, that a federal constitution for West Germany should be prepared, and that an international authority (excluding Russia) should control the distribution (though *not* the production) of coke, coal and steel from the Ruhr. Amid Soviet protests, this programme began to be effected. The Berlin crisis was triggered by the Western decision on 18 June to introduce the long overdue currency reform in the western zones of Germany.

On 23 June Sokolovsky declared that the new currency would not be allowed to circulate in West Berlin because 'Berlin is located in the Soviet zone of occupation and economically forms a part of that zone'.[7] Following this implied renunciation of the four-power control of Berlin agreed at

Potsdam, the Western powers decided to introduce the reformed currency in their zones of Berlin. The Russians thereupon imposed their blockade.

On 25 June the West faced several options: threaten war (which, because of Soviet conventional superiority, would almost certainly have to be nuclear); test the Russian will in some way, for example by pushing an armoured column towards Berlin; supply Berlin with essential materials by air as a stop-gap measure; or surrender Berlin to the Soviets and consolidate a more tenable position on the western side of the Iron Curtain.

In the House of Commons on 25 June Raymond Blackburn's private notice question sought an indication of which option Bevin was going to pursue. In reply Bevin read out a bald statement of events in Berlin, but when pressed for a definite assurance that the West intended to stay in the city he preferred not to add to the statement he had made, on the grounds that a 'delicate state of affairs' existed. Was he prevaricating here? Was the cast-iron guarantee of 4 May being re-examined in the Foreign Office? It would indeed be surprising if not, for the Pentagon on 25 June was anything but decisive.[8] On 28 June Truman resolved the indecision by deciding that America would stay in Berlin and that B29 bombers (capable of carrying atomic weapons) should be sent to Germany. The option of a temporary airlift had already been taken, and supplies were first landed on 26 July. But few seriously believed that the airlift would enable Berlin to survive for more than thirty days.

On 30 June, no doubt reassured by Yugoslavia's incredible defection from the Soviet camp, Bevin addressed the House of Commons on the subject of Germany. He removed any lingering doubts about British intentions in Berlin: 'We cannot abandon those stout-hearted Berlin democrats who are refusing to bow to Soviet pressure ... We recognise that a grave situation might arise, we shall have to ask the House to face it ... His Majesty's Government can see no alternative between that and surrender, and none of us can accept surrender.'[9] The last sentence was received with a great cheer. Bevin made it clear, therefore, that in defending Berlin, Britain was prepared to go to war. There would be no Munich this time. To strengthen the Western position he agreed, without delay, to the stationing of B29s on British soil.[11] On 3 July Sokolovsky made clear the primary purpose of the blockade; it would be lifted if the West abandoned its plans for West Germany. Russia was offering not to take the vulnerable pawn of Berlin as long as the position of the West's 'queen' was weakened.

On 6 July there was some indication, when heavy fighter activity took place near the air lanes, that the Soviets would interfere with the airlift. They did not advance beyond this, however. The Russians had raised the temperature to crisis point by blockading Berlin; the West had countered with the airlift, at first as a temporary expedient but increasingly, as its success was proved, as a realistic lifeline. The Soviet Union had not dared to raise the temperature beyond this, as it would have involved an unacceptable risk of war. Neither side wanted war, but both sides were prepared to risk the bluff that they were the less afraid of such an outcome. The airlift proved to be the perfect option; not so provocative as to precipitate a war and yet effective enough to enable Berlin to survive and thereby call the Soviet bluff. The blockade having failed in the short term, the communists stepped up their efforts to undermine the morale of the West Berliners, using a variety of intimidations and inducements.

The Social Democrats in the City Assembly, however, exerted powerful pro-Western leadership, and throughout the long siege the spirit of its citizens scarcely wavered. On the diplomatic level the West refused to negotiate until the blockade was lifted, but nevertheless diplomatic contacts at the ambassadorial level proceeded. On 2 August 1948 the three Western ambassadors met Stalin in Moscow. No agreement ensued. In early September the communists again increased their pressure and Truman feared that the world was once more 'very close to war'.[12] Bevin too was privately nervous, but publicly held firm:

We have to make our own position firm and secure. Berlin stands out as a symbol of resistance, a sort of salient. So far as I am concerned, I felt that when that blockade was put on that a great choice had to be made. We made it. It was either to stand firm there or turn south and go to another Munich.[13]

Some Conservative leaders, perhaps exicted by the Munich analogy, urged on him an even tougher policy. (On one occasion Harold MacMillan actually described the blockade as 'an act of appeasement'.)[14] In the Cabinet Bevin did not want for tough advice; Aneurin Bevan, the wartime champion of a Second Front to relieve the Russian war effort, favoured the strategy in the early days of the blockade of pushing an armoured column towards Berlin.[15]

Within the party the degree of consensus behind Bevin's handling of the crisis was massive. In the debate on 30 June it was the voices on the centre and right which dominated. F. J. Bellenger, for example, saw it as a Munich situation, a trial of strength in which the West must not possibly fail.[16] Richard Stokes,[17] John Hynd[18] and Reginald Paget[19] spoke in the same vein. On 27 July the National Council of Labour gave the official backing of the whole Labour Party to Bevin's foreign policy.[20] The *Daily Herald* recognised that since the beginning of 1948 an 'armed attack on Western Europe ... could no longer be ruled out of calculations'.[21] The editorial of 19 July, in welcoming the arrival on British soil of atomic-bomb-carrying B29s, judged it a fearful commentary on the Kremlin's 'dictatorial rule', a theme which the Labour daily developed, comparing Soviet tactics to the old Nazi methods.[22] The TUC was similarly solid behind Bevin and proceeded to 'declare war' on communists within its ranks.

Some elements on the left exhibited symptoms of hysteria during the crisis but other sections kept surprisingly cool. *Tribune* condemned the 'calculated barbarity' of the Russian action and strongly opposed any deal in which the future of Berlin would be traded; Henry Wallace's advice that the West should withdraw was condemned as appeasement. Laski also had no doubts whether the West should remain in Berlin. An audience of French socialists roundly cheered his assertion that Britain would stay in the city. 'We have the right,' he told them 'to stand up to the Russians on any question regarding the future of Germany.'[25] Crossman added his voice: 'Of course we are staying in.'[24] British policy in Germany over the previous six months had been 'completely right'.[25] The *N.S. and N.*, doubtless reflecting Crossman's informed arguments in editorial discussions, had consistently backed Bevin's German policy. An editorial on 17 April had, remarkably, forcast that the Russians would make a bid for Berlin when the West attempted to reform the currency, and, 'whatever the risks', Britain had to 'carry through the currency reform and set up a German government at Frankfurt'. On 12 June the *N.S. and N.* again expressed support for this policy, insisting that the government 'see it through'.

The *N.S. and N.*, however, took a long time to react to the Berlin crisis, devoting its 3 July edition to Tito's 'astonishing' defection, and when it came to express its views on Berlin its position was equivocal. On 10 July it feared that the West would ultimately have to use force to clear a route to the beleagured city; the airlift, as 'every expert knows', could not be anything other than a short-term summer expedient 'and inadequate at that'. On 17 July the journal began to describe the position as 'untenable' and urged that a face-saving formula be found. As usual it vacillated, not advocating withdrawal bur nervously reluctant to endorse a firm stand. This tendency persisted despite a severe deterioration in the editor's personal attitude towards Russia. On 4 September Kingsley Martin reported on his experiences at a Soviet-sponsored peace conference at Wroclaw in Poland. His article, was entitled 'Hyenas and other reptiles'.[26]

This conference had been an attempt to muster intellectuals in support of communist policies, yet it turned out to be a crude propaganda harangue. Martin was horrified at the way in which everyone who displayed even the slightest disagreement with the USSR, even sympathetic intellectuals like Sartre or Malraux, were automatically branded as hyenas or jackals. Martin's biographer believed that this episode more than any other 'finally disenchanted Kingsley about Soviet communism as an alternative to the capitalist economy'[27] and this judgement was borne out by Martin's own recollections in an interview with the author in 1968. In answer to the question 'When did you lose faith in Soviet communism?' he cited the Wroclaw conference and easily recalled the 'Hyenas and reptiles' article. Martin was thoroughly disillusioned, yet he must have known of these Soviet practices, for his journal frequently reported them. It was only when personally and unpleasantly confronted with the intractable reality of Soviet attitudes and behaviour that he was moved to speak out as strongly as he did. In the same interview cited above, he went on to say that, in retrospect, Soviet policy had been no different from British imperialist policy in the nineteenth century, but, as will be shown in a later section of this chapter, the editorial policy of the *N.S. and N.* was still a long way from such a position in the autumn of 1948.

Faced with the Berlin blockade, the former advocates of the Third Force remained silent. 'Keep Left', once the champion of a Third Force, also disintegrated during the summer of 1948. In a letter to *Tribune* Hugh Jenkins, MP, noted its demise and dryly observed that Crossman and Foot were now 'safe' centre men.[28] Crossman agreed that Keep Left had faded away, explaining that Russia's refusal to co-operate in the Marshall Plan had rendered obsolete Keep Left's proposals for an independent Third Force between Russia and the USA.[29] Crossman might have added that the Berlin blockade had made it clear that defence against the Soviet threat rather than neutrality towards both main powers was the first priority.

Labour pacifists were naturally desperately concerned over the dangers of war. Emrys Hughes eschewed criticism of Russian behaviour in favour of successive calls for a four-power summit, a world peace plan and a world recovery plan including Russia.[30] Hughes's reasoning was along the following lines. Do we want war? No. Do the Russians want war? No. There are no rational reasons why either side should go to war, and therefore all parties should meet to discuss their differences. There was no appreciation in this analysis of the complex issues that divided West from East or of the extent to which both sides, without desiring war, were willing to risk it in support of their objectives. Rhys Davies was similarly confused, expressing pained bewilderment at the actions of the Russian leaders, some of whom, he complained, he actually knew![31] *Reynolds' News* was scarcely less facile, urging blindly on 18 July that war 'cannot be allowed to happen'.

The voices of fellow-travellers in Parliament were surprisingly muted during the crisis. In the 30 June debate the Conservative MP A. C. M. Spearman noted that the fellow-travellers had been mostly absent, signifying 'the very great measure of agreement among members of the House on the subject of Russia'.[32] Hector McNeil noted in the same debate that only the communist Gallacher had offered criticism of Bevin. As in the crucial debates in the autumn of 1939, Gallacher's was the only voice to put forward the Soviet case, arguing on this occasion that Britain should leave Berlin, which was in the Soviet zone, break away from American monopoly capitalism and nationalise industry both in the UK and in the British zone of Germany.[33] Bevin dealt with Gallacher contemptuously (as indeed he did with all fellow-travellers and communists during these months), referring to him as a 'parrot' and reminding the House of the communists' conduct in 1940; their behaviour, Bevin dramatically stated, was 'burnt' into his memory.[34]

In the wake of the crisis the fellow-travellers confined themselves to minor acts of protest: Solley and Hutchinson joined the expelled Pritt and Platts-Mills in voting against Marshal Aid,[35] on 6 July Platts-Mills described as 'blackguardly' Richard Stokes's claim that seventeen million people were held in concentration camps in the USSR,[36] and in the 22 September debate Lester Hutchinson argued that Berlin was *not* a test case in relations with the Soviet Union, and that Britain should free itself from servitude to the USA.[37]

The Berlin blockade, therefore, coming as it did in the wake of the infamous Czechoslovak *coup*, weakened still further the scant remaining Labour sympathies for Russia. The attempt to starve out the population of two million West Berliners was a clever, even daring, political move, but it was one which in the public mind made heroes of the West Berliners and villians of the Soviet leaders in the Kremlin. During the crisis the traditional indulgence extended to Russia on the left was nowhere to be seen, and even the fellow-travellers forebore to criticise Bevin's firm stand. The dramatic airlift further improved America's image in a party which in the past had regarded America with a fair degree of hostility.

ii

In the autumn of 1948 the focus of diplomatic activity moved to the UN when America and Britain took the Berlin problem to the Security Council. Propaganda speeches were made. Bevin reiterated the usual list of Western camplaints: the USSR was pursuing Lenin's policy of inevitable and 'frightful collisions' with the bourgeois world. He accused the Soviet spider of wanting Greece within its web, of maintaining a threatening level of armaments, of secrecy, of censorship, of bad faith over disarmament proposals. Vyshinsky delivered the characteristic Soviet replies. Small wonder that Attlee commented in a broadcast that the UN 'often seems to be only a forum for the exhibition of differences'.[38]

One element in Vyshinky's speech presaged a new strand in Soviet policy: his offer of a disarmament plan. Over the next few months this tactic was to be used with increasing persistence. Bevin's instinct was to distrust plans which would weaken the West and did not allow for inspection of Soviet armament levels.

On 25 October nine members of the Security Council voted for a resolution calling for the immediate lifting of the Berlin blockade and the resumption of four-power talks on currency. Two negative votes were cast, those of the Soviet Union and the Ukraine. The *Daily Herald* noted that this was the twenty-eighth use of the veto by the Russians.[39]

Under the continuing stimulus of the Blockade and further tightening of the Soviet grip on Eastern Europe,[40] the Western allies drew yet closer towards giving independence to Western Germany and creating a North Atlantic mutual defence treaty. In the autumn delegates from the states of Western Germany met under the leadership of Konrad Adenauer to draw up a provisional constitution (or Basic Law, as it was called). Already the Soviet Union was denouncing the planned puppet government of American capitalism.[41] One disturbing aspect of the plans concerned the proposed international authority for the Ruhr. Aided and abetted by the American government, the Germans were keen to keep controls as weak as possible, and so the provisional agreement of 28 December envisaged a six-power authority (excluding the USSR of course) with only vague supervisory powers over the distribution of coal and steel; ownership of the Ruhr industries would return to private German hands. When considering these proposals on 21 December Bevin told a reluctant British Cabinet that it 'had to make up its mind whether it regarded Germany as still a danger or as an ally of Western Europe'.[42] The exhortation contrasted nicely with his statement in Cabinet in early 1947 when he judged that Germany rather than Russia represented the greater threat to the security of Europe.[43]

Western Europe itself, in the form of the Permanent Commission of the Brussels Pact, had already produced a draft Atlantic Pact on 10 December. During January and February the initiative passed to Acheson, who entered into discussions with Senate leaders and other departments of state. Bevin had explained his alliance strategy to Dalton when lunching at the Foreign Office on 15 October 1948.

Prophetically Bevin foresaw the achievement of a 'balance with Russia which will last a long time. We shan't reach an agreement but we shall live together.'[44] He was trying to organise the 'middle of the planet' — Western Europe, the Mediterranean and the Commonwealth. At the same meeting he allowed himself a fascinating piece of speculation; if Britain pushed ahead and developed Africa he believed she 'could have the US dependent on us and eating out of our hands in four or five years — the US is very barren of essential minerals and in Africa we have them all'. By any interpretation this was a strangely 'imperialist' line of thought for a socialist foreign secretary.⁴⁵

Labour Party images of Russia hardened still further in the winter months to the point where they resembled those of the winter of 1939–40. The *Daily Herald* suggested on 5 October that to criticise the Russians as 'Asiatic' or 'oriental' was to insult the peoples from the East. *Tribune* celebrated the thirty-first anniversary of the Bolshevik revolution with an article entitled 'A revolution betrayed'. *Tribune* was worried, however, whether the West would overreact to the Soviet threat in the form of a right-wing backlash. It anticipated some of the characteristic future criticisms of NATO in fearing that the USA would foist upon Britain such odious right-wing partners as a France led by De Gaulle or, worst of all, Franco's Spain.⁴⁶ The *N.S. and N.* seemed to share some of *Tribune's* disillusions with the Soviet system of government and also opposed the spread of communism in Europe (though not necessarily in Asia), but it insisted that Russia presented no military threat to the West and that Russia had not been 'guilty of military aggression at any time since 1945.'⁴⁷ The *N.S. and N.* was also, along with Labour pacifists and fellow-travellers, not to mention Harold Laski, fairly receptive to Soviet disarmament proposals and peace initiatives.⁴⁸ *Tribune*, however, sided with the *Daily Herald* and the Labour Party Secretary, Morgan Phillips, who warned the party against bogus 'peace conferences'.

At home the TUC intensified its campaign against communists who, the General Council maintained in a statement issued on 27 October, were attempting to wreck economic recovery 'in the interests of a foreign power'.⁵⁰ The call to all loyal trade unionists to resist communist sabotage was heard to some effect by the NUM; on 17 December its communist official, Arthur Horner, was upbraided by his executive for speaking at the CGT conference in Paris⁵¹ and for supporting French strikers.⁵² The TUC had more or less decided to pull out of the WFTU, now a hostile organisation effectively beyond its control.

Deakin foreshadowed this decision on 28 September. He described the WFTU as merely a platform for the Russians to engage in the glorification of Soviet life, and declared he was not prepared to see British trade union money spent upon such purposes.⁵³ In October 1948 the TUC decided to propose a suspension of the WFTU for one year, the reasoning being that a period of 'cold storage' might succeed in holding the organisation together.⁵⁴ At the 17 January meeting of the Executive Bureau in Paris, Deakin and Tewson moved their resolution. After two and a half hours' discussion Deakin moved a vote, whereupon uproar ensued. Deakin is said to have remarked cryptically, 'Well, the situation is clear,' before picking up his papers and walking out, followed by the Dutch and the Americans.⁵⁵

'So ends,' commented the *Daily Herald*, 'the latest and biggest of many attempts over the last hundred years to build an effective trade union international.' The *Herald* editorial had no doubt where to lay the blame. The basic aims of the organisation had been non-political — to improve the working conditions of workers in all lands — but the communists had persistently intrigued to make the organisation a tool for Moscow's political propaganda.[56] In retrospect it seems naive indeed that anyone could ever have regarded such objectives as non-political.

The WFTU continued in existence with its communist majority now uncontested. The Western organisational response, however, was not long in coming. On 7 December 1949 the International Confederation of Free Trade Unions was formed. The trade union world too now reflected the bipolar division of politics based upon the two post-war super-powers.

As British defence policy began to be overhauled in accordance with the needs of the emergent North Atlantic Pact, the *Daily Herald* resignedly accepted the new diversion of resources as inevitable, attributing the need purely to Soviet hostility. The *N.S and N.* attitude reflected the germ of future left-wing hostility to the expensive military aspect of NATO. The 25 September editorial deprecated what it saw as the beginning of an arms race between East and West. Britain needed Marshall Aid not for armaments but to rebuild her economy; this would be her best antidote to communism. 'Once we regard a hot war against Russia as inevitable,' the article concluded, 'we shall indubitably lose the cold war against communism.' In December the government introduced an amendment to the National Service Act, proposing that the period of National Service should be extended from twelve months to the eighteen which the government had originally envisaged. Some opposition was inevitable, but the government this time was firm, its resolution tempered, no doubt, by the threat of Montgomery and the other military members of the Defence Council to resign unless the measure was passed.[57]

In the debate on the second reading the opponents of conscription — Ellis Smith, Victor Yates, Rhys Davies — mentioned foreign affairs not at all, but the high proportion of 'Nenni' signatories among those who voted against the government (nine out of the forty-one, with the rest almost certainly deliberately abstaining) suggests that for the fellow-travellers the foreign policy implications of the extension of service were very much in their minds. Of the disbanded Keep Left group only Mikardo and Swingler voted against (Swingler had voted *for* conscription in April 1947), whilst Crossman, the central figure in the victory of the left in April 1947, now joined six other Keep Left members in supporting the policy he had previously opposed.[58]

iii

In a letter to Pierson Dixon on Christmas Day 1948, Bevin wrote, 'With all the difficulties, I am very hopeful for 1949. I want to speed on with the Atlantic Pact and with the unity of the West and the Commonwealth, this is the great combination that will save the world.'[59] Four months later, on 4 April, he appended his signature to the North Atlantic Pact.

The pact was indeed historic; in Dalton's words 'the final entanglement of America and Canada in Europe',[60] the institutionalisation of a rigid bipolar world, and the diplomatic wall of containment against communism.[61] Since 1939, as Harold MacMillan noted, the USSR had placed 24 million people and some quarter of a million square miles under its effective control. Following the signing of the pact, no further advances were made in Europe — indeed, on 12 May defeated by the airlift, Stalin raised his blockade of Berlin.

The key element in the treaty was embodied in the carefully worded Article 5, which stated that the signatory powers would 'assist' each other in the event of an external attack upon any of their number with 'such action as it deems necessary including the use of armed force'. In the debate upon the pact on 12 May, the same day the blockade was lifted, Bevin explained and defended the agreement, his speech, according to *The Times*, being punctuated by 'bursts of cheering'.[62] He recited the history of differences with Russia since the end of the second world war: Poland, elections rigged; Bulgaria, opposition destroyed; Rumania, government overthrown; Hungary, Smallholders' party undermined; Czechoslovakia, Soviet-supported *coup*; Greece, civil war fomented; Berlin, access blockaded; Marshall Aid, refusal to participate and an effort to sabotage. As on many other occasions, he invested heavily in the language of socialist foreign policy. The North Atlantic Pact was at heart an agreement by the most powerful country in the world to defend Western Europe from a threat perceived from the Soviet Union, yet it was presented by Bevin and other members of the government in anything but power-political terms. On the contrary, according to Bevin, support for the UN remained the basis of British foreign policy; the pact was simply a regional self-defence grouping under Article 51 of the UN charter, directed at no country. Furthermore it was in no way incompatible with the Anglo-Soviet alliance of 1942, which had commited Britain not to join an alliance that was directed against the Soviet Union. Bevin did stress, however, that the cultural and political tradition of Britain — respect for the individual, political freedom and so on — were at one with almost all the countries of the North Atlantic Pact and were alien to the Soviet bloc.[63]

Reactions within the party were enthusiastic on the right and centre. Bevin had received typical support from such MPs as Hynd, Paget, S. N. Evans and

Thomas Reid.[64] The *Daily Herald* hailed the pact as a 'tremendous forward stride' in the face of a Soviet threat to the whole of Europe and 'other continents besides'.[65] On the left, *Tribune* was highly resistant to the prospect of ever allying with Greece or Spain against Russia but it agreed that the pact was 'Made in Moscow', arguing that to oppose it was to betray socialism; it would now be a long hard trial of strength 'to prevent war and save freedom'.[66] The editors believed that neutrality was now a fantasy, but one member of the editorial board, Ian Mikardo, could not agree. He believed that the Third Force policy advocated by *Keep Left* was still a valid and credible objective. He was strongly opposed to the North Atlantic Pact, which involved a dangerous link-up with the USA and ignored the fact that the USSR was not at all interested in going to war with the West. Foot pointed out that a difference existed between 'the offer of dollars to governments, including socialist ones, by the USA and the provision of concentration camps and execution squads for the socialist victims of Soviet communism'.[67] Stephen Swingler, in supporting Mikardo's arguments, tartly reminded Foot that *Keep Left*, which Foot had helped to write, had said that it 'would be fatal to accept American leadership in exchange for dollars'.[68]

Laski was closer to Mikardo's position. For many years he had suffered on the NEC, debating whether to resign. He was deeply and primarily concerned with foreign affairs, particularly the problems of British attitudes to Palestine and the Soviet Union. On both these issues he was squarely opposed to government policy, but his minority case was regularly crushed by the steamroller of Bevin's support. He became convinced that Bevin was 'implacably hostile' to everything that Labour had ever stood for in foreign policy.

Laski's fight to alter Bevin's NATO policy of confrontation into one of co-operation with the USSR proved to be his last. On 13 February 1949 he wrote to a friend, 'Day by day I hear grim evidence of Ernest Bevin's continuing malice ... The last phase has had a grim effect on me, so deep that I have refused to be nominated for the Executive Committee of the Party.'[68] Laski departed from Labours national counsels in despair, taking his vanquished version of the 'socialist foreign policy' with him. Kingsley Martin (who briefly aspired to Laski's chair at LSE following his death in 1950) opposed NATO on similar grounds. Like Laski and Mikardo, he was convinced that Russia did not want war. He opposed NATO on the grounds that there was 'absolutely no evidence that the Soviet Union is threatening invasion';[70] that personnel changes in the Politburo (e.g. Vyshinsky succeeding Molotov) indicated a softening of Soviet foreign policy; that, bearing in mind Soviet military superiority, a nuclear response was the only credible one to a Soviet attack; and that the existence of NATO might provoke the very attack it was designed to prevent.[71] On 19 March the journal called for an immediate 'world truce' to pre-empt a costly arms race which would weaken the West economically and could only result in war. The cost of NATO was destined to become a crucial issue and one which, under Bevan's leadership, would unite the left in the early part of the next decade. The *N.S and N.* together with Crossman's speech at the Party Conference in June, anticipated some of these arguments.[72]

Pacifists were similarly disturbed by the danger of an ever-increasing arms race. Emrys Hughes and J. Rankin tabled an amendment to the motion to approve the pact, criticising arms spending at a time when the standard of life needed to be raised.[73] Hughes did not believe Russia had any aggressive intentions,[74] and feared that the formation of NATO presaged war.[75] And yet Hughes was inconsistent in being not entirely unhopeful of the pact's chances of success in deterring the Russians; if it did this, he believed, Bevin would go down as one of the greatest Foreign Secretaries of all time and would undoubtedly qualify for the Nobel Peace Prize![76] Rhys Davies, Hughes's inevitable fellow spokesman for the pacifist school of thought, had no doubt that Russia was in the wrong and that fellow-traveller criticisms of the USA were unjustified, but he could not embrace the idea of the pact, prefering to advocate the 'moral' leadership much favoured but little understood by the left. *Reynolds' News*, too, abandoned consistency in its attitude to the pact, which it denied had any aggressive intent and believed might have a stabilising influence.[77] The characteristic symmetry with fellow-traveller arguments was thus lost by the spring of 1949, but it may be that this change of policy was not unconnected with the action being taken against communists within the Co-operative movement.[78]

The fellow-travellers themselves criticised NATO vigorously; Driberg and Braddock chose the occasion of the signing of the pact to raise voices in Parliament which had been silent for many months. William Warbey spoke strongly against it in both March and May, condemning it as a traditional pre-1914 power-political alliance, a surrender of British sovereignty, a provocation to a basically peaceful Russia, a betrayal of socialism and a fulfilment of Fulton; Warbey at least remained true to the 1946 anti-Fulton petition of which he had been the sponsor.[79] Rather like Churchill, though for different reasons, Zilliacus was concerned to remind those in his party who had opposed Fulton: 'My honourable friends have been converted from the collective system to power politics.' He deployed the familiar objections to an American-dominated world-wide alliance against Russia and attempted to dispose of the claim that NATO qualified as a regional self-defence pact under the provisions of the United Nations charter. Article 53, he reminded the House, made it impossible for any action to be taken by regional agencies without the authority of the Security Council, except against ex-enemy States. Article 51 made it clear that aggression could be dealt with only by the Security Council, not by regional arrangements. Article 5 of NATO, by commiting signatories to collective action in the event of an attack, therefore represented a breach of the charter. It was stupid, Zilliacus concluded, to maintain this facade of legality.[80]

Zilliacus's argument was a powerful one. Article 51 does allow for 'collective self-defence measures' in the event of an attack, but only *until the Security Council has taken the measures necessary to maintain international peace and security*. Collective security action against an aggressor could be taken *only* by the Security Council, and Article 5 of NATO did indeed confer this right upon the 'regional arrangements'.[81] Zilliacus was joined by T. Braddock, Platts-Mills, Pritt, Gallacher and Piratin in the 'no' lobby; Emrys Hughes and R. Chamberlain were their tellers. The pact was approved by 333 votes to six.[82]

Churchill was able to note, with grim satisfaction, the silence of the vast majority of the 105 Labour MPs who had signed the motion of criticism on his Fulton speech in March 1946. Opposition had been whittled down under the pressure of the events Bevin had relentlessly listed; it seemed that the degree of consensus behind a policy which three years ago would have been condemned by a large section of the party as reactionary, was now overwhelming. But was it?

In his study of Labour Party foreign policy Gordon cites a poll taken in the late summer of 1949, which showed that 'whereas 81 per cent of Conservative voters favoured an alliance with the US, the comparative figure for Labour voters was only 69 per cent'.[83] Gordon concludes that party members were probably even less enthusiastic. He also uses the high number of Labour abstentions, over one hundred despite a three-line whip, as evidence of a lack of PLP enthusiasm for NATO. Gordon's first point cannot be refuted, but any widespread unease would almost certainly have been expressed at Conference in June. There was no such expression, in fact Dalton was moved to comment on the total absence of criticism of Bevin's foreign policy.[84] Contemporary assessments do not appear to sustain Gordon's second point, regarding abstentions. *The Times* referred to a 'small handful' of abstentions,[85] the *Daily Herald* made no comment; deliberate abstentions on this scale would surely have occasioned some comment. Gordon's assessment also ignores the fact that almost an equal number of Conservative MPs also neglected to vote. The most likely explanation of the low turn-out is that MPs correctly judged that opposition to the treaty would be minimal and that their presence in the division lobbies was not crucial. Who were the 'handful' of deliberate abstainers referred to by *The Times* report? This is difficult to decide, but the non-appearance of any Nenni telegram signatories suggests that most of their abstentions were deliberate. Driberg, Warbey and Mikardo almost certainly abstained deliberately, along with Maurice Orbach.[86] Over half Keep Left voted for NATO, but Crossman's abstention, together with the opposition of the *N.S. and N.*, suggests he too might have deliberately withheld his vote. The fact that twenty-five of the forty-one 'no's' cast against the December amendment to the Conscription Bill did not pass through the 'aye' lobby suggests that a fair proportion of the party's pacifist MPs were unhappy about NATO. Of the fifty-seven MPs who signed the amendment to the King's Speech way back in November 1946, however, nearly half now voted with the government, including such former critics as Maurice Edelman, Michael Foot and W. G. Cove.

Opposition to NATO, though slight, was significantly greater than the opposition to Bevin's policy over the Berlin blockade crisis, when even the fellow-travellers had remained silent. Explanations are provided by the fact that in the spring of 1949 the immediate threat to Western Europe had receded, indeed Stalin's emphasis upon peace initiatives took the edge off the perceived Soviet threat and probably helped to strengthen left-wing belief, typified by the *N.S. and N.*, that Soviet foreign policy was not at heart agressive. The North Atlantic Pact, moreover, represented a degree of intimate association with capitalist America which made many socialists uneasy. In the wake of the NATO debate, however, the Labour leadership set out to demonstrate that opposition to NATO did not pay.

Despite the excellence of Zilliacus's arguments, or perhaps because of them, he could not stop the Labour leadership moving against him and his close associate, Solley. The NEC refused to endorse their candidacies for the next election. A charge sheet of offences included participation in the communist-inspired World Peace Congress, articles in the *Labour Monthly* and *Daily Worker*, and attacks upon the Labour Party and the Atlantic Pact. Zilliacus claimed that a sub-committee had endorsed his position but that under Attlee's influence the NEC had overruled this judgement and therefore effectively expelled him.[87]

The Conference again refused to suspend standing orders to enable Zilliacus and Solley to speak (the vote was 3,000,023 to 1,993,000 against) but many spoke up for Zilliacus, who, after all, had a distinguished record as a supporter of collective security and as a formidable expert on foreign affairs. His defenders included Geoffrey Bing, Sidney Silverman and Ben Levy, but the trade union heavyweights Sam Watson and Arthur Deakin spoke, perhaps with some regret, in favour of his expulsion. Only 714,000 votes were mustered in favour of Zilliacus and Solley, whilst 4,721,000 endorsed the NEC decision.[88]

Both Solley and Zilliacus stood as independents in the 1950 elections along with Pritt and Platts-Mills, but all failed to be re-elected.[89] Zilliacus's career was not yet over. He established his credentials as a Titoist rather than a Stalinist and in 1952 was allowed back into the party, being narrowly elected MP for Gorton, Manchester, in 1955. It could be argued that, with the blockade lifted and the pact signed, the expulsion of Zilliacus and Solley was unnecessarily harsh. This view neglects the fact that many members of the Labour leadership would probably have expelled Zilliacus much earlier; it was not until 1949 that he was sufficiently isolated in the party for them to do so with impunity. Zilliacus was the powerfully articulate leader of a troublesome dissentient minority and was frequently regarded abroad as the leader of the Labour Party's left wing. The NEC's decision was a demonstration to the rest of the party and to the world that Labour would not tolerate a potential fifth column within its ranks. With the expulsion of Zilliacus the leadership attempted finally to exorcise the Bolshevik ghost from Labour Party foreign policy.

Notes

1 De Gasperi emerged victorious over the communists in the April elections in Italy.
2 In January 1948 Stalin told Yugoslavia to cease aiding the Greek struggle — M. Djilas, pp. 140–1.
3 W. Phillips Davison, *The Berlin Blockade: a Study in Cold War Politics*, p. 75. Most of the account of the Berlin blockade is based upon Davison's excellent study. See Eden for similar reasoning to Clay's, 452 *H.C. Deb.*, 2217, 20 June 1948.
4 450 *H.C. Deb.*, 1122, 4 May 1948.
5 For Bevin's explanation of this case, see 452 *H.C. Deb.*, 2229, 30 June 1948.
6 For an elaboration of this point, see *Tribune*, 9 July 1948.
7 Feis, p. 338.
8 452 *H.C. Deb.*, 1707, 25 June 1948, and Davison writes that on that day Washington had to be exhorted by Clay to stand firm, pp. 103–7.
9 452 *H.C. Deb.*, 2232–3, 30 June 1948.
10 See *The Times*, 1 July 1948.
11 Davison, p. 121.
12 Feis, p. 352.
13 456 *H.C. Deb.*, 910, 22 September 1948.
14 463 *H.C. Deb.*, 381, 23 March 1949.
15 Foot, *Bevan*, vol. II, *1945–60*; p. 230.
16 452 *H.C. Deb.*, 2247, 30 June 1948. According to Denis Healey, Bevin did not feel he could risk mankind even on a good chance that such a strategy would work. He preferred to place the initiative on the Russians, to 'dare them' to shoot down airlift planes. ITV programme, 9 September 1971.
17 452 *H.C. Deb.*, 2262.
18 *Ibid.*, 2290.

19 Ibid., 2307.
20 *Daily Herald*, 28 July 1948.
21 Ibid., 6 June 1948.
22 Ibid., 21 and 27 August 1948.
23 Ibid., 3 July 1948. Laski described Soviet policy as 'reckless' and as an encouragement to right-wing hawks in the Kremlin — *Forward*, 1 July 1948.
24 452 *H.C. Deb.*, 2238, 30 June 1948.
25 Ibid., 2243.
26 *N.S. and N.*, 4 September 1948.
27 C. H. Rolph. *Kingsley, his Life and Letters*, p. 298.
28 *Tribune*, 19 November 1948.
29 Ibid., 26 November 1948.
30 *Forward*, 1 July, 7 and 24 August 1948. Hughes told Attlee that there was grave national concern that 'we are going to war', 454 *H.C. Deb.*, 583, 22 July 1948.
31 456 *H.C. Deb.*, 941, 22 September 1948.
32 452 *H.C. Deb.*, 2298, 30 June 1948. Spearman also suggested that Labour Party members might desist from strike activities as this might encourage the Soviet Union to commit further aggression. On 30 June Zilliacus moved an amendment urging the settlement of the dispute by the Security Council (a forum controlled, of course, by the great power veto). He attracted the signatures of McGhee Chamberlain, E. Hughes, J. Hudson, T. Braddock, Capt. Field, Solley, Vernon, W. Griffiths, R. Sorensen and S. O. Davies.
33 452 *H.C. Deb.*, 2320, 30 June 1948.
34 Ibid., 2226.
35 The vote was passed by 409 votes to 12.
36 453 *H.C. Deb.*, 1396, 15 July 1948.
37 456 *H.C. Deb.*, 944, 22 September 1948, and 453 *H.C. Deb.*, 341–2, 6 July 1948.
38 *Daily Herald*, 25 October 1948. Bevin's speech was reported at length in *Daily Herald*, 28 September 1948.
39 Ibid., 26 October 1948.
40 On 19 November the *Daily Herald* reported the trials of Polish and Bulgarian social democrats.
41 *New Times*, 1 December 1948.
42 Dalton, *Diaries*, 21 December 1948. Also quoted in Feis, who records Dalton's reflection that this comment was a 'bad presage for the future', p. 369 and n.
43 See below, p. 150.
44 Dalton, *Diaries*, 10 September 1948.
45 Ibid. Written in Dalton's almost indecipherable handwriting, this extraordinary entry reflects the assumption of the time that British rule over Africa, as opposed to recently independent India, would be indefinite.
46 *Tribune*, 22 October 1948.
47 *N.S. and N.*, 9 October 1948.
48 For example see *N.S. and N.* 5 February 1949, in which the journal advised that the West had nothing to lose by testing Stalin's good faith.
49 See *Tribune*, 6 February 1949, and *Daily Herald*, 30 January 1949.
50 *TUCR 1949*, pp. 274–8. The General Council produced a further document on 24 November 1949, entitled *Defend Democracy*.
51 *Daily Herald*, 18 December 1948. On 14 March 1949 the TUC produced a

The genesis of NATO II 207

pamphlet entitled *The Tactics of Disruption*; *Daily Herald*, 15 March 1949.
52 *Ibid.*, 14 October 1948. Horner believed the right-wingers in the union were trying to get rid of him as part of their preparations for war; Horner, *Incorrigible Rebel*, p. 186.
53 *Daily Herald*, 29 September 1948.
54 *Ibid.*, 20 January 1948.
55 Windmuller, p. 143.
56 *Daily Herald*, 20 January 1949.
57 458 *H.C. Deb.*, 2123, 1 December 1948.
58 Jackson, *Rebels and Whips*, p. 61 n.
59 Dixon, p. 256.
60 Dalton reflected on the pact that 'It is the best we can do ... and of its kind it is very good in this miserable situation.' *Diaries*, 20 March 1949.
61 Already, on 23 March, Bevin could declare that communism was being 'contained' — 463 *H.C. Deb.*, 479–91.
62 *The Times*, 13 May 1949. The *Daily Herald* reported that the pact was received with the most magnificent cheer the House had ever given to a White Paper (19 March 1949). 464 *H.C. Deb.*, 2011–22, 12 May 1948.
63 McNeil's speech, similar in tone, in 463 *H.C. Deb.*, 391–402, 23 March 1949.
64 462 *H.C. Deb.*, 2539 and 2541, 18 March 1949; 463 *H.C. Deb.*, 408–10, 23 March 1949; 464 *H.C. Deb.*, 2051–60, 12 May 1949, respectively.
65 *Daily Herald*, 19 March 1949.
66 *Tribune*, 25 March and 4 February 1949. These comments were made, of course, before the pact was signed.
67 *Ibid.*, 20 May 1949.
68 *Ibid.*, 27 May 1949, p. 14, and p. 4 for Mikardo's article.
69 Kingsley Martin, *Harold Laski: a Biographical Memoir*, p. 190.
70 *N.S. and N.*, 12 March 1949.
71 *Ibid.*, 19 March 1949. Bevin too, it should be mentioned, was also aware of this danger; see Truman, *Memoirs*, vol. II, p. 282.
72 *LPCR 1949*, p. 193.
73 *The Times*, 11 May 1949. The amendment, together with four other critical amendments, was later withdrawn.
74 462 *H.C. Deb.*, 1571–2, 10 March 1949, and 462 *H.C. Deb.*, 511–13, 23 March 1949, respectively.
75 *Forward*, 26 March 1949.
76 464 *H.C. Deb.*, 2064–9, 12 May 1949.
77 *Reynolds' News*, 4 March 1949.
78 See *Daily Herald*, 7 July 1949.
79 464 *H.C. Deb.*, 2035–45, 12 May 1949.
80 *Ibid.*, 2073–83.
81 See Gordon, *Conflict and Consensus*, p. 126. Also Inis Claude, *Swords into Ploughshares* (London, 1965), pp. 115–23, and A. Wolfers, *Discord and Collaboration* (Baltimore, 1962) pp. 181–200, for the distinction between collective security and collective defence.
82 464 *H.C. Deb.*, 2127–30, 12 May 1949.
83 Gordon, p. 162 n.
84 *LPCR 1949*, p. 49.
85 *The Times* 13 May 1949.

86 Interview with author.
87 *The Times*, 19 May 1949; also see K. Zilliacus's pamphlet *Why I was Expelled*, 1949.
88 See *LPCR 1949*, pp. 119–27.
89 Lester Hutchinson also failed to return to Parliament when the NEC vetoed his candidature — see Jackson, *Rebels and Whips*, p. 212.

Concluding comments

To see what is in front of one's nose is a constant struggle. [George Orwell, in *The Collective Essays, Journalism and Letters of George Orwell*, ed. Sonia Orwell and Ian Angus, vol. IV, p. 154]

i

When Bevin signed the North Atlantic Pact on 14 April 1949 he remarked to a colleague that it was 'one of the greatest moments of my life.'[1] This pinnacle in his career also marks the coming of age of Labour's foreign policy. Lord Strang felt it was to the 'enduring credit' of the Labour government that it was able to eschew party doctrine and form policies 'suited to the strategic realities and to the national interest as traditionally understood'.[2] Bevin cut through Labour's heritage of radical internationalism and emotional pro-Sovietism to restore the balance of power in Europe. Throughout his career as a trade union negotiator he had been forced to recognise that parties to a dispute will, in the last resort, use or threaten to use their power to harm one another. As Foreign Secretary he applied the same appropriate logic. Few employers could have been tougher to deal with than Stalin and Molotov. At the 1949 Conference Dalton neatly summed up the Labour leadership's conclusions after four years of dealing with the Russians. 'I would say, and Dick Crossman and anybody with any knowledge of the Russians will agree — that the Russians have no respect for weakness of any kind. But they understand strength and so, I hope, do we.'[3] In June 1949 only a tiny minority disagreed with him. Since the heady days of wartime comradeship, support for Russia had ebbed away, to be replaced by a spirit reminiscent of 1940 rather than 1943. Beneath the cloak of a collective security agreement in harmony with the UN and the Anglo-Soviet treaty, power politics had triumphed over traditional notions of socialist foreign policy.

It has been one of the purposes of this study to show how Labour experience of the Soviet Union was the principal vehicle by which this transition took place. It has traced and attempted to explain how the intense admiration of Russia first arose, was then modified by reports of police repression and later sustained by the need to co-ordinate opposition to Hitler. Stalin's apparent collaboration with the common enemy during the autumn of 1939 was a blow which left the Labour Party breathless; his attack on Finland compounded a bitter disillusion which lasted until June 1941. Thereafter enthusiasm was renewed, albeit with a slightly hysterical edge, and went on to reach unprecedented heights. This tremendous groundswell of support washed into the early years of the new Labour administration, creating intractable problems between the party leadership and its backbench supporters. The essence of Labour's post-war conflict over foreign policy lay in the differing conceptions held by government and backbenchers upon two crucial issues; the nature of Soviet intentions and the nature of international politics itself. Bevin, with the support of all but a small proportion of the trade unions assured, had to overcome the arguments and influence of three main opposition groups in the PLP and the party in the country: the fellow-travellers, the pacifists and the radical idealists.

The fellow-travellers managed to survive the period up to 1949, their image of Russia more or less intact. They never began to convince Bevin, and he did not succeed in moving them; they remained in 1949 as the rump of the opposition which had threatened to shake the government in October 1946. However, in 1949 they were isolated and the leadership felt safe enough to expel some of their number from the PLP. The pacifists in the party were never fully convinced that the Soviets posed a threat. They tended to see a more peaceful and constructive Russia than Bevin, principally because it accorded with their vision of what they wanted to see; it could be used as an argument against government conscription policies and what they regarded as potentially dangerous counter-measures against Soviet pressure. Their influence, however, was slight and their victory over the National Service Bill in 1947 short-lived. The radical idealists offered the most substantial opposition. The *N.S. and N.* was well informed, perceptive and commanded a wealth of journalistic talent unequalled on the left. However, its judgement was muddled, vacillating and often contradictory; it was prepared to censure the USSR for its misdeeds but never to endorse a firm stand against its foreign policy. The MPs associated with these journals, including R. H. S. Crossman, the nearest thing to a leader on the left before the emergence of Bevan in 1951, were the architects of the persuasive Third Force idea. This school of thought commanded a great deal of support within the centre of the PLP well into 1947, but after the Marshall Aid programme most of these MPs closed ranks with the trade unionist-dominated right wing of the party, which, along with the Cabinet, viewed Russia through the lens provided by Ernest Bevin. Under the editorship of Postgate and Bevan *Tribune* moved from a crypto-communist position in 1939 to a clear-eyed stance nearer the centre of the party. After the war it strongly advocated the Third Force idea, but after Marshall Aid vociferously supported Bevin. *Tribune's* analysis of international affairs was profound, perceptive and extremely well informed; its record on most issues survives the test of time well.

The Labour leadership had learnt much of the international facts of life as members of the wartime coalition government — not only Bevin and Dalton, the pre-war realists, but also the pro-Soviet rebel Sir Stafford Cripps. What separated the realism of Bevin from the idealism of dissenting groups within the party, however, was an argument not so much about the future shape of society as about the most prudent way of advancing towards it. Bevin agreed with the need for disarmament but was not prepared to disarm unilaterally as the pacifists demanded; he agreed with the radical idealists upon the need for an international peace-keeping organisation and collaboration with social democrats abroad, but he would not prejudice national interests in the process; he would have liked to co-operate with Russia as the Marxists urged but not whilst Stalin demanded an unacceptable price. Despite his constant use of the term, Bevin knew that, far from putting your 'cards on the table face upwards', in dealing with other countries, particularly the Russians, you tried to build the strongest possible hand and kept it close to your chest. If this is the way everyone behaves in international diplomacy —and indeed it is — the adoption of less cautious strategies might invite damage by default to the national interest.

It took time for Bevin to educate the party along these lines — a process made even more protracted by the fact that he often chose to deliver his lessons in the language of idealistic socialist foreign policy. Conceptual confusions abounded. Bevin's political lexicon was crammed with emotively laden phrases like 'democracy', 'equality', 'freedom', 'economic justice', 'world government' and so on, which lent themselves easily to the interpretation his audiences chose to give to them and which consequently caused misunderstandings to multiply.

The rearguard action in defence of a socialist foreign policy provided the only substantial opposition he had to face, but it is worth noting that had Churchill been in power post-war the inevitable Soviet pressure upon a weakened Britain would almost certainly have produced a swift resort to a 'Fultonite' policy. This would have been much more difficult for the left centre and right of the Labour Party to accept, and the degree of parliamentary conflict would consequently have been much more intense.

The left wing of his own party may have been Bevin's only effective opposition, but had the Conservatives been in power support for British policy towards Russia would have been far less bipartisan.

It was not, of course, merely the force of Bevin's arguments which eroded and finally overcame the opposition; Stalin himself was the sternest of tutors in the business of *Realpolitik*. In the post-war years it is almost possible to discern a pattern of disillusion. Firstly, persecution of Eastern European social democrats revived memories of the Moscow trials and reinforced doubts long harboured about Soviet political and legal methods. The next stage was disappointment with Russian unwillingness to co-operate internationally; a realisation grew that Russia was pursuing narrow national interests rather than a peaceful internationalist policy. Ultimately a conviction grew that Russian foreign policy was scarcely different from tsarist imperialism. For his final disenchantment the socialist tended to turn his attention back to the Soviet homeland, when he perceived the Russian economic system, her irreducible claim to be a socialist State, to be unequal and unfair. Not every member of the party, of course, traversed the whole spectrum from enchantment to total disillusion. W. N. Ewer, the *Daily Herald*'s foreign affairs correspondent, was one who did; his disillusion began in the late 'twenties and reached its conclusion in the late 'forties. Maurice Orbach, on the other hand, developed his enthusiasm in the 'thirties and sustained it in some measure even after 1949, right up to 1956; even then retaining a respect for Soviet economic organisation.[4] Nor should it be thought that this process was consistent; it followed the ebb and flow of events and fluctuated accordingly.

One other characteristic is worth noting. When the image was not reinforced by strong ideological assumptions it could change very quickly, as war time experience showed; when it was, it proved remarkably resistant to change. This last point is illustrated by Laski and Cole, who both subscribed to Marxist assumptions; they found it very painful, traumatic almost, to abandon their preconceptions about Russia. Others, like Cripps and Tawney, whose socialism owed more to Christian values, were not affected in this way.[5]

Until the advent of the Cold War, however, admiration for Russia in the Labour Party united Marxist with social democrat. To be pro-Soviet was regarded as one of the credentials of being on the left. The period covered in this study has illustrated the problems this caused. Abroad, it entangled the Labour Party with the international position of the Soviet Union and, at home, with the activities of the CPGB. In the light of the Labour Party's entwined relationships with Russia it seems almost appropriate that Hector

McNeil's private secretary, Guy Burgess, should have turned out to be a Soviet agent.

In January 1948 the *N.S. and N.* called for an end to this 'Russia complex'; within the body of the party it had already effectively passed away. Indeed, by 1949 the distinction between British social democracy and communism, Soviet or British, was infinitely clearer than during the 'thirties. Attlee made the point explicitly in *The Times* on 11 April 1949. 'There are some of our own people who still think that the communists are the left wing of the socialist movement. They are not. The socialist movement was always a movement for freedom.' Its Soviet experience was salutory to the Labour Party in the domestic field as well as in foreign affairs. It revealed that approaches to politics based upon logic and reason, however brilliantly conceived and elaborated, do not necessarily coincide in practice with the infinite complexities of social reality. It reinforced the traditional British disinclination to fuse violence with political change. For the reformist Labour Party, Stalinism was a sharp reminder that revolutions are too important to leave to revolutionaries.

The Cold War period, in fact, had the effect of discrediting left-wing socialism; during the 'fifties British Labour's rethinking was done by the right and not by the left (as often happens to a left-wing party in opposition). The architects of this change were predominantly anti-Soviet realists, men like Dalton, Healey and Gaitskell. Trade unions too were dominated during the 'fifties by right-wing anti-communists who rose to power in the shadow of Ernest Bevin and the Cold War. The story of Labour's disenchantment with Russia, therefore, is closely bound up with the evolution of British socialism itself.

The rehabilitation of left-wing ideas into Labour Party thinking in the era of *détente* has likewise been no coincidence; when in opposition between 1970 and 1974 the party swung sharply to the left. It is interesting to note that such leftward swings in opposition also occurred in the early 'twenties, the early 'thirties and in the early 'forties, all partly under the influence of favourable images of Russia. The most recent swing to the left, however, cannot in any way be attributed to favourable views of Russia but rather to an absence of negative ones. By 1970 the backlash against the Soviet Union had worked itself through, and British socialism is now developing in an atmosphere virtually free from Soviet influence. This is not to say that the Labour leadership does not still worry about the strength of Marxism in the party, but now it is either a modified British version or an international variety owing a greater debt to Trotsky — a renegade from Moscow — rather than to Moscow itself.

ii

In his study of dissent in British foreign policy A. J. P. Taylor records the opinion of Lord Bryce that dissenters are often proved right in the light of history.[6] The 'revisionist' school of Cold War historians has reassessed Soviet intentions in the post-war period in ways which have a rough congruence with contemporary left-wing analyses.[7] American foreign policy after the war, the argument runs, was just as provocative as Russia's, if not more so. Russia was not interested in communising Western Europe and wanted Eastern Europe's friendship as a guarantee against a future attack from the West; Russia, after losing twenty million lives, was understandably paranoid about the threat of Germany; she was intent upon reconstruction at home and was in any case far too weak to contemplate an imperialist policy. Have the left wing views been rehabilitated? Undoubtedly they have for some.

There can be little doubt that the Soviets were pathologically afraid of West Germany and wished to build up Eastern Europe as a defensive barrier. Russia was weak, obsessed with reconstruction and in no shape to sustain successfully an imperialist policy in Western Europe for any length of time. And yet, despite all these facts, her post-war foreign policy in Eastern Europe bore many of the repugnant hallmarks of Hitler's policy of aggrandisement. The Soviet-supported *coup* in Czechoslovakia and the Berlin blockade were provocative acts by a power whose massive land armies were a source of constant apprehension to the West. Bevin noted the paradox in his *tête-à-tête* with Molotov in December 1947: 'You know you cannot stand a war,' Bevin told him, 'but you are risking one.'[8]

These words go right to the heart of the debate about Soviet intentions. Revisionists concentrate upon proving the first part of the statement — that rationally Russia could not afford, could not sustain and therefore did not want war. They neglect to realise that Soviet policy had all the *appearances*, however irrational, of expansionism. If Bevin, Bidault and Marshall had ignored these signs and taken no precautions they would have been extremely poor Foreign Secretaries. Given their recent experience of Hitler, the fact that Europe was unarmed and Russia still militarily strong, and the propensity Stalin had shown for moving into contiguous power vacuums and exerting near-total control, they could not afford to take the risk that he meant them no harm. Even if his intentions had initially been peaceful the temptation to move into Western Europe, had it remained weak, might eventually have proved irresistible. The revisionist school has reinforced some of the contemporary left-wing analyses — and persuasively — but it cannot, in the present writer's view invalidate the alliance policy of the Western countries.

Perhaps history will justify Labour faith in the Soviet economic, social and political systems? Again, it seems highly unlikely. Rather, the history of the Soviet experiment will be seen to illustrate the fatal flaws in Marxism-Leninism, particularly its assumptions about human nature. Marx believed that defects in human nature were the reflection of an unjust economic system. If the system were transformed, it followed that the defects would be eliminated. The problem, however, lies in the process of transition. According to Marx, this should be the task of the communist parties: the elite members of the working-class who were educated in the economic laws of history. On to this precept Lenin built the idea that a small section of that elite should impose a period of iron control while a socialist economic system was being fashioned: in other words, the dictatorship of the proletariat. Once socialism was achieved, the dictatorship could be dismantled and the machinery of the State would ultimately wither away. But what if society proved resistant to the imposition of socialism and what if members of the working-class elite proved to be less than incorruptible?

Koestler describes how the early Bolsheviks justified the use of violence in the suppression of resistance to their programmes of economic reconstruction. Rubashov saw himself as the instrument of inevitable historical forces beside which conventional scruples were irrelevant — antithetical, even. As the vehicle of rapid social change a breed of men was produced who specialised in intimidation, psychological vivisection and liquidation. Under the guidance of the man who had gained control of and developed this machinery of oppression the new Bolsheviks consumed the old; thus did Rubashov spawn his own destroyer, Gletkin. Few can believe that the Gletkin generation will willingly wither away. Bolshevism, as refined by Stalin, had not only reflected the natural tendency to authoritarianism in Russian political culture but developed it to an unprecedented degree. Instead of being the noble crusade many Western socialists initially believed it to be, Stalin's leadership of the first socialist State reads like a particularly bloody chapter out of the history of the Mafia. Marx had predicted and prescribed drastic social engineering; his mistake was to overlook the shortage of the right kind of social engineer. He failed to appreciate, as Herzen did, that 'we are not the doctors, we are the disease'.

Perhaps the future will justify the excesses of the Stalinist period, for the present cannot. Even a cursory glance at the relative position of the Soviet and American worker does not indicate that sixty years of communism have secured any spectacular advantages. Communism, to be sure, succeeded within a generation in bringing the Soviet economy to the front rank from a position of great backwardness; its ability to withstand the onslaught of Hitler was testimony to this. But Japan, with fewer natural resources, can boast a similar transformation via the free enterprise system. Whatever the iniquities of capitalism in the Western world, Soviet communism has not produced advantages which can reasonably justify the privations suffered in its name by the Russian workers. As John Strachey, the foremost British Russophile of the 'thirties, finally came to conclude, 'The means have been terrible; the result commonplace.'[9]

Indeed, it is not the heralds of the new Utopia who are remembered from the period — Strachey, the Webbs, Hindus, Fischer — but the prophets of disillusion; Bevin, Healey, Koestler, Orwell. If Koestler came closer than most to explaining the birth of totalitarianism in Russia, then Orwell, of all the commentators, ultimately came closest to explaining the hold it came to exert over the British Labour Party. Labour's pro-Sovietism, he believed, was due 'much more to the need for an external paradise than to any real interest in the Soviet regime, and it cannot be counted by an appeal to the facts even when they are known'.[10] The British, in any case, simply could not conceive of millions enslaved in camps, mass deportations and the brutal suppression of minority views, and Labour Party members were consequently easy prey for the reassuring certainties of Soviet propaganda.[11] Orwell could see that the totalitarian State could not be satisfied with anything less than infallibility. It demanded total belief in its constantly changing distortions of the present and its rewritings of the past. Ultimately it challenged the validity of objective truth itself.[12] Orwell's contempt was total for anyone who propagated the sophistries of the Soviet State — whether they believed them or not — but he reserved his most vitriolic condemnations for the British rather than the Soviet intellectuals. For intellectuals in Stalin's Russia it was fear of physical reprisals which turned them into liars; for intellectuals in the West it was merely the fear that their dreams were not true.

Orwell's self-appointed task of destroying the 'Soviet mythos' in the Labour Party was virtually complete by the time of his death in 1950, but had he lived he would have derived little satisfaction from its repercussions. He had believed his objective to be essential if the socialist movement were ever to be revived, but the destruction of faith in Russia scarcely realised this hope.[13] The reason was partly that socialism and Russia *were* interrelated ideas and the discrediting of one damaged the other, and partly that Cold War reactions to Soviet pressure strengthened the right and weakened social democracy all over the world. A final irony was that although Orwell's bitter indictment of totalitarianism, *Nineteen Eighty Four*, was written from a left-wing standpoint, it was widely cited against left-wing arguments by right-wing Cold Warriors.

This book has attempted to show the diverse ways in which the Russian revolution has influenced the British Labour Party. From the first, the Soviet Union was a source of hope and idealism; it was a distant champion of socialism to be supported against its capitalist enemies. Later, when capitalism appeared to falter fatally, it became a potent vision of a highly successful planned economy and a classless society imbued with socialist values. Those who visited it returned, mostly, to declare that the future was wonderful and it worked. Labour's left wing became heavily influenced by the CPGB, and the example of the USSR nourished the development of a socialist foreign policy dedicated to peace, collective security, support for socialists abroad and opposition to imperialism and fascism. In the 'thirties socialists looked at Stalin's portrait and saw the modest proletarian leader of a great revolution, his face wearing a benign, sagacious half-smile. By the end of the next decade the same smile seemed to indicate a cosmic contempt; socialists now saw an imperialist dictator, heartlessly indifferent to the death or imprisonment of millions. The USSR, once the source of so much idealism in the Labour Party, had fostered a corresponding cynicism. In addition it had destroyed any chance of the CPGB ever had of becoming a mass party or of affiliating to Labour; helped to usher in an era of moderation in the Labour Party and the trade unions; etiolated the concept of 'socialist foreign policy' and nurtured support for a return to a traditional balance-of-power policy. Perhaps the final word is best left to a Labour MP, Ernest Fernyhough, who lived through the period in question and had a strong empathy with the Soviet Union. 'The real tragedy of the Russians is that they blindly squandered the goodwill that existed towards them in the West. They seldom did anything to evoke a response in the thousands of people over here who were sympathetic to the Russian cause.'[14]

It can be strongly argued that the Russian experiment in socialism has done a great disservice to Marxism in that it has discredited a system of ideas which potentially has much to contribute towards the achievement of fairer and more just societies in many parts of the world. It is still too early to judge, but perhaps the happier adaptations of Marxist ideas we are witnessing in Cuba and China will correct this imbalance. Are we then to see the growth of a new enchantment? David Caute has prophesised that *détente* with China will make it the destination for 'a flood of inquisitive Western tourists ... discharging the fraternity and goodwill which has for so long been damned up'.[15] This may well prove to be the case, perhaps deservedly so, but ironically it seems unlikely that China will ever occupy the revered position in the Labour Party once held by Stalinist Russia. Disillusion has been such that it is improbable that a comparable enthusiasm will emerge in the future; the Soviet Union was Labour's last Utopia.

Notes

1. F. Williams, *Ernest Bevin*, p. 270.
2. Quoted in Gordon, *Conflict and Consensus*, p. 118.
3. *LPCR 1949*, p. 197.
4. Interviews with W. N. Ewer and Maurice Orbach.
5. See, for example, Ross Terril, *R. H. Tawney and his Times*, p. 238.
6. A. J. P. Taylor, *The Trouble Makers* (London, 1957), p. 16.
7. E.g. Gar Alperovitz, *Atomic Diplomacy and the American Confrontation with Soviet Power* (London, 1966); David Fleming, *The Cold War and its Origins, 1917–1960* (London, 1961); David Horowitz, *From Yalta to Vietnam: American Foreign Policy in the Cold War* (London, 1967).
8. Nicolson, vol. III, *1945–62*, pp. 115–16.
9. John St Loe Strachey, *The Strangled Cry*, p. 21.
10. Sonia Orwell and Ian Angus, *The Collected Orwell*, vol. III, p. 438.
11. Ibid., vol. III, p. 458.
12. Ibid., vol. IV, p. 84.
13. Ibid., vol. III, p. 458.
14. Interview with Mr Fernyhough.
15. Caute, *The Fellow Travellers*, p. 380.

Selective bibliography

Interviews were conducted with the following (relevant biographical details given):

H. L. Beales. Reader in Economic History, University of London (1936–56). Editorial adviser to Penguin Books to 1945.

V. Bernard. formerly chairman of the International Committee of the Czechoslovak Parliamentary Party, 1945–48, and for many years Secretary of the Socialist Union of Central and Eastern Europe.

Lord (Fenner) Brockway. Political Secretary of the ILP, 1939–46. Editor, *New Leader* 1931–46. Joined Labour Party in 1946, and MP for Eton and Slough after 1950.

Dame Margaret Cole. journalist, author, wife of G. D. H. Cole and sister of Raymond Postgate.

Ernest Davies. MP, Enfield, 1945–50. PPS to H. McNeil, 1946–50. Parliamentary Under-Secretary to the Foreign Office, 1950–51.

T. E. N. Driberg. MP (Independent), Malden, 1942–45, and (as Labour) 1945–50. Member of NEC, 1949.

W. N. Ewer. Diplomatic correspondent of *Daily Herald* throughout most of the period studied.

Ernest Fernyhough. MP for Jarrow from 1947.

Michael Foot. MP, Devonport, 1945–50. Assistant editor, *Tribune*, 1937–38. Acting editor, *Evening Standard*, 1942. Editor, *Tribune*, 1948–52.

John Lee. Labour MP, Reading, 1966–70, and Handforth, Birmingham, from 1974.

Kingsley Martin. Editor, *New Statesman and Nation*, 1930–60.

Ian Mikardo. MP, Reading, 1945–50.

Maurice Orbach. MP, Willesden East, 1945–59.

John Parker. MP, Romford, 1935–45, and for Dagenham from 1945. Closely associated with Fabian Society. Junior Minister, Dominions Office, 1945–46.

Raymond Postgate. Editor, *Tribune*, 1940–42.

D. N. Pritt. KC, MP, North Hammersmith, 1935–50 (as Independent after 1945).

Andrew Rothstein. Historian, Librarian, Marx Memorial Library, and prominent member of CPGB.

Lord (Reginald) Sorensen. MP, West Leyton, 1935–50.
George Strauss. MP, North Lambeth, 1934–50. Junior Minister of Transport, 1945–47. Minister of Supply, 1947–51.
Tudor Watkins. MP, Brecon, 1945–70.

Correspondence was also exchanged on specific points with Lord Citrine and the late Raymond Postgate.

Hazelhurst and Woodward (see below) have confirmed the scarcity of private papers belonging to Labour Cabinet Ministers, but the Dalton diaries, held at LSE, proved to be an invaluable source of original material. The papers of the Labour backbencher R. W. G. Mackay, also at LSE, were of peripheral relevance only. Professor Hugh Berrington kindly allowed me access to his copies of parliamentary early day motions put down during the period of the Labour government, 1945–50.

A wide range of newspapers and journals have been consulted for this study, including the *Daily Herald, Daily Worker, Forward, Manchester Guardian, News Chronicle, New Leader, New York Times, Times, Reynolds' News, Left News, Labour Monthly, New Statesman and Nation, Socialist Commentary* and *Tribune*.

The annual Labour Party and TUC Conference reports were also extensively used, together with the House of Commons Debates, fifth series.

What follows is a selection of the most useful secondary sources consulted. It does not include the more standard reference works on the Labour Party and the Soviet Union.

Attlee, C. R., *The Labour Party in Perspective*, Gollancz, London, 1937.
Berrington, Hugh B., et al., *Backbench Opinion in the House of Commons, 1945–55*, Pergamon Press, Oxford, 1973.
Brockway, Fenner, A., *Inside the Left*, Allen and Unwin, London, 1942.
— *Outside the Right*, Allen and Unwin, London, 1963.
Bullock, A., *The Life and Times of Ernest Bevin, 1881–1940*, Heinemann, London, 1960.
Carpenter, L. P., *G. D. H. Cole: an Intellectual Biography*, Cambridge University Press, Cambridge, 1973.
Caute, D., *The Fellow Travellers: a Postscript to the Enlightenment*, Weidenfeld and Nicolson, London, 1973.
Citrine, Walter M., *I Search for Truth in Russia*, Gollancz, London, 1936.
— *Two Careers*, Hutchinson, London, 1967.
Cole, G. D. H. *Europe, Russia and the Future*, Gollancz, London, 1941.
— *Labour's Foreign Policy*, N.S. and N. pamphlet, 1946.
— *A History of the Labour Party from 1914*, Routledge, London, 1948.
— *A History of Socialist Thought*, Macmillan, London. Vol. IV, *Communism and Social Democracy* (1958). Vol. V, *Socialism and Fascism* (1960).
Cole, Margaret (ed). *Twelve Studies of Soviet Russia*, New Fabian Research Bureau, London, 1933.
— *The Diaries of Beatrice Webb*, Longmans, London. Vol. I, *1912–1924* (1952). Vol. II, *1924–1932* (1956).
— *The Life of G. D. H. Cole*, Macmillan, London, 1971.
Coates, W. P. and Zelda, *A History of Anglo-Soviet Relations*, Lawrence and Wishart, London, 1943.
Cockburn, Claud, *I Claud*, Penguin, 1968.

Cooke, Colin, *The Life of Sir Stafford Cripps*, Hodder and Stoughton, London, 1957.
Conquest, R., *The Great Terror: Stalin's Purge of the Thirties*, Macmillan, London, 1968.
Crossman, R. H. S. (ed.), *The God that Failed: Six Studies of Communism*, Hamilton, London, 1951.
Crossman, R. H. S., Foot, M., and Mikardo, I., *Keep Left*, 1947.
Dalton, Hugh, *Call Back Yesterday: Memoirs, 1857–1931*, Muller, London, 1953.
— *The Fateful Years: Memoirs, 1931–1945*, Muller, London, 1957.
— *High Tide and After: Memoirs, 1945–1960*, Muller, London, 1962.
Davis, S., 'The British Labour Party and British foreign policy, 1933–39', unpublished Ph.D. thesis, LSE Library, 1950.
Davison, W. Philips, *The Berlin Blockade: a Study in Cold War Politics*, Princeton University Press, Princeton, N.J., 1958.
Deane, H. A., *The Political Ideas of Harold J. Laski*, Columbia University Press, New York, 1955.
Deutcher, Isaac, *Stalin: a Political Biography*, Oxford University Press, London, 1948.
Dixon, Sir Pierson, *Double Diploma: the Life of Sir Pierson Dixon, Don and Diplomat*, Hutchinson, London, 1968.
Djilas, Milovan, *Conversations with Stalin*, Pelican, London, 1962.
Dowse, Robert, *Left in Centre: the Independent Labour Party, 1893–1940*, Longmans, London, 1966.
Durbin, E. F. M., *The Politics of Democratic Socialism: an Essay on Social Policy*, Routledge, London, 1940.
Epstein, Leon, *Britain — Uneasy Ally*, Chicago University Press, Chicago, 1953.
Feis, Herbert, *Churchill, Roosevelt and Stalin: the War they Waged and the Peace they Fought*, Oxford University Press, London, 1957.
— *From Trust to Terror: the Onset of the Cold War, 1945–50*, Anthony Blond, London, 1970.
Fleming, D. F., *The Cold War and its Origins, 1917–1960*, Allen and Unwin, London, 1961.
Foot, M., *Aneurin Bevan: a Biography*, Davis Poynter, London. Vol. I, *1897–1945* (1963). Vol. II, *1945–1960* (1973).
Fitzsimmons, M. A., *The Foreign Policy of the British Labour Government, 1945–51*, University of Notre Dame Press, Indiana, 1953.
Gollancz, Victor, et al., *Betrayal of the Left*, Gollancz, London, 1942. — *Reminiscences of Affection*, Gollancz, London, 1968.
Gordon, Michael R., *Conflict and Consensus in Labour's Foreign Policy, 1914–1965*, Stanford University Press, Stanford, Cal., 1969.
Gould, Barbara, et al., Letter to the Prime Minister on Foreign Policy, October 1946, LSE Library.
Graubard, S. R., *British Labour and the Russian Revolution, 1917–1924*, Harvard University Press, Cambridge, Mass., 1956.
Haseler, S., *The Gaitskellites: Revisionism in the British Labour Party*, Allen and Unwin, London, 1960.
Hazlehurst, C., and Woodward, C., *A Guide to the Papers of British Cabinet Ministers, 1900–1951*, Royal Historical Society, London, 1974.
Healey, D., *Cards on the Table*, 1947.
Hobson, J. A., *Imperialism: a Study* (third edition), Allen and Unwin, London, 1961.
Horner, Arthur, *Incorrigible Rebel*, MacGibbon and Kee, London, 1960.

Hyde, Douglas, *I Believed*, Heinemann, London, 1950.
Jenkins, Roy, *Mr Attlee: an Interim Biography*, Heinemann, London, 1948.
— *In Pursuit of Progress*, London, 1956.
Jones, W. D. A. 'The Labour Party and the Soviet Union, 1939–1949', unpublished Ph.D. thesis, National Library of Wales, 1975.
Jupp, M., 'The left in Britain, 1931–41', unpublished M.Sc. (Econ.) thesis, LSE Library, 1956.
Kennan, G., 'The sources of Soviet conduct' (under pseudonym 'X'), *Foreign Affairs*, July 1947.
— *Memoirs, 1925–1950*, Little Brown and Company, Boston, Mass., 1967.
Koestler, A., *Darkness at Noon*, Penguin, 1969 (first published, Jonathan Cape, 1940).
Labour Party, *Labour's Russian Policy: Peace with Soviet Russia*, 1920.
— *Finland: the Criminal Conspiracy of Stalin and Hitler*, 1939.
— *Is this an Imperialist War?* 1940.
— *The Communist Party and the War: a Record of Hypocrisy and Treachery to the Workers of Europe*, March 1943.
— *The International Post-war Settlement*, 1944.
— *Let us Face the Future* (election manifesto), 1945.
— *The Secret Battalion*, 1946.
Laski, Harold J., *Communism*, Williams and Newgate, London, 1927.
— *Faith, Reason and Civilisation*, Gollancz, London, 1944.
— *The Webbs and Soviet Communism*, The Webb Memorial Lecture, 4 June 1947.
Maddox, W. P., *Foreign Relations in British Labour Politics*, Harvard University Press, Cambridge, Mass., 1934.
Martin, B. Kingsley, *Harold Laski, 1893–1956: a Biographical Memoir*, Gollancz, London, 1953.
— *Father Figures: a First Volume of Autobiography, 1987–1931*, Hutchinson, London, 1964.
— *Editor: a Second Volume of Autobiography, 1931–1945*, Hutchinson, London, 1968.
Meehan, Eujene J., *The British Left Wing and Foreign Policy: a Study of Influence and Ideology*, Rutgers University Press, New Brunswick, New Jersey, 1960.
Miliband, Ralph, *Parliamentary Socialism: a Study in the Politics of Labour*, Allen and Unwin, London, 1961.
Muggeridge, Malcolm, *Winter in Moscow*, Eyre and Spottiswood, London, 1934.
— *The Thirties, 1930–1940, in Great Britain*, Collins, London, 1967.
— *Chronicles of Wasted Time*, Vol. I, Collins, London, 1972.
Naylor, John F., *Labour's International Policy: the Labour Party in the 1930s*, Weidenfeld and Nicolson, London, 1969.
Nove, Alex, *The Soviet Economy*, Allen and Unwin, London, 1965.
Orwell, George, *Nineteen Eighty Four*, Secker and Warburg, London, 1949.
Orwell, Sonia, and Angus, I., *The Collected Essays, Journalism and Letters of George Orwell* (4 vols.), Penguin, 1971.
Parkinson, Roger, *Blood, Toil, Tears and Sweat: the War History, from Dunkirk to Alamein, based on War Cabinet Papers of 1940 to 1942*, Hart Davies, MacGibbon and Kee, London, 1973.
Pelling, Henry, *A Short History of the Labour Party*, Macmillan, London, 1962.
— *The British Communist Party: a Historical Profile*, Black, London, 1958.
Pritt, D. N., *The Zinoviev Trial*, Gollancz, London, 1937.
— *Light on Moscow*, Penguin, 1939.

Selective bibliography 223

— *The Autobiography of D. N. Pritt*, Lawrence and Wishart. Vol. I (1965). Vol. II (1966).
Read, B., and Williams, G., *Denis Healey and the Politics of Power*, London, 1971.
Rolph, C. H., *Kingsley: the Life, Letters and Diaries of Kingley Martin*, Gollancz, London, 1973.
Rose, Richard, 'The relation of socialist principles to socialist foreign policy, 1945-51', unpublished Ph.D. thesis, Bodleian Library, Oxford.
Solzhenitsyn, Alexander, *The Gulag Archipelago, 1918–1956*, Fontana, 1974.
Strachey, John, St Loe, *The Theory and Practice of Socialism*, Gollancz, London, 1936.
— *The Strangled Cry*, Bodley Head, London, 1962.
Taylor, A. J. P., *English History, 1914–45*, Oxford University Press, London, 1965.
— *The Trouble Makers*, Hamilton, London, 1957.
TUC, *Russia and International Unity*, 1925.
Ulam, Adam, *Expansion and Coexistence: the History of Soviet Foreign Policy, 1917–67*, Secker and Warburg, London, 1968.
Webb, Sidney and Beatrice, *Soviet Communism: a New Civilisation?* (2 vols.), Gollancz, 1936 (second edition 1937, third edition 1941).
Werth, Alexander, *Russia at War, 1941–45*, Barrie and Rockliff, London, 1964.
Williams, Francis, *Ernest Bevin: Portrait of a Great Englishman*, Hutchinson, London, 1952.
Windmuller, John P., *American Labour and the International Labour Movement, 1940–53*, Ithica, N.Y., 1954.
Wood, Neal, *Communism and British Intellectuals*, Gollancz, London, 1959.
Woodward, E. L., *British Foreign Policy in the Second World War* (3 vols.), HMSO, London, 1971.

Index

ACHESON, DEAN, 171n
Acland, Sir R., 127
Adenauer, K., 183
Advisory Committee on International Questions (ACIQ), 4, 5, 9
Albania, 150
Alexander, A. V., 176, 183
Angel, N., 1
Anglo-American Loan, 106
Anglo-Soviet Friendship Committees, 64
Anglo-Soviet Public Relations Committee, 65
Anglo-Soviet Trade Union Committee, (1941), 66, 69, 82–84, 85, 96, 107
Anglo-Soviet Trade Treaty (1947), 167
Anglo-Soviet Treaty (1942), 66, 78, 148
Anglo-Soviet Advisory Trade Union Committee, (1925), 8, 23
Anglo-Soviet Parliamentary Committee, 15
'Arcos Raid', 8
Atomic weapons, 107, 117
Atlantic Pact, 177; *see also* NATO
Attlee, Clement, 12, 56, 58, 62, 63, 75, 79, 85, 104, 109, 138, 143, 185, 213; chooses Bevin as Foreign Secretary, 110; replies to Crossman's criticisms, 141

BACON, A., 131
Baltic States, 62
Bartlett, Vernon, 40, 45
Beaverbrook, Lord, 85
Bell, Clive, 68
Berlin Blockade, 190–200
Bevan, A., 29, 51, 61, 63, 65, 79, 80, 81, 82, 86, 91, 93, 104, 105, 142, 183, 211; autum of 1939, 40–41; compared with Kingsley Martin, 100–1; editor of *Tribune*, 78; Second Front, 74
Bevin, Ernest, 75, 85, 95, 103, 143, 144n, 159, 165, 169, 174, 185, 193, 196, 200, 201, 210, 214, 216; Anglo-Soviet Treaty, 148; Berlin Blockade, 191–96, 205n; bipartisan foreign policy, 109; Bournemouth Conference, 128–129; chosen as Foreign Secretary, 110–111; compared with MacDonald, 111; continuity in foreign policy, 116, 127; critics in the party, 117, 118, 120n, 211; European Recovery Programme, 176; Foreign Ministers Conference, Paris, 130–131; Fulton speech, 125; internationalisation of Ruhr, 197; Keep Left, 156–7; *Jolly George*, 5; Labour Foreign Policy, 209; London Foreign Ministers Conference, 115; Marshall's speech, 160–61; New York, 147; Potsdam, 113–114; 'realism', 166; on Soviet Union, 123; talks to Dalton on foreign policy, 197, 206n; UN General Assembly, 122; unveils Western union, 175
Bidault, G., 160
Bing, G., 104, 152
Blackburn, R., 89
Blackpool Conference, 103
Bolshevik Revolution, 1
Bor, General Komarovski, 92, 93
Braddock, T., 202
Brailsford, H. N., 3, 5, 10, 27, 99; compared with D. N. Pritt, 40–42
Brest Litovsk, Treaty of, 5
British Socialist Party (BSP), 1, 4
Brockway, Fenner, 40
Brown, G., 140
Buchanan, G., 46
Burgess, Guy, 213
Buxton, C. R., 2
Byrnes, James, 130, 131

CAMPBELL, J. R., 9, 38
Cards on the Table, 155, 156, 166
Castle, Barbara, 104

Chamberlain, Neville, 28
Chamberlain, W. H., 22
Churchill, Winston, 67, 75, 76, 80, 81, 91, 94, 95, 103, 104, 109, 115, 117, 123, 124, 202, 203; attacked by left in war, 78
Citrine, Sir Walter, 36, 54n, 66, 82, 89, 95, 108, 162; Nazi-Soviet Pact, 34–35; Russian calls for Second Front, 83; visits Russia, 24, 82–83; World Federation of Trade Unions, 95–96
Clay, H., 131, 157–8
Clay, General Lucius, 190–91
Clynes, J. R., 3
Coates, W. P., 15
Cobden, Richard, 1, 2
Cockburn, Claud, 14, 23, 48
Cocks, S., 117, 134, 145n, 151
Cold War, impact on British Socialism, 213, 214
Cole, G. D. H., 16, 70, 73n
Cole, Margaret, 10
Cominform, 161
Comintern, 6
Communism, fidelity to Moscow line, 42–43; influence in thirties, 12; and intellectuals, 10, 13–14; Labour leaders' attitudes towards, 9; and social democracy, 7
Communist Party of Great Britain (CPGB), 27, 85, 188, and autumn of 1939, 37–40; formed in 1920, 7; and Labour left, 217; membership in thirties, 14; rebuffed by Labour Party, 7, 64, 108; and trade unions in war, 86
Confédération Général du Travail, 162, 198
Cooper, Duff, 68
Conscription, 132, 153, 199
Conservative Party, 23, 118
Convention Movement, *see* People's Convention
Councils of Action, 6
Cove, W. G., 106
Cripps, Sir Stafford, 12, 16, 29, 44, 47, 58, 63, 77, 86, 105, 169, 173n; ambassador in Moscow, 61–62; and

Russia, 86
Crawley, A., 158
Crookshank, Capt. H. F. C., 142
Crossman, R. H. S., 13, 50, 100, 116, 137, 139, 143, 154, 180, 195, 199; and 'Third Alternative' speech, 140
Curzon Line, 94
Czechoslovakia, 29, 160, 174–187

DAILY HERALD, 34, 36, 59, 66, 67, 71, 77, 78, 93, 95, 98, 122, 123, 139, 152, 171, 179, 183, 193, 197
Daily Telegraph, 156
Daily Worker, 49, 60, 71n, 93, 184
Dallas, G., 90
Dalton, Hugh, 6, 63, 63, 75, 84, 85, 131, 142, 150, 169, 173n, 181, 197, 200, 209, 213; foreign policy, 119n; Nazi-Soviet Pact, 35; and NATO, 206n; as potential Foreign Secretary, 110; talk with Bevin, 206n
Davies, Ernest, 128, 195
Davies, H., 158
Davies, Rhys, 177, 181
Deakin, Arthur, 198
Dickinson, Lowes, 2, 3
Dieppe, 80
Dimitrov, G., 184
Dixon, Sir Pierson, 117, 143, 184, 200
Downie, J., 36
Driberg, Tom, 14, 80, 152, 158, 202
Dukes, C., 82
Dunkirk, 58
Duranty, W., 13
Durbin, E. F. M., 109
Dutt, R. Palme, 48

EASTERN EUROPE, 114, 132–3, 155, 167
Eastman, Max, 27
Economist, 142
Edelman, M., 45, 104, 134, 143
Eden, A. C., 93, 117, 124, 162, 166
Edwards, Ebby, 107
Eisenstein, S., 13
European Recovery Programme, 160–1, 176, 177
Evans, S. N., 163
Ewer, W. N., 34, 36, 40, 93, 158, 159, 165

FABIANS, 16, 17–22
Fabian International Advistory Committee, 151, 163
Feather, V., 82
Fellow-travellers, 14, 95, 132–3, 139, 155, 163, 182, 188, 195, 202, 210
Fernyhough, Ernest, 217
Finland – Winter War, 34
Fischer, Louis, 26, 27, 45, 216
Five Year Plan, 12
Foot, Michael, 63, 65, 67, 88, 104, 108, 111, 126, 130, 157, 179, 180, 185
Foreign Ministers' Conferences, 115, 130–31, 121, 147
Foreign Office personnel, 127–8
Forward, 45, 92, 95, 97, 124, 181
Frankfurter, F., 165
Freeman, J., 127
Fulton Address, 124–5

GAITSKELL, H., 213
Gallacher, W., 38, 39, 63, 108, 157, 196
General Strike, 8
Germany, 96, 97, 158, 114, 130, 148–49, 197
Gide, André, 27
Gollancz, Victor, 27, 49, 51, 52, 59, 65–66
Gooch, G. P., 2
Greece, 94, 95, 149
Greenwood, Arthur, 34, 35, 145n
Grenfell, David, 35
Griffiths, J., 61, 63
Gusev, F., 93

HAIRE, J., 163
Haldane, Charlotte, 43
Haldane, J. B. S., 14, 38
Hale, L., 104
Halifax, Lord, 62, 109
Hartshorn, 48
Healéy, D., 106, 156, 205n
Henderson, Arthur, 3, 144n
Hewlett, Johnson, 14, 39, 52, 59
Hindus, Maurice, 13, 216
Hitler, A., 33
Hobson, J. A., 2, 3
Hodges, F., 7
Horner, A., 38, 199, 206n

Hudson, J., 142
Hughes, E., 95, 123, 132, 181, 185, 195, 202
Hutchinson, L., 196
Hyde, Douglas, 85
Hynd, J. B., 117, 144n

INDEPENDENT LABOUR PARTY, 3, 4, 6, 37, 69, 97, 181
India, 127
International Brigade, 25
International Sub-committee (of NEC), 90
Internationale, 68, 73n
Intourist, 13
Iran, 122, 126
Izvestia, 123

JEGER, S. W., 107
Jenkins, H., 195
Jolly George, 5, 112

KAGAN, J. W., 128
Katyn massacre, 90
Keep Left, 154–59, 162, 179–80, 185, 199
Kennan, G., 150, 170
Keynes, J. M., 46, 81
King-Hall, Commander Stephen, 76
King's Speech (1946), 139
Koestler, A., 27, 51–52, 185, 215–6
Kuusinen, Otto, 34

LABOUR PARTY, and 1945 election, 103–4; delegation to Finland, 36–37; idealised view of USSR in thirties, 11; images of Russia, 107, 198, 212–213, Orwell's views on, 216; mission to Moscow, 131; and new MPs in 1945, 104; reactions to Fulton, 125; reactions to NATO, 200–204; and socialist foreign policy, 52, 84, 105, 109, 118, 209–211; and world government, 106
Lansbury, G., 12, 153
Laski, Harold, 15, 50, 52, 53, 69, 79, 85, 89, 90, 106, 127, 128, 131, 135, 156, 165, 168, 178, 206n
Lawson, J., 182

Index   227

League of Nations, 3, 24
Lee, J., 155
Leeds Convention (1917), 1
Lees-Smith, 75
Left, attitudes to USA, 129; and CPGB, 217; left 'revolt', 137–143; and NATO, 199; send letter to Attlee, 138
Left Book Club, 27–28, 49, 50
Left News, 65
Lenin, N., 6, 7, 9, 36, 215
Levy, B., 104, 180
Libya, 79
Lillienthal Report, 128
Litvinov, 34
Lloyd-George, D., 5, 6, 46
Loughlin, Dame Ann, 166
Lublin Poles, 91, 94, 98, 99

MACAULAY, ROSE, 85
MacDonald, Ramsay, 3, 6, 9, 12, 111
Mack, J. D., 108
Maclean, Brigadier Fitzroy, H. R., 118
MacMillan, Harold, 123, 200
Maisky, I., 34, 51, 64, 80
Mallalieu, J. P. W., 104
Manchester Evening News, 89
Manchester Guardian, 140, 142
Manning, Mrs Leah, 151
Martin, Kingsley, 25, 40, 45, 61, 65, 66, 100, 164, 172, 180, 194–195, 201
Marshall, Secretary of State, 160
Masaryk, J., 175
Maxton, J., 37
Mayhew, C., 148
McGovern, J., 37, 39, 97, 124
McNeil, H., 174
Meany, G., 108
Mellor, W., 10
Metro-Vick trial, 75
Mikardo, I., 94, 178, 185, 199
Mikolajczyk, S., 92, 99
Milne, J. Wardlaw, 79
Molotov, V., 79, 115, 167, 174, 214
Monckton, W., 62
Montgomery, Field Marshal, 148
Moore-Brabazon, 69
Morel, E. D., 2
Morrison, Herbert, 65, 90, 184

Moscow Trials, 20, 21, 25–27
Mosley, O., 12
Muggeridge, M., 13, 23
Munich, 28

NALLY, W., 140
National Conference for Anglo-Soviet Unity, 65
National Council of Labour (NCL), 28, 36, 62
National Executive Committee (NEC), 7, 61, 64, 182
National Service Act, 153–4, 199
Nenni telegram, 153, 188n
New Economic Policy, 12
New Statesman and Nation (N.S. and N.), 26–27, 45, 46, 47, 61, 67, 77, 79, 81, 91, 93, 98, 99, 106, 123, 125, 126, 130, 136, 137, 138, 153, 164, 168, 170, 180, 184, 198, 201–202, 208
New York Times, 139
New Leader, 97
Nicolson, H., 151, 157
Noel-Baker, P., 36, 79, 90
North Atlantic Treaty Organisation (NATO), 174–205, *passim*, 209

ORBACH, MAURICE, 1, 212
Orwell, George, 25, 43, 46, 62, 67, 86, 89, 92, 104; and Soviet mythos in the Labour Party 216
Owen, F., 65, 78

PACIFISTS, 24, 132, 142, 153, 168, 181, 199, 202, 208
Peart, T. F., 106
People's Convention, 42, 59–60
Petherick, M., 97
Pethick-Lawrence, W., 94
Phillips, Morgan, 131, 183
Piratin, Philip, 108, 139, 198
Platts-Mills, J., 14, 104, 139, 182, 183, 196
Poland, 5, 33, 89–101 *passim*, 151, 160
Polish Committee of National Liberation (PCNL), 91
Polish Provisional Government, 98
Pollit, H., 38
Popular Front, 24, 27, 52, 65

Postgate, R., 10, 48, 55n, 56, 211
Pravda, 148, 159, 160
Price, M. P., 123, 152
Pritt, D. N., 26, 42–43, 51, 52, 87, 139

RADICALS, 168–69, 186, 201, 210
Rainboro, Thomas, 79
'Realism' and foreign policy, 28, 109, 166, 168–9, 209–10
'Red Letter', 9
Reuter, 82
Revisionist historians, 214
Reynolds' News, 92, 98, 152, 182, 202
Ribbentrop, 29
Robertson, A., 39
Rothstein, A., 55n, 64, 66–67
Ruhr, 197
Rumania, 174
Russell, B., 9–10, 101
Russia, *see* Soviet Union
'Russia complex', 213
Russia Today Society, 15
Rust, William, 38

SAILLANT, L., 162
Sargent, Sir Orme, 113
Schevenels, 162
Second International, 2, 37
Second Front, 74–87, *passim*
Shaw, G. B., 17–18, 46, 61, 184
Shinwell, E., 75, 105
Shvernik, 84, 131
Sikorski, General, 90
Silverman, J., 130
Silverman, S., 68, 184
Sinclair, Upton, 81
Snowden, Philip, 3, 6
'Socialist' foreign policy 1–4, 105, 125, 126, 127
Socialist League, 27, 30n
Solkolovsky, V. D., 191–2
Solley, L. J., 104, 205
Sorensen, R., 68
Sosnokowski, K., 93
Soviet Union, 63, 68; Councils of Action, 6; and Eastern Europe, 114, 130, 160–62, 167; and economy, 12; foreign policy, 24, 28–29, 116, 118, 214–215; invades Poland and Finland, 33–34; and Labour Party, 11, 107; and Marshall Aid, 160; Wartime literature on, 72n; and Webbs, 18–22
'Soviet Wives', 151, 184
Spanish Civil War, 24–25
Spender, S., 27
Stalin, J., 35, 58, 61, 67, 81, 96, 115, 131, 169, 174, 212; and CPGB, 217; and Stalinism, 215; and Warsaw Uprising, 92–94
Stewart, M., 46, 158
Stockholm conference (1917), 3
Stokes, Richard, 91, 97, 196
Strachey, E. J. St. Loe, 14, 15–16, 47, 49, 51, 52, 53, 56, 56n, 57, 60, 105, 216
Strang, Lord, 113
Strauss, G., 29, 105
Swingler, S., 56, 199

TANNER, J., 82, 158
Taylor, A. J. P., 84, 214
Tewson, V., 178, 198
The Week, 61
Thomas, J., 8
'Torch', 81, 84
Toynbee, P., 14, 49
Trade Union Congress (TUC), 8, 23, 28, 34, 82, 84, 93, 96, 107, 166, 198
Third Alternative, 140, 143
Third Force, 154–59, 164
Tribune, 6, 62, 65, 69, 78, 81, 82, 90, 97, 98, 104, 106, 107, 130, 134, 163, 168, 185, 195, 198, 201, 208; editorial crisis (1939), 48–49, 56n; Fulton, 124; Nazi-Soviet Pact, 44–47 *passim*; People's Convention, 59; Poland, 91, 93; Soviet Foreign Policy, 124, 179; supports Bevin, 178–79; Truman Doctrine, 153
Truman, Harry, 107, 114, 144n, 147
Truman Doctrine, 150–153
Turkey, 149

ULBRICHT, W., 40
Unemployment in 'thirties, 11
Union of Democratic Control (UDL), 2, 4, 70

Union of Polish Patriots (UPP), 40
United Front, 27
United Nations, 106, 109, 114, 117, 141–2, 121, 126
United Europe Committee, 158
United Socialist States of Europe (USSE), 180–181
United States of America, 106, 129, 143, 158–9, 163, 185
Usborne, H., 139

'VIGILANS', 47
Vyshinsky, 122

WALKER, P. GORDON, 109
Warbey, W., 202
Warriner, D., 151
Warsaw Uprising, 92–94

Watkins-Tudor, 143
Webbs, Sidney and Beatrice, 4, 18–22
Wedgwood, J., 76
Wilkinson, E., 10, 44
Wintringham, T., 80
Woolf, L., 3, 164
World Federation of Trade Unions (WFTU), 96, 117, 178, 198–99

YALTA, 97, 113
Yates, V., 142, 145n
Younger, K., 158
Yugoslavia, 192

ZILLIACUS, Konni, 44, 47, 55n, 104, 107, 108, 153, 157, 166, 172n, 177, 182, 202–3, 204–205, 206n
Zhdanov, A., 161